The President as Prisoner

i

**SUNY Series in The Presidency:
Contemporary Issues**
John K. White, EDITOR

THE PRESIDENT AS PRISONER
A Structural Critique of the Carter and Reagan Years

WILLIAM F. GROVER

STATE UNIVERSITY OF NEW YORK PRESS

Published by
State University of New York Press, Albany

For Information, address State University of New York
Press, State University Plaza, Albany, NY 12246

Library of Congress Cataloging-in-Publication Data

Grover, William F., 1956-
    The president as prisoner.

    (SUNY series in the presidency)
    Bibliography: p.
    Includes index.
    1. Presidents—United States. 2. Pressure groups—United States. 3. Carter, Jimmy,
1924-   . 4. Reagan, Ronald. 5. Industrial safety—Law and legislation—United
States. 6. Industrial hygiene—Law and legislation—United States. 7. MX (Weapons
systems) 8. United States—Economic policy. 9. United States—Military policy.
I. Title. II. Series.
JK516.G76 1989   353.03′13   89-11518
ISBN 0-7914-0090-5   ISBN 0-7914-0091-3 (pbk)

10 9 8 7 6 5 4 3 2 1

For Pat, who lovingly endured,
and for Sam and Luke,
that they may have a more
liberated vision of the possible.

CONTENTS

ACKNOWLEDGMENTS

I have accumulated many debts in the course of writing this book. The project began in graduate school at the University of Massachusetts, Amherst, where Glen Gordon, Jerome Mileur and, especially, Dan Clawson deserve much credit for their thoughtful guidance and general encouragement. Glen and Lewis Mainzer were instrumental in helping me obtain a Political Science Department grant for research at the Jimmy Carter Presidential Library in Atlanta, Georgia, for which I am grateful. Moreover, I deeply appreciate the efforts of Kathleen Kelly, Bruce Miroff, Gary Olson and Joe Peschek for reading and providing critical comments on the manuscript. Their thoughtful consideration has improved the book in many ways. All of these people share in whatever virtues this work may have, although they are of course absolved of any responsibility for its shortcomings.

I am indebted to the St. Michael's College Faculty Council for granting me a reduced teaching load for two semesters to provide additional time to work on the book in its latter stages. John White provided considerable insight as editor of the State University of New York Press series in the presidency. His enthusiasm for the project helped keep me going at various points along the way. SUNY editors Peggy Gifford and Bernadine Dawes, and the SUNY Press staff, also were extremely helpful in seeing the project through to its completion.

No one would be happier to hear of the publication of this book than my late grandfather Frank Burd. Although he passed away when the book was in its infancy, our many discussions and friendly disagreements about politics and presidents will always remain a fond memory. I would also like to thank my parents, James and Margery Grover, for their constant support.

Finally, but foremost, I want to express my love and thanks to my wife Pat Troxell, and to my sons Sam and Luke, who were born at different times during the life of this project. Without their patience and unfailing sustenance the effort needed to complete this book simply would not have been possible. It is dedicated to them.

Those who lead the country into the abyss
Call ruling too difficult
For ordinary men.

—Bertolt Brecht

The Voluntary Captive

Energy in the executive is a leading character in
the definition of good government.
>   —Alexander Hamilton, Federalist
>   No. 70.

This country cannot prosper unless business
prospers. This country cannot meet its obligations
and tax obligations and all the rest unless business
is doing well. Business will not do well and we
[will not] have full employment unless they feel
there is a chance to make a profit. So there is no
long-run hostility between business and
government. There cannot be. We cannot succeed
unless they succeed.
>   —John F. Kennedy, at a press
>   conference, 1961.

I understand this is where I was supposed to come
to restore business confidence.
>   —Jimmy Carter, joking to a
>   meeting of the Business Council,
>   December, 1977.

On June 1, 1987 Paul A. Volcker resigned as chairman of the
Federal Reserve Board, leaving President Reagan to appoint
someone to take over as, arguably, the most powerful central
banker in the world. As it was, he chose conservative economist,
and former business consultant, Alan Greenspan to succeed
Volcker. Having served as chairman of the Council of Economic
Advisers under President Ford, the free-market Republican was
familiar and well-connected in both Wall Street and Washington
circles. He was expected to continue his predecessor's eight-year
legacy as a single-minded crusader against inflation as the
nation's economic public enemy number one.[1] There was nothing

1

particularly remarkable about Reagan's decision to name
Greenspan as the Fed chief. Apart from continuing the
administration's steady second-term tilt away from its earlier
supply-side agenda, Greenspan represented an unexceptional
choice (albeit a less respected figure within the international
financial system than Volcker) to manage corporate-banking
policy.

But suppose, for the sake of argument, President Reagan—
or any president, for that matter—had a dramatic change of heart.
Perhaps he perceived the overwhelming bias of his presidency
toward capital and the wealthy—a bias possibly unmatched since
the presidency of Calvin Coolidge—and decided to make an
eleventh hour move to present the appearance of fairness and
balance in his administration. Thus guilt-laden, he now wanted
to select someone dedicated to altering the Fed's secretive control
over interest rates and the buying and selling of government
securities—policy tools known collectively as monetary policy—in
the interest of promoting the agenda of people *other* than bankers,
corporate executives and related dominant players in the
economic system. Insulated from public pressure and existing
outside normal avenues of democratic accountability, the central
bank is an antidemocratic center of power, an "uncomfortable
contradiction with the civic mythology of self-government" not
responsible to the electorate.[2] It has enormous power to decide
who the winners and losers of economic policy will be. As
William Greider notes, concerning the Fed's historic role, "The
governors of the Federal Reserve decided the largest questions
of the political economy, including who shall prosper and who
shall fail, yet their role remained opaque and mysterious."[3] If
a president wanted to fundamentally change the structure of,
and interests behind, the nation's monetary policy, could it be
done?

Setting aside, for the moment, President Reagan's obvious
ideological aversion to anything not in accord with his near-
worship of the "free-market"; and assuming further the virtual
impossibility of the Senate confirming such an appointment, the
question becomes—could the president have undertaken the
radical reform of appointing, say, a progressive or socialist
economist to run the Fed? Technically, of course, the president
can name anyone he wants. Under the Federal Reserve System

created in 1913, the president has the authority to appoint all seven members of the Fed's Board of Governors to 14-year terms, subject to Senate confirmation, and to elevate one of them to the position of Chair for a four-year term. A left-wing professor with scholarly experience in issues of international economics and banking would be formally qualified. But what would happen if the president actually made such an unorthodox appointment?

The surest outcome would be immediate and widespread panic in the national and international business community. Stock prices would plummet and the overall level of business confidence would hit rock bottom as financial markets reacted with swift negative signals. Over the long term, such a reform would ensure that businesses, fearing market instability and suspicious of inflationary pressures, would dramatically restrict investment and employment, giving rise to higher unemployment and economic stagnation. In short, a presidential initiative of this type would trigger a reaction known as "capital strike."[4] Shattered business confidence would result in a swift rebuke to the president with results manifesting themselves in the form of punishment inflicted on the economy, and hence, on peoples' economic well-being.

The ability of corporate capital to register its displeasure with government policy toward the Fed (or any other government policy) involves what political scientist Charles Lindblom has termed the "automatic punishing recoil" of the market economy.[5] The interests of business necessarily predominate within this scenario due to government's dependence on the private sector for the maintenance of a healthy economy. Public policy-makers, chief among them the president, are publicly accountable for the performance of the economy, even while the health of the economy is dependent on the perceptions and actions of largely unaccountable private individuals. As Lindblom explains, "When a decline in prosperity and employment is brought about by decisions of corporate and other business executives, it is not they but government officials who consequently are retired from their offices."[6] Business thus holds a kind of veto power over public policy, repressing (if not outright preventing) change. Businesses occupy a "privileged position" within capitalist economies, and the resulting situation of the president and other policy-makers is comparable to that of a prisoner—they are, in effect, prisoners of the market.[7]

This, very briefly, is one of the crucial constraints faced by all presidents. It is a constraint peculiar to capitalist democracies, a structural feature of their natural operation, and it raises fundamental and troubling questions about the scope and limits of "democracy," when coupled with capitalist economic structures. And it gives rise to the imperative of elected political leaders, whether reformist or not, necessarily attending to the needs of capital before the needs of all other groups making claims on the state or risk the evaporation of business investment, the precondition of capitalist economic vitality.[8] Despite their constitutional and statutory power to make policy choices, who and what they choose is confined within the boundaries of acceptablity as defined by the business community, especially the corporate sector, whose investment and employment decisions can quickly affect millions of workers and the overall state of the economy. Thus President Reagan, in a flight of fancy, would not move to change the basic rules of the game at the Federal Reserve Board. Such an action would be tantamount to political suicide. It could only be undertaken within a climate of popular insurgency aimed at changing the very nature of the American political economy—and even then it would confront the formidable power of capital to resist such plans.

As the quotes from Presidents Kennedy and Carter above suggest, American chief executives typically are quite comfortable with the goals of business as the general goals of political and economic life. Indeed it is doubtful they could conceive of things being any other way. Rare are the times a president might perceive his options as being imprisoned by the needs of a capitalist economy. President Reagan, for instance, if informed of this status as a prisoner, likely would extol the virtues of blissful incarceration behind the walls of the "magic of the marketplace." Voluntary captivity most accurately describes the plight of the American presidency.

To be sure, there are different degrees of captivity. President Carter and other more liberal-leaning chief executives may have policy agendas that put pressure on corporate profitabilty, in the areas of environmental regulation and provision of social welfare, for example. Yet liberals and conservatives alike are dependent upon a level of economic stability driven by national and international decisions lodged in the private sector. In the end, and indeed throughout, presidents and the public they serve are imprisoned. The servitude to private capital may be less voluntary with some presidents, but it never is involuntary. It is one key dimension of the structure which defines the office itself.

The image of the president as prisoner flies in the face of much of the conventional wisdom about the chief executive, with its Hamiltonian roots. Alexander Hamilton was ahead of his time. The twentieth century has seen his conception of the presidency become a celebrated maxim of political science. Yet his late eighteenth century advocacy of broad executive power— expressed, though in somewhat muted terms, in the famous passage from *Federalist* No. 70 above—did not fit the theory and practice of the next hundred years.[9] This is not to say that his vision of modern commercial expansion and American empire was absent from the nineteenth century scene. On the contrary, these objectives were pursued with vigor.[10] But the notion of the presidency as the locus of institutional initiative for political-economic ends—joining his theory of the executive and his vision of what kind of society America should be—did not gain wide acceptance until after the Spanish-American War. The preceding decades, with the notable exception of the Civil War period, generally are characterized by political scientists as the era of "congressional government."[11]

The shift in power and importance from Congress to the presidency can be demonstrated in the writing of Woodrow Wilson. In 1885 the young Princeton professor's classic work, *Congressional Government*, was published. In it he argued that "the actual form of our present goverment is simply a scheme of congressional supremacy."[12] "Congress [is] the dominant, nay, the irresistable, power of the federal system. . . ."[13] The president, according to the early Wilson, was a comparatively minor official whose business, though "occasionally great, is usually not much above routine," not much more than "mere administration, mere obedience of directions from the masters of policy, the Standing Committees."[14] By 1908, however, his thinking had changed considerably. Reflecting on Theodore Roosevelt's tenure in the White House, the rise of the regulatory function of the state, and the enhanced stature of the U.S. in the world, he revised his earlier assessment. The thrust of his *Constitutional Government In The United States* concerns the political supremacy of the president, who he now saw as "at liberty, both in law and conscience, to be as big a man as he can."[15]

> The President can never again be the mere domestic figure he has been throughout so large a part of our history. The nation has risen to first rank in power and resources. The other nations of the world look askance upon her, half in envy, half in fear, and wonder with a deep anxiety what she will do with her vast strength. . . . Our President must always, henceforth, be one of the great powers of the world, whether he act greatly and wisely or not . . . We can never hide our President again as a mere domestic office . . . He must stand always at the front of our affairs . . .[16]

Here is a thoroughly Hamiltonian view of the presidency, with the chief executive constituting the unifying force of the government, since "there is but one national voice in the country, and that is the voice of the President . . . Only the President represents the country as a whole."[17]

By the time Wilson himself reached the White House the presidency thus had risen dramatically as an institutional component of the government. Yet for all the heightened attention given to the office as a practical focal point for policy leadership, it did not receive a concomitant amount of attention as an area of study within political science. That change took place only in light of the lengthy tenure of Franklin Roosevelt, the chief executive who, in the words of one historian, "re-created the modern presidency."[18] Emboldened by crisis conditions, Roosevelt operated in highly personal terms. He oversaw the unprecedented expansion of the federal government directly into the everyday lives of Americans. As Theodore Lowi aptly puts it, the Roosevelt years inspired "the new sense that the president is the government."[19] FDR also bequeathed to American politics an institutional and ideological apparatus that has been termed the welfare-warfare state. His successors inescapably have had to come to grips with the rich stylistic and substantive heritage of the activist Rooseveltian approach to the office. Describing this legacy, historian William Leuchtenburg argues that all postwar presidents have labored "in the shadow of FDR."[20]

Not only presidents have been shaded by Roosevelt, however. Subsequent scholarship has been profoundly affected as well. In the postwar period studies of the presidency became something of a growth industry in political science. Much, if not most, of this writing touts the beneficence and efficacy of the office. Thus, for example, we learn of Clinton Rossiter's "own feeling of veneration" for "this astounding institution" in his seminal 1956 text on the presidency.[21] While not all theorists shared Rossiter's effusiveness—he characterized the president as "a kind of magnificent lion"—they were by and large sanguine about the prospects of activist chief executives. And perhaps rightly so. For the chief executive analysts had uppermost in their minds when they examined the modern office almost invariably was FDR—a paragon of presidential power and authority. Add to this the fact that the U.S. emerged from World War II as the globally preeminent political, economic and military power and we have a confluence of forces that encouraged heady optimism about American political institutions.

The reality of the postwar period was, of course, much more sobering. U.S. hegemony in the world's political economy did not go unchallenged. When the tapestry of economic and military superiority began to unravel in the late 1960s and early 1970s, American superpower status, and the power of the presidency as the guarantor of both national and economic security, were severely tested. Vietnam and Watergate in particular, and economic stagnation in general, combined to help turn sour the dominant opinion of the presidency. Electorally, one candidate based his campaign for the office on the belief that people had lost confidence in their government. "It is obvious that the best way for our leaders to restore their credibility is to be credible, and in order for us to be trusted we must be trustworthy!" wrote Jimmy Carter in 1975.[22] More than halfway through his presidency he still felt the need to warn the public about the "crisis of confidence" in the American spirit which loomed as "a fundamental threat to American democracy."[23] And in political science, paeans to presidential power were replaced by more cautious assessments that the presidency had become "imperial," "a puzzle," "an illusion," "rhetorical," "impossible," and "plebiscitary."[24]

This shift in conventional thinking about the nature of presidential power serves as the focus of Chapter One of this study.

Two main schools of thought have dominated the discourse on the postwar presidency. One school—the *expansivists*—generally held sway from the time of FDR through the late 1960s. Tracing their twentieth century origins back to Wilson and Theodore Roosevelt, expansivists were energized by FDR's leadership. They celebrate the ideal of the purposive, active, power-wielding, yet benevolent chief executive, and tend to downplay the threat of a president amassing too much power. Though they are aware of the need for countervailing power within the mix of governmental institutions, expansivists clearly endorse a political system within which the president has the upper hand. The other school of thought—the *restrictivists*—are a more recent phenomenon within the discipline, although they do include some theorists who wrote with FDR's years fresh in mind. Their twentieth century roots are most firmly planted in William Howard Taft's relatively narrow conception of the office. Restrictivists are wary of the growth in presidential power, and point to the excesses of the Johnson and Nixon presidencies for confirmation of the danger inherent in such growth. They seek a restoration of balance between the executive and legislative branches. And they hope to deflate public expectations about what any president can reasonably be expected to accomplish, given the constraints of today's world.

By contrasting the expansivist and restrictivist approaches I want to illuminate the range of debate and analysis that dominates prevailing notions of the presidency within political science and to argue that this range is woefully inadequate to the task of explaining the dynamic forces buffeting the chief executive. Specifically, the conventional literature has three major interrelated deficiencies. The first shortcoming of mainstream theories is the narrow scope of debate they foster. Such a confined intellectual space provides little room for orientations that seek to question the assumptions and settled understandings upon which previous theories have rested. Second, conventional accounts of the presidency are fixated on institutionalism. They focus primarily on the institutional balance of power between the president and Congress, making their difference one of degree, not one of kind. Finally, such orientations are intoxicated with process, tending to treat presidential power as a problem of means, not ends. They view the office as a management issue, contending that the complexities of the world have made the job of achieving the nation's goals too big for any one person. While this may be true, the goals themselves are taken for granted. Seldom are the ends of presidential power critically questioned, or seen as contributing to the difficulties confronting the president.

While not dismissing the two leading approaches—indeed acknowledging some debt to particular aspects of them—Chapter Two widens the scope of inquiry to move toward an alternative framework that highlights the relationship between the presidency and the structure of the American political economy.[25] This *structural* approach is differentiated from what passes for "structural" anaylsis within orthodox political science. The two dominant models of the presidency view structure in a shallow sense, as a reflection of *constitutional* structure. The balance of forces between the established political institutions, particularly between the executive and legislative branches, is accorded analytic primacy. Such conventional notions thus regard events like Watergate or the Iran-contra scandal as indicative of the most profound dangers facing American democracy. Yet while undoubtedly important, these political crises can obscure more basic systemic ills. The shallow notion of structure fails to analyze the core assumptions and interests *underlying* governmental institutions and their periodic instability. It cannot see the forest for the trees. Structure understood in the deeper, more fundamental sense intended in this work, by contrast, explores and questions these basic principles which typically are taken as givens, directing the focus of study to the context of the political economy of liberal democratic capitalism.

Used in this deeper sense of the term, structural analysis of the presidency draws much of its sustenance from the large body of work concerned with the theory of the state. For if Lowi is correct that presidents now view their office as the "state personified," it makes sense to explore the imperatives of the capitalist state to discover the dynamics of presidential action.[26] The chapter considers three major variants of non-pluralist theories of the state which, despite their important divergence in emphasis, focus on the structural continuities among all presidents that transcend whatever differences they may have over party, policy or personality. Conventional theories of the presidency place great weight on these differences; structural theory focuses on the deeper continuities.

While analysts seldom attempt to place the presidency within the context of state theory, when this encounter has been forged, two intertwined priorities of the state—promoting economic growth and national security—have commanded attention for their centrality to the president's issue agenda, regardless of who occupies the White House.[27] How the provision of these societal goals is defined and pursued, and on whose terms, are questions absolutely paramount to an understanding of the modern chief executive. As provision of growth and security has become increasingly problematic in light of changes in the context of U.S. postwar economic and military supremacy, however, both the state and the presidency have been in crisis. Structural theory thus can help us sketch the contours of a critical perspective on the office in general, and particularly in an era of declining hegemony, the setting inherited by Presidents Carter and Reagan.

The importance of this changed context cannot be over-emphasized, although mainstream theories of the presidency typically underemphasize, or disregard, its basis in the altered dynamics of the capitalist political economy.[28] America's postwar position of hegemony within the restructured global political economy carried with it new powers and responsibilities for the president. The postwar period paved the way for a transformed terrain of executive action, necessitating increased state intervention to pursue the domestic prosperity and international commitments (both economic and military) accompanying the nation's new status. A close connection was forged between hegemony and executive power, rooted in in the creation of domestic and international institutions to foster the simultaneous achievement of economic expansion and military power.[29]

For roughly a quarter-century the connection held. From the late 1940s through the early 1970s the government pursued a policy of political economy that can be described as ''cold-war liberalism.'' This policy mix entailed a welfare-warfare combination of limited endorsement of liberal social programs via the welfare state, coupled with rigid anticommunism at home and expanding military involvement abroad. A rapidly expanding economy served as the precondition for such an alliance. During the watershed years of 1973–1975, however, these preconditions collapsed under the accumulated weight of the interplay of factors which included, briefly, deep economic recession and inflation; the defeat of America in Vietnam and the concomitant erosion of the postwar foreign policy consensus; the diverse emergence of the third world as a political and economic force, punctuated by though not limited to the 1973–1974 OPEC-led oil crisis; the rebound of Europe and Japan as major players in international economics; and the diminishment of America's lead in the arms race with the Soviet Union.

The next two chapters are policy case studies that employ the structural approach to assess the efforts of Carter and Reagan to pursue the fundamental imperatives of growth and national security within this new setting. Chapter Three examines occupational safety and health policy as an example of how the two administrations confronted the problem of reconciling the mandate of the Occupational Safety and Health Act of 1970 with the pursuit of economic growth. The story of these administrative attitudes toward OSHA policy reveals much about the pressure business priorities—especially those of corporate capital—put on presidential policymaking. What is sacrificed and what is preserved in the name of promoting economic growth has important consequences for the workers of America. And the tradeoffs involved in OSHA policy are especially troubling because they can create a situation where worker safety and health is subordinated to the quest for corporate profitability and the health of the free-market system, a cruel twist of logic for those on the receiving end of presidential power.

Chapter Four focuses on national security through the issue of the MX missile. Like OSHA, the MX is a program with a relatively short history involving consequences that literally can affect life and death. And like OSHA, the MX also has been a lightning rod for intense debate over the direction of national policy. One of the most controversial weapons systems of the 70s and 80s, the MX has had a rocky, almost bizarre history. Both Carter and Reagan spent considerable time and energy trying to justify the need for this counterforce, war-fighting weapon. The extent and quality of their efforts at justification reveal quite a bit about how leaders view the connection between our security and our military capabilities. Moreover, the MX debate demonstrates how little difference there is between competing postwar definitions of national security within the mainstream of "responsible" thought. Thus, as with OSHA and the imperative of economic growth, the MX debate illustrates the narrow nature of the range of the possible for presidential policy, and the overriding continuities between administrations with ostensibly different political agendas.

The fifth and final chapter draws conclusions about the presidency from the policy experiences of the two administrations. Of central importance here is the extent to which each chief executive came to terms with a job constrained by the dual imperatives of the state. For Carter, and his version of the liberal agenda, this was an especially painful process. After roughly two years in office he embarked on the domestic and foreign policy course that would lay the groundwork for Reaganism. The similarity between the two presidencies is at times striking, as is the very different public perception of them. The point in looking at these similarities and differences is to highlight the dilemma faced by Carter, Reagan and future presidents who are judged by criteria that are increasingly difficult to fulfill.

What are the prospects for a presidency whose power appears structurally directed toward the ends of economic growth and national security as they are conventionally understood? How are these imperatives affected as the political economy undergoes major transformation? What are the implications of a citizenry whose desire to hold its president accountable for policy failures varies depending on the strength of its basic need to believe in the efficacy of the office? How might the legitimacy of the office (and the state) be affected if its imperatives could not be met without fundamental change in the political economy? These and corollary queries lie at the heart of the final chapter. My contention is that the two leading theories of the presidency cannot adequately confront such basic issues because neither is capable of questioning the premises of the political-economic system within which the president operates.

A structural approach makes a break from the prevailing theories. It critiques the fundamental dynamics and ideological values that exist *independent* of the president at any given time. And it squarely confronts the possibility that the current crisis of the political economy may require a serious rethinking and redefinition of the guiding priorities of liberal democratic capitalism. In that sense, it is a radical theory. With this in mind, we should be less concerned with the interesting but relatively comfortable question of what kind of president our society needs, and more attuned to the unsettling yet urgent question of what kind of society we want to be.

— CHAPTER ONE —

The Rise and Decline of Presidency Fetishism

The day of enlightened administration has come.
— Franklin D. Roosevelt

In 1941 Henry Luce proclaimed the dawning of the "American Century." With political science in mind, he might have heralded the "Presidential Century."

Franklin Roosevelt's tenure stimulated a veritable love affair between political science and studies of the presidency. The "Roosevelt revolution" not only overturned entrenched notions of the relationship between government, economy and society. It also refocused the vision of American government scholars. His handling of the dual crises of depression and world war permanently elevated the office to heights unimagined in the nineteenth century, save for periods of temporary urgency. With the coming of the Roosevelt administration, political scientists spent considerable time gazing up at the heights, often in semi-awe. The era of presidential government had arrived.[1]

Like any historic change, however, the rise of the presidency was not without its antecedents. While FDR routinely is credited with creating the modern office of the presidency and solidifying its activist character, Theodore Roosevelt is thought to be the first chief executive who legitimately can be termed "modern" in outlook.[2] His view of the office was filled with Progressive Era notions of the president as the guarantor of reform and innovation. There is, in fact, a direct link between Theodore Roosevelt's enlarged conception of the office and the expansion of the modern positive state, whose interventions to rationalize the economy preceded similar New Deal efforts by several decades.[3] Roosevelt explains his energized view of the presidency in his autobiography. The section where he enunciates his "stewardship" theory is worth quoting at length:

The most important factor in getting the right spirit in my Administration, next to the insistence upon courage, honesty, and a genuine democracy of desire to serve the plain people, was my insistence upon the theory that the executive power was limited only by specific restrictions and prohibitions appearing in the Constitution or imposed by the Congress under its Constitutional powers. My view was that every executive officer. . .was a steward of the people bound actively and affirmatively to do all he could for the people, and not to content himself with the negative merit of keeping his talents undamaged in a napkin. I declined to adopt the view that what was imperatively necessary for the Nation could not be done by the President unless he could find some specific authorization to do it. My belief was that it was not only his right but his duty to do anything that the needs of the Nation demanded unless such action was forbidden by the Constitution or by the laws. Under this interpretation of executive power I did and caused to be done many things not previously done by the President and the heads of the departments. I did not usurp power, but I did greatly broaden the use of executive power.[4]

Roosevelt's expansive theory of the president's powers gave the chief executive wide latitude to pursue his idea of the public good, unless prohibited by specific legal barriers. On this reading of the presidency, the White House could become the "bully pulpit" Roosevelt relished. "I believed in invoking the National power with absolute freedom for every National need," he asserted, while maintaining high regard for the Constitution as a tool for social progress, "not as a straightjacket cunningly fashioned to strangle growth."[5]

Roosevelt contrasted his theory of the presidency—what he termed the "Jackson-Lincoln" school—with the more circumscribed vision of the "Buchanan-Taft" school. The latter outlook held the "narrowly legalistic view that the President is the servant of Congress rather than of the people, and can do nothing, no matter how necessary it be to act, unless the Constitution explicity commands the action."[6] Roosevelt's successor upheld this second, more confined notion of the presidency. William Howard Taft saw great danger of "executive domination" in Roosevelt's stewardship theory. In addition to encouraging presidents to hold inflated opinions of their own worth—he chided Roosevelt for equating himself in any way with Lincoln—Taft believed that making the president responsible for the general welfare of the nation stretched the power of the chief executive well beyond reasonable limits, establishing him as a "Universal Providence" whose judgments are beyond reproach. Roosevelt's view of "ascribing an undefined residuum of power to the President is an unsafe doctrine," Taft reasoned, one that "might lead under emergencies to results of an arbitrary character, doing irremediable injustice to private right."[7] A far safer notion of executive power would limit the scope of presidential discretion, as Taft here asserts:

The true view of the Executive functions is, as I conceive it, that the President can exercise no power which cannot be fairly and reasonably traced to some specific grant of power or justly implied and included within such express grant as proper and necessary to its exercise. Such specific grant must be either in the Federal Constitution or in an act of Congress passed in pursuance thereof. There is no undefined residuum of power which he can exercise because it seems to him to be in the public interest. . . . The grants of Executive power are necessarily in general terms in order not to embarrass the Executive within the field of action plainly marked for him, but his jurisdiction must be justified and vindicated by affirmative constitutional or statutory provision, or it does not exist.[5]

It was FDR's presidency that ensured the triumph of the earlier Roosevelt's conception of the office in the expectations of postwar America. Coming to power in the wake of three passive Taft-like chief executives, Franklin Roosevelt stood for virtually everything the more restricted model opposed. He had an abounding faith in the stewardship approach, believing in presidential leadership as the best hope for the material and spiritual revival of the country. On the eve of the election of 1932 he offered this well-known assessment of the historic role of the presidency:

The Presidency is not merely an administrative office. That's the least of it. It is more than an engineering job, efficient or inefficient. It is preeminently a place of moral leadership. All our great Presidents were leaders of thought at times when certain historic ideas in the life of the nation had to be clarified.[9]

Henceforth, the presidency would be both enormously expanded in its scope of operation—the government would take on a host of functions previously either beyond its purview altogether or not formally institutionalized—and greatly enhanced as a source of affirmation for society's basic principles. The president would provide the enlightened administration espoused by FDR, the chief executive who, in the words of one observer, "first made the office 'real' in the daily lives of Americans."[10]

The broad vision of Theodore Roosevelt, as etched into American political life by FDR, and the narrower view of Taft, both have since served to delimit the range of thinking about the presidency. Political scientists typically locate the office, analytically and normatively, somewhere between the poles articulated by these two presidents. The former position endorses an active chief executive who expands the reach of the office for the sake of achieving widely shared programmatic goals. This *expansivist* view is presidency-weighted, regarding the maximization of presidential power as virtually the sine qua non of American politics. The latter perspective seeks to rein in presidential power, viewing a relatively restrained chief executive as more closely attuned to the intentions of the framers of the Constitution and less prone to abuses of authority. Greater balance between the branches of government, particularly the executive and legislative, forms the basis of this *restrictivist* position.[11] Versions of these approaches have survived in the wake of FDR, right on through the presidency of Ronald Reagan. This chapter surveys some major works within these two schools of thought, beginning with the expansivists—those analysts who sought to consecrate in theory, what the presidency had become in practice.

Expansivist theories of the presidency

Scholarly doubts about the ascendancy and virtue of presidential initiative in postwar American politics were few and far between. By the early 1960s the expansivist view of the office as an engine for the pursuit of the liberal agenda seemed firmly entrenched in political science. One can get a sense of the spirit and substance of the expansivist outlook from the work of James MacGregor Burns. In *Presidential Government*, Burns develops a model of the modern presidency rooted in the ideas of Alexander Hamilton. The Hamiltonian model "implied a federal government revolving around the Presidency, and depending on energy, resourcefulness, inventiveness, and a ruthless pragmatism in the executive office. . . ."[12] He hopes such a model might serve as an antidote to the "delay and devitalization" of government he discerned in an earlier work analyzing the "deadlock" built in to the constitutional machinery of American democracy.[13]

For Burns, Lydon Johnson represented the glory of presidential government. Writing at the outset of Johnson's Great Society program, Burns confidently claims the presidency to be "at the peak of its prestige." Johnson's tenure marks the "triumph of presidential government," a kind of government geared to the achievement of new qualitative goals of liberalism which FDR, another Hamiltonian chief executive, had failed to achieve. These goals include "a concerted and sustained and expensive effort to impart values like those of Johnson to the barren lives of millions of Americans, middle class as well as deprived," accompanied by the diversion of "the kind of resources into cultural, recreational, and educational acitvities that we have in the past poured into economic recovery, or even into national defense."[14] Burns wrote, of course, before the massive pouring of resources into the effort of imparting "values like those of Johnson" to the "barren" lives of millions of Vietnamese.

At times, Burns' affection for presidential assertions of power goes even farther—perhaps too far. It reaches nearly absurd proportions in his reflections on an earlier progressive president, Theodore Roosevelt. He laments:

> For a man with Theodore Roosevelt's need for personal fulfillment it was a sort of tragedy that he had no war—not even a Whiskey Rebellion. Not only would war have given him immense psychological gratification, it would also have brought his means and ends into better relation.[15]

This regret is offered for the needs-gratification of a president who unflinchingly championed the use of America's Big Stick to achieve its supposed destiny as the global policeman. It takes little imagination to think of the means Roosevelt would have employed to secure his ends, given his record of allowing U.S. military interventions short of war to defend the "civilized world's" standards of law and order. His racist, patronizing attitude toward the "damned dagoes" of Columbia, or the "Chinese halfbreds," "Malay bandits," "savages, barbarians, a wild and ignorant people" of the Philippines provides a hint on this score.[16]

Despite his exalted view of presidential government, Burns admits Americans generally are ambivalent toward an energized, expansivist administration like that of the Hamiltonian Johnson (or Roosevelt), ambivalence rooted in the fear that "a current or future strong man in the White House might threaten American democracy." However, such fear has been misplaced, Burns reasons, for as it turns out, "presidential goverment, far from being a threat to American democracy, has become the major single institution sustaining it—a bulwark of individual liberty, an agency of popular representation, and a magnet for political talent and leadership."[17] When tempered by an abiding concern for Jeffersonian purposes, a key for Burns, this situation can endure to the benefit of the office and the public.

Burns saw an entire "epoch" of presidential government on the horizon. His endorsement of the expansivist view proved to be especially ironic, though, since Johnson's presidency marks the beginning of the decline—if not the end—of expansivist theories in postwar political science. To appreciate the precipitousness of this decline it is useful to examine some of the major theorists whose tracks Burns followed. Harold Laski, Clinton Rossiter and Richard Neustadt will be the focus of my attention. They certainly do not exhaust the supply of expansivist writers, nor do they include all the variations on the expansivist theme.[18] But they do represent classic defenses of this major approach to the presidency.

British political scientist and Labor Party leader Harold Laski was one of the first analysts to posit the unique character of the presidency. His 1940 book *The American Presidency* shuns any simple comparisons between the chief executive and institutions of European parliamentary systems.[19] Believing the essence of the presidency to be its organic development within an American environment and historic traditions, Laski contends that there is no foreign institution against which it can be compared "because, basically, there is no comparable foreign institution." The presidency is novel: "The president of the United States is both more and less than a king; he is, also, both more and less than a prime minister."[20] The special nature of the office places an enormous burden on its occupant. Citizens expect direct thought and action from the president on the key issues of the day, since the officeholder symbolizes the entire nation. But while embodying the hopes and dreams of the people as the head of state, the president stands alone as head of the government, shouldering the responsibility for the success or failure of government policies. "In England, we blame an anonymous entity 'the Government' if thing go wrong, or a mistake is made," Laski points out, whereas "in the United States it is the president who is blamed."[21] Hence, Laski sees an unusual degree of risk for presidents who would be bold and innovative.

More than this risk, though, Laski everywhere sees limits to the expansion of presidential influence. He has these constraints in mind when he states that "the day of a successful election is the day on which the president ceases to be a free man." Setting aside for now the question of the freedom of a person *before* being elected, among the many contstraints on the officeholder is the deep-seated American aversion toward strong governmental leadership. Laski notes Americans' traditional fear of centralized authority, manifest in the scheme of federalism and checks and balances established by the framers of the Constitution. The institutionalized fragmentation of power and authority has long been noted as one of the defining features of democracy in the U.S. Laski takes a dim view of such impediments to coherent leadership. In particular, he finds Congress an annoying barrier to presidential action. The oppositional role of the U.S. legislature (unlike the unified parliamentary government in Britain), combined with its sectional orientation and its will to assert its own power, makes for factionalized politics. Summing up the relationship between the two branches of government, Laski is unambiguous about his opinion of Congress. "Its own instinctive and inherent tendency is, under all circumstances, to be anti-presidential," he says, adding that it constantly seeks ways to differ from the president, for in so differing it is "affirming its own essence" and "exalting its own prestige."[22]

Along with the divisive role of Congress, Laski cites the power of big business as especially troublesome for presidents. He contends that the "interstitial connections between business and politics in the United States" color every facet of the context of political life. Congress is affected, directing its energy to the maintenance of "those conditions of confidence which business men approve." Parties are equally deferential to the business ethos: "[S]ince the Civil War the dividing line between them has never been real. . . . The truth is, I think, that these major parties have been essentially the agents of the property interests of the United States. . . ."[23] And, of course, the president must "pay continuous attention to the attitude of business itself." Laski writes: "The president who arouses the suspicion that he is not a 'sound' man from the angle of business philosophy is bound to run into heavy weather."[24] Forms of "heavy weather" can vary, but he clearly has in mind some kind of investment strike on the part of capital, with the attendant "rapid repercussion upon unemployment and the standard of life." The general idea here simply is that any government program for innovative social reform must prove acceptable to big business, or risk confronting business efforts to undermine the conditions of economic health upon which such reforms must rest.

Aligned against the risk of presidential initiative, the historic distrust of centralized power, and the effective veto power of the business community is what Laski sees as the modern imperative of the positive state, directed by strong presidential leadership. Citing the presidencies of Washington, Jefferson, Lincoln, Wilson and FDR, Laski argues that strong executive leadership has occurred in the U.S during periods of crisis. Indeed, it is a measure of the beauty of the American political system that "so far, it is clear, the hour has brought forth the man." His point is that the time has come for the *sustained* exercise of presidential initiative. "America has now entered the epoch where the requirements of the positive state can no longer be denied," he writes. Political, economic and social forces have made a strong president a necessary and enduring part of the nation's future. And there is no question that he thinks of Franklin Roosevelt and the New Deal as the kind of president and program such conditions demand.

For Laski, the first 100 days of FDR's term stand as the greatest example of presidential leadership ever, including wartime. Roosevelt was a positive president with a gift for knowing how to "prick men into thought" and into enthusiastic support for his programs. But because the tradition of negative government is so entrenched in the U.S., once the most immediate dangers of depression had passed, congressional and other opponents of the New Deal were able to constrain the Roosevelt administration in numerous ways, especially during his second term. Laski wants America to overcome this cyclical, boom-bust quality of assertions of executive power through the establishment of strong, unified, presidentially-led government. For as he contends, "a government does not prove its adequacy because it can transcend its own principles in an emergency; its adequacy is born of its ability to prevent the outbreak of emergency."[25] Central to this goal is a "radical realignment of parties" in America. Absent the formation of a truly progressive party, the "forces of privilege" will continue to dominate the scope of political choices. But with disciplined parties a strong president will find the institutional support, especially in Congress, for executive leadership. No longer would parties simply "enthrone the conservative forces in permanent power."

Such a shift ultimately depends on popular support among the people, however, and it is here that Laski looks for the real staying power of a president's claim to enhanced authority. Again with FDR as the model, he asserts the need for presidents to draw upon the vigor of movements for social and economic change to ensure a constituency for reform. Roosevelt's passion for change aroused the "dynamic of democracy," a dynamic with "an energy. . . more powerful and more pervasive than the dynamic of any other form of state."[26] Laski claims that unleashing such a powerful democratic force is the answer to the problem of generating the presidential leadership necessary for the nation in the difficult times ahead. It can spark the interest and moral concern of an ordinarily uninterested populous. The concerns of the common person, and the object of broad executive initiative for future generations, will center on the expansion of the positive state. Expanded presidential power will be the vehicle for its realization. A weak presidency will not suffice. As Laski explains:

A weak president, in a word, is a gift to the forces of reaction in the United States. It enables them to manipulate and maneuver between every difference that is provoked by the absence of a strong hand at the helm. It arrests the power to transcend the negativism which the scheme of American government so easily erects into a principle of action. A weak presidency prevents that transcendence of the limitations of 1787 which the compulsions of our generation demand.[27]

It is, finally, in this potential transcendence that we can locate the essence of Laski's case for the expansion of the presidency. Only a president with broader power can confront the problems plaguing the nation. Only a president can rise above the pervasive obstacles to progressive reform. Laski is mindful of the possible dangers of increasing the power of the chief executive. The temptation to abuse is great. Yet he sees power as an opportunity as well, an opportunity that must be granted if the country is to achieve its highest aspirations. "[G]reat power alone makes great leadership possible" he concludes; "it provides the unique chance of restoring America to its people."[28] This argument for the transcendent ability of the office (elsewhere referred to as the ability to "suspend the normal assumptions of the American system") seems thin, though, upon closer examination. Two weaknesses are particularly damaging to his argument.

First, Laski offers no critical assessment of the dynamics of U.S. foreign policy and how they impinge upon a president's power. He is correct to point out that in matters of international affairs the president has a "decisive hand." He informs us that "in no other part of American political life has the separation of powers counted for so little as in the definition of this part."[29] True enough. But he proceeds to accept without a note of dissent the proposition that the U.S. had developed, even before the Spanish-American War, a "consciousness of a world-destiny" which the presidency reflects and pursues. Apparently this American outlook is unproblematic—no need for presidential transcendence here. It is puzzling, though, why someone who grounds his analysis of the domestic side of the office in some kind of moral framework would accept without qualification the premise of American empire. Moreover, even if he is simply expressing an implicit hope for American resolve and aid in the face of growing tension in Europe over the expansion of Nazi Germany (and it is not clear that he is), he should not ignore altogether the connection between U.S. foreign policy and the domestic economy, particularly the interests of big business. If these interests constrain the president in the domestic sphere, as he suggests, it bears notice how they do so in the foreign sphere.

This raises a second, more significant, weakness of Laski's analysis. While it may be true that a strengthened president

working within an invigorated party system might provide the
unified leadership the framers tried so hard to foil, it is less clear
how such unity could elude the reach of big business, whose
powerful position he contends has given it "an economic and
psychological authority unexampled. . . . in any country in the
world." Laski repeatedly refers to the maintenance of business
confidence as imperative for the realization of reform. Yet he also
wants activist presidents—emboldened by the ongoing equivalent
of crisis conditions and rooted in popular support—to overcome
the interests of privilege and the propertied classes in order to
extend the positive state. He makes no attempt to resolve this
tension. Hence his prescription for the presidency rests on too
sanguine a view of the possibilities of reform.

Systemic reforms can have a tremendous impact on people's
lives. The New Deal experience has taught us that. But the limits
of reformism stop well short of the transcendence of the basic
structure of the political economy, which is another New Deal
lesson. After all, it was FDR—Laski's model of liberal reformism—
who offered perhaps the most lucid summary of the status quo
bounds of such a philosophy. "The most serious threat to our
institutions comes from those who refuse to face the need for
change," he declared while campaigning for reelection in 1936.
"Liberalism becomes the protection for the far-sighted conservative. . . . 'Reform if you would preserve.' I am that kind of
conservative because I am that kind of liberal."[30] The consequences
of these limits affect both presidents and programs they would
pursue. They are explored in the rich literature of the "corporate
liberal" perspective on 20th century history.[31] Laski anticipates
no such obstacles to political change; he overstates the efficacy
of a popular president infected with the reforming spirit.

Whatever the shortcomings of Laski's work, he at least thought
it important to grapple with the issue of how the political economy
constrains the scope of presidential initiative. Clinton Rossiter's
1956 book *The American Presidency* gained a far wider audience
and much more praise while providing less analytic content. It
is perhaps a testament to how little the expansivist, usually liberal,
New Deal presidency actually challenged the basic interests of
American business that by the 1950s a leading conservative, like
Rossiter, could champion its power as well. Rossiter applauds

the accretion of presidential power since the founding of the
nation, while describing in near-worshipful tones the contributions of individual chief executives to that increase. His sketches
of the most influential presidents (e.g. Washington, Jefferson,
Lincoln, FDR) at times approach hagiography. Of this tendency,
we are forewarned: "I would be less than candid were I not to
make clear at the outset my own feeling of veneration, if not
exactly reverence, for the authority and dignity of the
Presidency."[32] Rossiter's influential text thus has a civics book
quality about it, which may, in part, account for its popularity.[33]

Rossiter describes the president as a man wearing many
"hats." The hat imagery aptly summarizes the thrust of the book,
for his purpose is to explain the many roles a president must,
by necessity, play upon assuming office. This emphasis on the
president's roles proved so popular an approach that it could be
written that it constituted "the most prevalent and academically
respectable way of viewing the presidency. . . . [I]t may be dubbed
the received view of the office."[34] Rossiter catalogs presidential
roles, or functions (he uses the terms interchangeably), in order
to draw attention to "the staggering burden he bears for all of
us." In all, ten major roles are discussed. The first five roles
comprise the "strictly constitutional" functions of the office, and
include chief of state, chief executive, commander-in-chief, chief
diplomat, and chief legislator. Many provocative themes can be
found here. For instance, being the head of both state and
government—fusing "the dignity of a king and the power of a
prime minister"—carries with it complex issues of accountability
of power. Likewise, the historically controversial commander-in-
chief position poses fundamental problems not only with
Congress, and its competing authority to declare war, but also
with the people, who in the nuclear age must face a president
swollen to "nothing short of a 'constitutional dictator' " in
wartime. Yet as pressing as these issues are, Rossiter makes no
attempt to scratch below their surface. He is enumerating, not
analyzing.

Together these five roles give the president formidable political
muscle. Citing Harry Truman, Rossiter says the responsibilities
"form an aggregate of power that would have made Caesar or
Genghis Khan or Napoleon bite his nails with envy."[35] But these
do not exhaust a president's arsenal. To the original five Rossiter

adds five additional functions he believes round out a realistic assessment of the president's job: chief of party, voice of the people, protector of the peace, manager of prosperity and world leader.[36] These roles have arisen from historic exigency, not constitutional design. The manager of prosperity role stems from the need for overall economic stability to prevent depression, the role of world leader from our post World War II stature, and so on. Nevertheless, he accords them equal status with the constitutionally-grounded functions.

Having briefly touched upon the ten presidential roles he then steps back to see what they add up to. He finds a "seamless unity," "something more than the arithmetical total of all its functions," a single office that is the presidency itself. He is almost giddy with this finding: "I feel something like a professor of nutritional science who has just ticked off the ingredients of a wonderful stew."[37] Sometimes the ingredients do not mix well with one another, however, causing presidents to use their leadership to find the proper balance between them. Rossiter shifts metaphors to make this point:

> If the Presidency is a chamber orchestra of ten pieces, all played by the leader, he must learn for himself by hard practice how to blend them together, remembering always that perfect harmony is unattainable. . . .[38]

Such a blending of musical instruments, or stew, adds a tremendous administrative responsibility to the already "monstrous" burden resting on the president's shoulders. That burden is made more manageable by the vast executive bureaucracy which has flourished in the twentieth century. But it is not removed. The office remains a "one-man job." Truman's famous sign on his desk—"The buck stops here"—captures the essence of the presidency for Rossiter.

Despite great power and responsibility the president is not a free agent. Rossiter follows his account of the president's roles with a discussion of the limits that balance these powers, serving as safeguards that "keep the President's feet in paths of constitutional righteousness." He highlights seven major centers of power restraining the chief executive. Congress, the Supreme Court, the federal bureaucracy and political parties offer a check on the level of national government, while individual states, free enterprise and public opinion present other potential barriers. Most of the seven provide partial restraint, or serve only as an irritant. The Supreme Court, for example, usually ends up "rationalizing most pretensions" of presidents, amounting to "one of the least reliable restraints" on executive behavior. Free enterprise—broadly defined to include, among others, corporations, small businesses, consumer groups and, somewhat oddly, unions—similarly plays a modest part in checking the president. To be sure, a president must seek the support of this "fabulous galaxy" of free enterprise organizations. But beyond that Rossiter does not explain the nature of the relationship involved, except to criticize the performance of labor free enterprisers, John L. Lewis ("the last of the robber barons") and Philip Murray.

The two centers of countervailing power that actually play a significant ongoing role are Congress and public opinion. Congress is a "fiercely independent" institution that vigorously wields its many weapons to check and confine presidential initiative. Yet while Congress is the most reliable constraining force, public opinion constitutes, "over the long run," the "most effective check upon the President." Granting the chief executive's power to shape public sentiment, Rossiter thinks there is a point beyond which the public will not be led. That point marks what he several times calls the "grand and durable pattern of private liberty and public morality." By this he intends to draw attention to the importance of ends and means that are "within the common range of expectations," namely ends and means which "at least do not outrage the accepted dictates of constitutionalism, democracy, personal liberty, and Christian morality."[39] While Rossiter is vague on what these terms entail—they essentially represent his version of an American consensus on liberalism—he does single out those who contend that Roosevelt should have nationalized the banking system in 1933 as holding a view that would have fallen outside an acceptable range of liberty and morality.

Even allowing for the efficacy of an aroused public voicing its opinions through countervailing centers of power, however, Rossiter finds the ultimate limit on the chief executive to be internally generated, not externally imposed. Personal beliefs, conscience, and a sense of history together form the human constitution that ensures a president will act in accord with established norms. These self-limitations, in conjunction with the more formal barriers, thus keep the American presidency moving "with the grain of liberty and morality." The imagery we are left with after this exposition of the interplay of presidential power and its limits is vintage Rossiter:

> [T]he President is not a Gulliver immobilized by ten thousand tiny cords, nor even a Prometheus chained to a rock of frustration. He is, rather, a kind of magnificent lion who can roam widely and do great deeds so long as he does not try to break loose from his broad reservation.[40]

Rossiter's ensuing account of the history of the presidency amounts to a celebration of those who have roamed widely and done very great deeds. With George Washington in mind as the person who would be chosen as the first U.S. president, the authors of the Constitution made a series of key decisions enabling a strong executive to emerge from the proceedings in Philadelphia. Since then, Rossiter perceives a steady (though not unbroken) upward trajectory for the status of the chief executive, propelled by exigent forces of history that have left the office "a hundred times magnifed." By themselves, these historical factors would not necessarily have strengthened the office if the challenges they ushered in were not met by leaders willing and able to exercise authority with resolve. Fortunately for the nation we have been blessed with exceptional presidents when the times called for them. Here he echoes Laski's "the-hour-has-brought-forth-the-man" thesis. He counts eight presidents who merit the adjective "great," and six other "notable" ones, who together helped build the "office of freedom." His brief portraits of these men offer tribute to their legendary achievements, achievements that Rossiter stands in awe of as he glorifies them:

> Each is an authentic folk hero, each a symbol of some virtue or dream especially dear to Americans. Together they make up almost half of the company of American giants, for who except Christopher Columbus, Benjamin Franklin, Daniel Boone, Robert E. Lee, and Thomas A. Edison in real life, Deerslayer and Ragged Dick in fiction, and Paul Bunyon and the Lonesome Cowboy in myth can challenge them for immortality? Washington the spotless patriot, Jefferson the democrat, Jackson the man of the frontier, Lincoln the emancipator and preserver of the Union, Theodore

Roosevelt the All-American Boy, Wilson the peacemaker—these
men are symbols of huge interest and value to the American
people.[41]

Myths and symbols certainly play an important role in any
society. No one would argue with that. But Rossiter nearly leaves
the realm of earthy existence in lavishing praise on these
luminaries. Myths seem to be an end in themselves when he
writes, "The final greatness of the Presidency lies in the truth
that it is not just an office of incredible power but a breeding
ground of indestructable myth." Are there any drawbacks to the
preservation of a mythical aura surrounding our most elevated
political figure? Apparently not. Even the presidents that
historians and political scientists routinely cite as the worst—
Franklin Pierce, James Buchanan, Ulysses S. Grant and Warren
Harding—receive, as consolation of sorts, kind words: "a man
of rich experience," "a gentle man," and so on.[42] This hero worship
confirms a "cardinal fact" of historical scholarship: "American
history is written, if not always made, by men of moderate views,
broad interests, and merciful judgments."[43] A critical temper, it
appears, would be almost unpatriotic.

The merciful judgments continue for the three figures Rossiter
examines at some length in a section on the modern presidency—
FDR, Truman and Dwight Eisenhower.[44] All three contributed to
presidential modernization, which entailed the incorporation of
five key changes (on top of the ones listed earlier) over the quarter-
century since Roosevelt first took the oath of office. The first
change is the further erosion of congressional power vis-a-vis the
executive branch. New Deal economic management, in particular,
solidified expectations that the president would play a crucial role
in the legislative process, virtually becoming a "third House of
Congress." This blossoming responsibility was aided by the
concomitant development of radio and television, the second
dimension of the modern office. The "miracles of electronics"
opened up the channels of communication that put the president
in touch with the people in a more intimate and sustained way.
Henceforth, the president would mold public opinion as never
before.

A third change is the increased use of the president as
"Protector of the Peace," one of the ten original roles that define

the office. The citizenry now demands the president be a "one-man riot squad" able to go anywhere and do anything necessary to maintain domestic tranquility. Although numerous applications come to mind, the one Rossiter is most clearly pleased with—and one that underscores his conservative bias—is the president's power to intervene, with bloody force if need be, to resovle labor disputes.[45] He applauds the executive's willingness, both pre- and post-Taft Hartley Act, to quell strikes, the gravest threat to liberty and morality from Rossiter's perspective. Rounding out the modern alterations are presidential efforts on behalf of civil rights and civil liberties, and the conversion of the office into a bureaucratic structure of the Executive Office of the President. The former development establishes the president more firmly as "a friend of liberty;" the chief executive has no choice but "to serve as the conscience and strong arm of American democracy." The bureaucratic evolution institutionalizes the office, surrounding the presidency with the personnel to carry out its burgeoning duties.

What are we left with, then, after Rossiter's discussion of the roles of the presidency and the men who filled them? His own final reflection is one of conservative (in the sense of conserving the status quo) contentment, expressing his "deep note of satisfaction" with the office and predicting "a long and exciting future for the American Presidency." His expansivist optimism rests on his belief that "all the great political and social forces that brought the Presidency to its present state of power and glory will continue to work in the future," ensuring that "we will turn to the President. . . . for help in solving the problems that fall thickly upon us."[46] The strong, active chief executive, reminiscent of the great ones who have come before, is a certainty: "There is a Presidency in our future, and it is the Presidency of Jackson and Lincoln rather than of Monroe and Buchanan, of Roosevelt and Truman rather than of Harding and Coolidge."[47] Persistent and vigorous presidential leadership thus serves as both description and prescription for Rossiter, who opposes any effort to weaken the institutional centrality of the office. The stakes are simply too high:

> [A]ny major reduction now in the powers of the President would leave us naked to our enemies, to the invisible forces of boom and

bust at home and to the visible forces of unrest and aggression abroad. In a country over which industrialism has swept in great waves, in a world where active diplomacy is the minimum price of survival, it is not alone power but a vacuum of power that men must fear.[48]

The presidency Rossiter endorses with a shamelssly uncritical eye represents "a choice instrument of constitutional democracy." It is ascribed totemic qualities. To tamper with this "peculiar treasure" in any fundamental way is to court disaster. "Leave Your Presidency Alone"—this is Rossiter's fundamental counsel.

Though Rossiter's stature in the field of presidency scholarship has endured, the evolution of discourse on the presidency veered away from his approach with the publication in 1960 of *Presidential Power*, perhaps the most influential book ever written on the topic and certainly the most forceful statement of the expansivist position. Written by Rossiter's friend and colleague Richard Neustadt, the book represents a self-conscious attempt to break with the hitherto dominant way of conceptualizing the office. Rather than adopting a traditional constitutional orientation to the presidency, viewing it as an amalgam of formal roles to be carried out within a matrix of competing institutions, Neustadt sought to see it as a more unified whole with one major purpose—to wield power.[49] He writes:

My theme is personal power and its politics: what it is, how to get it, how to keep it, how to lose it. My interest is in what a President can do to make his own will felt within his own Administration... .[50]

He has written what amounts to a prescription for presidential power (his first working title for the book was "Primer for Presidents") broadly defined as "personal influence on government action." Drawing on case studies of the Truman and Eisenhower years, he proceeds by examining examples of presidential weakness and contrasting them with the type of executive behavior he believes could have resulted in more effective policy outcomes. The latter are reinforced by examples of successful presidential action in roughly similar circumstances, with FDR often serving as the model efficacious actor.

For Neustadt, the essence of presidential power is the power to persuade. The extent of this power depends upon the ability to influence the behavior of people in government, with such influence becoming the measure of presidential leadership. However, Neustadt sees a problem with a president's power to persuade; it is not simply an automatic ability acquired once in office. Formal constitutional "powers" do not guarantee power in the day-to-day affairs of the president. For a chief executive to turn formal power and status into an operative political tool for achieving desired results, more must be done than issuing commands from on high. Presidents must engage in earthly give-and-take of the persuasive endeavor, in effect bargaining with various constituencies which include executive officialdom, Congress, party officials, citizens at large and citizens abroad.

The connection between persuasion and bargaining is central to Neustadt's thesis. He locates the imperatives of this nexus in the Constitution, which created a government of separate institutions sharing powers. This relationship of reciprocal need among separate institutional actors defines the parameters within which the president must persuade. Of course, the authority inherent in the job enhances a president's persuasiveness. An enormous amount of respect and esteem come with the territory. Yet as Neustadt stresses, a president also depends upon those who must be persuaded; their authority and power are necessary for effective presidential leadership. Thus, in Neustadt's view, the operation of government hinges on "relationships of mutual dependence." As he summarizes:

> Persuasion is a two-way street....
> The power to persuade is the power to bargain. Status and authority yield bargaining advantages. But in a government of "separated institutions sharing powers," they yield them to all sides.[51]

Given an environment of pressures and counter pressures, of interaction among influential people with differing vantage points, how does a president wield influence and garner support for programs? How does a president persuade? One method, least desirable from Neustadt's perspective, is through command. As shown in the case of Truman's dismissal of MacArthur, his seizure of the steel mills, and Eisenhower's dispatch of troops to Little

Rock, a president can on occasion command certain actions that
result in quick compliance. From a presidential perspective, these
three cases involved orders which were self-executing. Yet despite
the fact that commands can work, Neustadt says they do so only
under certain circumstances. Conditions under which the necessary factors combine to produce compliance are relatively rare.
Moreover, cases of command typically occur as a last-ditch effort
after all other options have failed or been discarded, in sum
constituting political failure rather than success. Results may be
produced, but the quality of the result is strategically poor, often
inconclusive and usually costly to future programmatic aims.
Neustadt concludes that anything accomplished via the persuasion mechanism of command necessarily will prove to be
transitory.

As a means of effective persuasion, Neustadt prefers the
aforementioned technique of bargaining. The need for bargaining
in the formulation of government policy stems from the
underlying motive of persuasion: self-interest.[52] Because policy
actors have differing outlooks and loyalties, a president seeking
to persuade must convince them "to believe that what he wants
of them is what their own appraisal of their own responsibilities
requires them to do in their interest, not his." People with
divergent interests must come together and hammer out policies
that not only embrace their desire objectives, but also appear in
a form consonant with their individual situations. Truman's
handling of the Marshall Plan is used to illustrate the meshing
of policy form and content, the need for bipartisan policy
agreement and the success such accommodation can produce.
And this also serves as an example of how a president can best
protect the chances of achieving favorable policy results. Such
protection, Neustadt postulates, can be obtained only through
the choices a president makes. Power to persuade is thus intertwined with choices, for "a President's own choices are the only
means in his own hands of guarding his own prospects for
effective influence." Yet to understand how a president can guard
personal power in bargaining relationships through specific
choices, one must first touch upon the two other key power
sources: professional reputation and public prestige.

For Neustadt, a president's professional reputation (reputation
within the Washington community) is a central factor in the

exertion of influence because the power to persuade depends upon what other people who share governing power have come to expect of the chief executive. A president's reputation is always evolving. Accordingly, attention must be paid to presenting an overall image of "tenacity" and "skill." Mistakes are inevitable, but the impression of recurring inconsistency and poor judgment must be avoided at all costs. Of course, a positive reputation in Washington does not guarantee effective persuasion. But it can make life at the top much smoother. Neustadt emphasizes that the responsibility for reputation is almost entirely a president's own affair. Since words and actions can damage one's professional image, the responsibility is fraught with risks. The point, though, is that a president's reputation is not immutable. It can change, as Eisenhower changed his in 1959 with the emergence of a purposeful "New Eisenhower" following more than a year of equivocation over budgetary matters. It is this potential to alter a reputation through executive decisions which lies at the heart of a president's opportunity as a reputation-builder.

Public prestige offers another measurement by which the Washington community gauges a president's performance. Personal power depends on the president's standing outside Washington as well as within. Neustadt terms a president's popularity among the citizenry "a jumble of imprecise impressions held by relatively inattentive men." Yet this disparate collection of subjective judgments directly influences the responsiveness of policy actors to the president's programmatic aims. A president's prestige as an element of influence, Neustadt contends, is comparble to that of his professional reputation—neither one may decide the outcome of a particular situation, but both may have an impact on the possibilities in those situations and thus are pivotal to power prospects.

To protect public prestige a president must not merely be concerned with people's perceptions of the presidential personality; the image of the office itself, and what it ought to be, must be protected. He emphasizes this connection between popular prestige and people's notions of the role of the presidency because he believes the private lives of citizens—their personal dreams and anxieties—greatly color their expectations of the president. Popular discontent weakens one's public image. Therefore, to protect public prestige a president must be attuned to their hopes and the objective conditions of their real world existence, such as "paychecks, grocery bills, children's schooling, sons at war" and other concerns of Main Street America. Unable to control all these elements of people's lives, the president must become a teacher of the public through words and, more importantly, actions, in effect convincing people to "accept the hard conditions in their lives, or anyway [to] not blame him."

Given that tactical choices provide the most essential means of guarding a president's three power sources—bargaining relationships, professional reputation and public prestige— Neustadt turns to an analysis of how the chief executive can gain the greatest benefit from these choices. His advice hinges on the simple proposition that a president makes the most of available choices by first comprehending the power stakes involved and acknowledging their implications. A president must perceive the possibilities of power and influence: "Before power can be served, it must be seen."[53] Here Neustadt definitely means for the president to undertake these activities personally. These are not tasks for advisers: "Nobody and nothing helps a President to see save as he helps himself." As the examples of Eisenhower's budget-day fiasco in 1957 and Truman's Korean War strategy shift in 1950 display, when a president neglects personal power stakes the policy results can seriously erode executive influence. Presidents should be wary of relying exclusively on the advice of experts and advisers, even when the issues are far removed from their experience. Only the president is an expert in the field of personal power. By developing "a consciousness of power stakes" a president will protect self-interest, clarify vision and improve the capacity to make choices, thus standing ready to decisively plan the course of government action.

Having discussed the philosophy behind, and importance of presidential choice-making, Neustadt asks how a president actually operationalizes his suggestions. A fundamental ingredient of self-help for the chief executive is information. By information, Neustadt does not simply mean the policy briefings and other routine data produced by advisers. Presidents need all this, but also need more. They need to stay abreast of "the odds and ends of tangible detail that pieced together in his mind illuminate the underside of issues put before him." Being generally informed is not enough for the power-seeking president. Knowledge of the nitty gritty substance of policy formulation is the key. This implies the president should shy away from delegating all the dirty work of information gathering to advisers who report back only a clean, capsulized version of reality. Presidents need the dirt too. They ought to be their "own director of [their] own central intelligence." As Neustadt explains:

> Presidents are always being told that they should leave details to others. It is dubious advice. Exposure to details of operation and of policy provides the frame of reference for details of information. To be effective as his own director of intelligence, a President need be his own executive assistant. He need be both, that is to say, if he would help himself.[54]

Time constraints, of course, incessantly impinge upon a president's ability to secure such a broad view of government operations. But Neustadt believes it is possible for a president to deal with time pressure and still attend to personal power stakes. He grounds this belief in the figure of Franklin Roosevelt and his competing advisers, self-created deadlines and other administrative devices. Roosevelt's use of power and extraordinary administrative success, according to Neustadt, depended upon the development of his "interior resources," comprised of his acute sense of power, his abounding self-confidence and his sense of direction.

Neustadt concludes his study of presidential power by stressing the increasing need of the chief executive to bring to the office the qualities of government experience and an intense drive for personal power. Although he thinks that expertise and ambition, to be effective components of power, must be kept in perspective by the proper temperament, he still reduces presidential efficacy to the extremely personal pursuit of power. The power-seeker must be able to accept the inevitable frustration of the job. Save for that qualification, the chief executive's "unremitting search for personal power" remains the engine of enlightened administration. When it comes to American presidents who have searched unremittingly for power, the exemplary case for Neustadt (as it is for Laski and Rossiter) is FDR, the president whose call for enlightened administration frames this chapter at the outset. Of FDR, Neustadt writes:

No President in this century has had a sharper sense of personal power, a sense of what it is and where it comes from; none has had more hunger for it, few have had more use for it, and only on or two could match his faith in his own competence to use it. Perception and desire and self-confidence, combined, produced their own reward. No modern President has been more nearly master in the White House.[55]

Elsewhere he commends FDR's qualities, his insatiable appetite for power, as the cornerstone of presidential greatness, citing the fact that he "wanted mastery," "wanted power for its own sake," brought a "taste for power," to the job, and so on.

Just what a president is supposed to do with all this personal power once the thirst for it has been quenched is not clear from Neustadt's discussion. He does equate the determined quest for power with the attainment of "viable" public policy, primarily because the president's political vantage point is so broad he should naturally pursue balanced, feasible policy directions. But the terms "viable," "balanced," and "feasible" seem hopelessly vague. Indeed, the language he employs to clarify such terms sounds reminiscent of Rossiter's ambiguous words, particularly when Neustadt (twice) tells us the president should be certain administration policy moves with "the grain of history," an especially obscure phrase. Disappointment awaits anyone hoping to discover an *analysis* of the *ends* of presidential power.[56] Neustadt has collapsed questions of ends into the quest for "viability." Presidential power is thought of in purely instrumental terms. What is doable is what should be done.

In sum, Neustadt wants his readers to follow him in placing their faith in the president as the political system's "Great Initiator." The job of the "President-as-expert" is to reconcile the seemingly irreconcilable factors which the nation's problems entail, a task the chief executive is suited to perform if an awareness of power stakes and viable policy is maintained. While a president's expertise through experience and consciousness of personal power provide no panacea for the country's ills, they offer our best hope for "effective" policy. If there is any danger in all of this it "does not lie in our dependence on *a* man; it lies in our capacity to make ourselves depend upon a man who is inexpert." "Inexpert" performers in the White House are what Neustadt fears most. American democracy is addicted to expertise at the top, expertise available only from a small group of "experienced politicians of extraordinary temperament." Such proficiency ensures the status quo will not be disturbed, for

> [Presidential] expertise assures a contribution to the system and it naturally commits him to proceed within the system. The system after all, is what he knows. The danger lies in men who do not know it.[57]

Neustadt ends his original edition of *Presidential Power* with these thoughts on the need for expertise at the commanding heights of the political system. Subsequent editions have added three chapters of "Later Reflections," covering the presidency from John Kennedy through Jimmy Carter, but leaving the original study intact. In no significant way do they enhance or shed new light on his original thesis. Only in his comments on the demise of Carter's presidency—with its roots (for Neustadt) in the "hazards of transition" to office which gave rise to the resignation of his Budget Director Bert Lance—does he suggest that presidents might be done in by something larger than particular incidents or personal weaknesses. He argues that Carter was a victim of expectations, in particular the expectations of Washingtonians. People expected too much of him, and continue to expect more than *any* president can deliver. But if this note of caution in his work has the ring of special pleading on behalf of politicians he personally supports, it is because the trajectory of his thesis has not prepared us for such a revision. Indeed, *Presidential Power* contributed significantly to the kinds of expectations Neustadt begins to view as in some way undermining the presidency itself. He is caught in a bind he helped create and of which he is only dimly aware.

> In a relative but real sense one can say of a President what Eisenhower's first Secretary of Defense once said of General Motors: what is good for the country is good for the President, and vice versa.[58]

This thought—especially the "vice versa"—perfectly captures the spirit of Neustadt's classic text. It is the expansivist clarion call.

The restrictivist reply

Neustadt's eleventh-hour second thoughts about the wisdom of the expansivist outlook give a hint that something went awry

along the way to the enchanted land of presidential government.
By the late 1960s and early 1970s, defectors from this perspective
were legion. It is common for political scientists to credit the twin
debacles of Vietnam and Watergate with providing the impetus
for the intellectual retreat. Erwin Hargrove's comments on the
"crisis of the contemporary presidency" are representative of the
changed climate in the aftermath of these two events:

> If this chapter were being written in 1960 by a political scientist
> of liberal persuasion it would surely eulogize presidential power.
> But today [1974] the words do not come.... Our optimistic
> assumptions about the happy fusion of power and purpose have
> been exploded. It is not only that power has been abused but also
> that we trusted too much in it.[59]

Reflecting on the terms of Johnson and Nixon, Hargrove warns,
"we must not be beguiled again by men of power."

Others more explicitly sought to refute the expansivist notion
of presidential government as an enduring chapter in American
political history. "The 1970s marked the end of the presidential
era in American politics," writes Lester Salamon in an essay
directly addressed to the kind of position Burns endorsed so
enthusiastically. He continues,

> [T]he illusory quality of presidential government ceased being a
> cause for concern and became instead something to be applauded.
> The reason: for a brief period, the illusion of presidential
> government came close to being translated into reality, and the
> results turned out to be far different, and far more frightening,
> than its champions had expected.[60]

Clearly the times warranted some measure of rethinking on
the part of presidency scholars. In the face of presidential excess
and abuse of power, the idea that the reach of the office should
be restricted gained credence.

It would be shortsighted, however, to consider the restrictivist
orientation as simply a reaction to the strife of the 60s and 70s.
In fact, its intellectual origins can be found decades earlier in the
work of Edward S. Corwin. Written in 1940, with numerous later
editions, *The President: Office and Powers* expressed Corwin's
concern that the office has become dangerously personalized,
its powers enlarged to the point of resembling, on occasion, a

"primitive monarchy." Corwin contends that the deliberately loose grant of "executive power" in Article II of the Constitution has been stretched by the combined impact of the handful of truly great presidents who have occupied the office, especially those of the twentieth century. He thus finds that, "Taken by and large, the history of the presidency is a history of aggrandizement."[61] The fruits of aggrandizement are passed on from strong chief executives to less dynamic ones through the "accumulated tradition of the office," hence "precedents established by a forceful or politically successful personality in the office are available to less gifted successors, and permanently so because of the difficulty with which the Constitution is amended."[62] For this reason, the potential threat posed by such presidents as FDR is not likely to diminish over time.

Corwin brings a legalistic approach to the study of the office. He focuses much attention on Supreme Court cases which contributed to the evolution of the president's constitutionally granted powers from 1787 onward. We get, for example, a discussion of the president in the role of "organ of foreign relations." Here we see the founding fathers issuing "an invitation to struggle for the privilege of directing American foreign policy," the struggle taking place between the chief executive and Congress. While such power is formally divided, the president's portion has waxed inexorably for a host of reasons, leaving the office with "the lion's share" of responsibility for shaping the substance of foreign policy. The disparity in power is even more pronounced during wartime as the president assumes the commander-in-chief role. Then the executive benefits from the accretion of inherent powers lodged in the leadership position of a sovereign state.

As a result of this growth in presidential prestige, people come to view the chief executive as the architect of the nation's every circumstance, "looking upon the Chief Executive as the author of peace, prosperity, and good crops, or, in the alternative, of war, depression, and famine." Even in light of the institutionalization of much of the administrative dimension of the job, "the office remains highly personal." For Corwin, personalization signals the dominance of a conception of the office as an autonomous center of activity, with the citizenry *embodied* in the executive. The casualty of this supremacy is legislative power and the notion of the people being *re-presented* in Congress. Ironically, the legislature has collaborated in its own evisceration, delegating vast amounts of power and responsibility to the president in the name of meeting the demands placed on the modern state by the public. Presidential aggrandizement therefore encourages the marasmus of the most cherished constitutional principle for Corwin, and for all restrictivists—the separation of powers.

Corwin insists upon the need to stabilize the relationship between these two branches of government. The presidency has encroached too deeply into American political life, a problem made no less troubling by the knowledge that it has come, by and large, with the blessing of popular opinion. While not certain the encroachment poses a threat to personal liberty, he remains wary of its advance. It is this sense of unease that restrictivists share. Corwin's writing thus led the way for what later became a parade of scholars seeking to restrain, in some measure, the political dominance of executive authority. What follows is an exploration of three represenattive members of this bandwagon— Arthur Schlesinger, Jr., Thomas Cronin and Theodore Lowi.

The first thing to note about Schlesinger is how fitting it is to picture him climbing aboard a bandwagon in writing his renowned book *The Imperial Presidency*. He was not always given to cautious appraisals of the scope of presidential power, serving as the "official historian" of the Kennedy administration, to use Noam Chomsky's apt phrase connoting his criticism of Schlesinger's generally effusive praise for Kennedy's presidency and his uncritical attitude toward the administration's foreign policy initiatives, especially in Vietnam.[63] For his part, Schlesinger admits a degree of complicity in the furtherance of expansivist notions of the office. Lamenting the "rise of the presidential mystique," he faults political scientists and historians, including himself, for giving "historical sanction" to an "uncritical cult of the activst presidency" in postwar scholarship.[64] We should think of him, then, as a sort of born-again restrictivist.

Schlesinger's shift away from the expansivist school was prompted by his revulsion against what he saw as the deformation of the Constitution caused by the growth of presidential power, especially in foreign policy. The specific deformation—the underlying theme of the entire book—is the extent to which postwar presidents have besieged the separation of powers. While many factors contributed to the historic destabilization of the institutional balance of power between the president and Congress, they seemed to coalesce in a White House fueled by President Nixon's "compulsive internal drives." Vietnam and Watergate drew attention to the glaring decay of presidential accountability which, under the intense pressure of worldwide crisis, created the imperial presidency. Schlesinger's only explicit definition of the "imperial presidency" comes in an epilogue to a mid-1974 edition, where he says that it "may be briefly defined as the condition resulting when the balance between presidential power and presidential accountability is destroyed."[65] It is absolutely crucial to note that what concerns him throughout is the draining of countervailing centers of power (most notably congressional powers) out of the political system. The problem is an *institutional* one. The *presidency* has run amok. Hence the title of the book tells the story: the office has become imperial, not the nation's foreign policy or the political economy it supports.

Schlesinger's work traces the history of changes in the balance of power between the president and Congress, with the modern period marked by an outright presidential "appropriation" of powers granted the Congress in the Constitution. This appropriation is particularly striking in foreign affairs, the aspect of political life that provided the "decisive impetus" to the imperial presidency. However difficult it might be to ascertain the intent of the framers, Schlesinger points out that they surely intended to divide control over the war powers. Yet it is this division that has come under attack since the early days of the republic.

The increase in the occurance of "presidential war" has not been a steady one. It can be seen more accurately as a cycle of action and reaction: the president engages in some type of military activity which leaves the office with the upper hand in foreign policy matters, and then Congress tries to recoup some of the power taken by the president. The key is that the power lost by Congress is never completely recovered. And each new presidential recoil against congressional reassertions of power elevates the office in the conduct of international relations. The result is an upward trend by fits and starts. Thus we have the nineteenth century examples (there are dozens more) of presidential war in the case of the bloody annexation of Texas, the destruction of San Juan del Norte (Greytown), Nicaragua, and the Civil War. Each of these assertions of presidential war-making power came at the expense of a serious congressional role in these matters.

The case of the leveling of San Juan del Norte in 1854 is instructive for what it says about both U.S. foreign policy (especially given the Reagan administration's eight-year war against the Nicaraguan government) and about Schlesinger's approach to his thesis. The U.S. naval bombardment of the town came as an act of revenge after an incident in which an American official was insulted. Not wanting to back down to pressure from Congress and Britain, President Franklin Pierce eventually defended this wanton destruction by defining the inhabitants of the town as, after all, only a "camp of savages" living in a "pretended community." The incident speaks volumes about the U.S. attitude toward Latin America, and toward the rest of the world we define as the Other when it suits our global ambitions. It is an antecedent of the kind of foreign policy the nation would carry into the twentieth century as well. But for the purposes of Schlesinger's analysis the incident serves only as another case where Congress was denied a role in authorizing military conflict. The issue for him is an institutional one concerning process.

Institutional jockeying continued after the Civil War, when Congress "makes a comeback," asserting its power in the areas of treaty-making and requests for executive information. But the congressional star fell once again with the Spanish-American War and the proliferation of executive agreements under William McKinley and Theodore Roosevelt. Also, Congress generally took a back seat during the strong tenures of Roosevelt and Wilson, provoking "the inevitable reaction" of congressional resurgence between the time of the Versailles Treaty and Pearl Harbor. With the coming of the Second World War, though, the institutional ebb and flow begins to diminish, in part because of unfavorable reaction to congressional neutrality legislation which had tied Franklin Roosevelt's hands in the critical years leading up to the war. In trying to act as a check on the executive, Congress instead had acted as a "straightjacket" on the nation's foreign policy, leaving "the verdict of history" to be one of congressional failure. "No one for a long time after would trust Congress with basic foreign policy," Schlesinger writes. "Congress did not even trust itself."[66]

Against this backdrop, the build up of presidential power in foreign affairs became nearly irresistible. The bombing of Pearl Harbor facilitated a major shift in FDR's conception of presidential power. Prior to the war, he sought congressional collaboration for most of his New Deal and foreign policy initiatives. But after Congress declared war, he used his commander-in-chief powers to expand the unilateral use of executive authority. As it had so often in the past, Schlesinger asserts, "war nourished the presidency." Schlesinger's concern is with the unilateral aspect of the president's power, since its growth was accompanied by a corresponding decline in legislative power. But as with his earlier articulation of this procedural position, he forecloses many fundamental issues. For instance, his preoccupation with purely tactical questions leads him to obscure the importance of policies such as the decision to intern Japanese-Americans during the war (Schlesinger chooses to refer to their "removal," a curiously sanitized word choice). Here a "shameful" policy decision received the approval of Congress and the Supreme Court, leaving in doubt the salience of his thesis on the centrality of the separation of powers issue. Is the emergency power of the president the basic question at stake when a segment of the population is put in prison camps, or is there also a crucial question about the nature of U.S. foreign policy and the ideology that underlies it at home? Schlesinger confines his criticism to the first issue.

Indeed, Schlesinger consciously tries to sidestep questions about the values and interests behind policy decisions of the government. Thus in a section on postwar America he admits that in order to secure congressional passage of aid for Greece and Turkey, Truman used the tactic of trying to "scare the hell out of the country" with appeals to anticommunism and international peril. But some 30 pages later, assessing the national climate in the wake of the Korean War and the crisis atmosphere of threats to "national security," the fact that the Soviet threat was to a great extent simply a promotional strategy aimed at the American public is no longer of importance. Of the cold war, he writes:

> It is not necesary here to argue whether crisis was real or imagined and the foreign policy decent or imperialistic. Surely all those adjectives applied at one time or another. . . . But whatever the

motives and merits of American foreign policy in these years, our
present analysis requires us only to assess the impact of that policy
on American political institutions.[67]

The resulting elevation of "national security" to a "supreme value"
certainly merits attention, as does the concomitant expansion of
executive prerogative to combat alleged threats. But since
Schlesinger can offer no evidence that Congress—the branch
losing power in the face of an inexorable executive power grab—
could have responded to a *different* set of imperatives or would
have offered a *different*, less contrived account of Soviet foreign
policy aims in particular and the world situation in general, his
unwillingness to question "the motives and merits of American
foreign policy" during this formative cold war period weakens
his argument considerably. He ignores the deeper level of analysis
for the sake of an exclusively institutional focus.

Schlesinger continues to confine his inquiry to procedural
questions in his analysis of Nixon's presidency, especially his
handling of Vietnam and Watergate. Fed by Kennedy's "brilliance"
during the missile crisis, and Johnson's use of executive power
to order troops into the Dominican Republic and again to manufacture the circumstances surrounding the Tonkin Gulf resolution,
the presidency becomes "rampant," "revolutionary," and an
outright threat to democracy under the sway of Nixon's "agitated
psyche." "By the 1970s the title Commander-in-Chief had acquired
almost a sacramental aura," according to Schlesinger, "translating
its holder from worldly matters into an ineffable realm of higher
duty."[68] Nixon basked in the aura to defend his unilateral
assertions of power in Vietnam and Cambodia, using the phrase
commander-in-chief "as if it were an incantation." But Schlesinger
is not without his own enchanted language, with "separation of
powers" casting its spell of constitutional closure on the issues
involved. For it is, we must keep in mind, the "legal need to go
to Congress before leading the nation into war" that Nixon's
presidency so brazenly ignores. The *presidential* nature of Nixon's
"presidential war" offends Schlesinger most profoundly, not the
war itself or the dynamics that engendered it. As Schlesinger
frames the problem:

> The Nixon theory of presidential war...had effectively
> liquidated the constitutional command that the power to authorize

war belonged to the Congress. Nixon had thereby erased the most solemn written check on presidential war.[69]

Though clearly rooted in foreign policy, Nixon's assault on the balance of power between the executive and legislative branches eventually found domestic equivalents. His efforts to control appropriations through impoundment and his enlargement of claims of executive privilege stand as two examples of Nixon's desire to "make Congress as impotent in domestic affairs as it had come to be in foreign affairs." Reinforced by a host of other historic forces tending to transfer political power to the executive, Nixon's personal compulsions drove him to seek ever-greater control of national priorities. He sought, Schlesinger asserts, nothing short of a revolution in American politics, its essence being "power to the presidency." What this would have entailed was the establishment of a "plebiscitary presidency"— since Nixon personified the majority of the citizenry, his own beliefs about the best interests of the nation justified any course of action he deemed necessary, accountability coming only at election time. This type of personal rule renders any opposition inherently undemocratic. And its logic legitimizes the types of illegal activities the administration undertook in the Watergate affair.

Fortunately for the nation, Watergate eventually put a halt to the advance of Nixon's revolutionary agenda. The other institutions that are supposed to play a vital role in the polity— the judiciary, the press, Congress, and executive agencies—"all drew new confidence as institutions from the exercise of power they had forgotten they possessed." With constitutional vigor restored, the nation is still left to grapple with the question of the relationship between democracy and foreign policy. For Schlesinger this question boils down to an old argument over "the location of the war-making power." The problem turns on the precise distribution of power between the two branches that are supposed to share this authority, with the distribution meant to ensure that no one person exercises such monumental power.

In searching for a solution Schlesinger provides a glimpse of a critique that moves beyond the bounds of his procedural orientation. The answer, he finds, "lay not in machinery but in policy." Perhaps we need to rethink the "messianic globalism"

traditionally associated with our foreign policy. Perhaps it is time
for a "redefinition of American interests abroad" to diminish
America's "will to unlimited global intervention." "If such things
took place," he speculates, "then the imperial heat would be off,
and Congress would have the opportunity. . . .to reassert its role
in the constitutional scheme."[70]

The feebleness of Schlesinger's commitment to such major
foreign policy revisions quickly becomes evident, though. To
begin with, his principle objection to American pursuit of empire
is that it tends to "deform and disable the Constitution,"
centralizing power where he prefers to see power shared.
Moreover we learn that it was the *Nixon* administration that
fumbled the opportunity to do the basic rethinking and
redefinition necessary to change U.S. international objectives, as
if the major practitioner of the imperial presidency would be
predisposed to challenge the foundations of imperial logic and
interest. Finally he argues that to regain democratic control over
foreign policy, the "ultimate answer lay in the restoration of the
constitutional comity so badly breached by the imperial
Presidency and so nearly destroyed by the revolutionary
Presidency."[71] The rebirth of comity calls for such measures as
the revival of the State Department, the reassertion of Congress
as at least a junior partner in the formulation of policy, and a
loosening of the "secrecy sytem" that gives the executive branch
such a tight hold on information. While these moves might help
the president understand that "foreign policy was not his personal
property," Schlesinger gives us no grounds for reasonably
expecting that if it became shared property—with Congress or
the State Department or anybody else—decisions would be based
on anything other than status quo assumptions about national
security and the national interest which have proven so
compatible with the imperial presidency. His call for a rethinking
of "messianic globalism" thus seems purely rhetorical, divorced
as it is from any sustained, penetrating analysis of the historic,
systemic roots of such motives.

Looking to the future of the presidency, Schlesinger foresees
not only the need for constitutional comity, but also the need
to foster a less deferential public attitude toward the chief
executive. "[W]hat the country needs today is a little serious
disrespect for the office of the Presidency," he contends, calling

for "a decline in reverence" to reverse the decline in presidential accountability. Seen in this light, Nixon's dark tenure had a very bright side to it—"Watergate was potentially the best thing to have happened to the Presidency in a long time." If the right lessons are learned, then the Nixon years will be viewed as "a culmination" of American society's "compulsion toward presidential power." The chief lesson is the need to strike a balance between an energetic chief executive and a constitutional one. If such a balance can be restored, he feels people will come to speak not of "the shame of Watergate," but "the glory of Watergate." The glory, of course, lies in the conclusion that the nation's democratic institutions work. Bad guys eventually get caught.

Schlesinger's misgivings about the relative growth of presidential power and his advocacy of greater accountability and constitutional balance are standard fare for the restrictivist school of thought. His special place in the literature comes from the urgency of his message. The pharase "imperial presidency" became something of a rallying cry for those concerned that the nation's institutional integrity was at stake in the swirl of events of the early 1970s. It was one of his subthemes, though—the necessity of diminishing public reverence for presidential authority—that received fuller development in the writing of Thomas Cronin, particularly his *The State of the Presidency*. Published in 1975, Cronin's book posed a major challenge to orthodox scholarship on the presidency.[72] He charged the academy with presenting a standard, hopelessly idealized version of the office, which fostered exaggerated public expectations about presidential efficacy. His contribution to the restrictivist cause was to make a case for lowering substantially those expectations.

Writing at a time of heightened public awareness of the dangers of executive usurpation of power, Cronin sets out to explain "the presidential puzzle." Noting a marked drop in public confidence in the credibility of presidents, he warns of widespread cynicism and confusion if the veil of illusions and misplaced hopes surrounding the president is not lifted. From the outset he makes his pitch for realism:

> To understand the presidency, we need to appreciate the limits of the presidency, the constraints on presidents, and the

exaggerated expectations we visit on both. We overestimate powers
of the office, and underestimate the economic, social and cultural
factors that shape presidential performance.[73]

Healthy skepticism is in order if the office is to be brought back
in to some kind of reasonable focus.

At the root of the puzzle, Cronin finds a series of paradoxes
born of public expectations and demands which place presidents
in no-win binds. These binds have grown especially confining
in recent decades, as the public came to expect presidents
routinely to live up to the Rooseveltian image of bold, innovative
leadership, while simultaneously not overstepping the limits of
acceptable constitutional behavior.

> The modern (post-Franklin Roosevelt) presidency is bounded
> and constrained by various expectations that are decidedly
> paradoxical. Presidents and presidential candidates must
> constantly balance themselves between conflicting demands. . . .
> [I]t could well be that our paradoxical expectations and the
> imperatives of the job make for schizophrenic presidential
> performances.[74]

Public expectations which are "exaggerated or hopelessly
contradictory" create a climate conducive to presidents attempting
to reach too far, thus leaving them subject to criticism when they
inevitably come up short.

Cronin cites a dozen such presidential paradoxes, with the
idea that "a more sophisticated and tolerant consideration" of the
office might lift a portion of the disabling burden from presidents'
shoulders. It is not necessary to delve into all of them; a sampling
conveys the thrust of his argument. For instance, the public
demands a president be "the decent and just but decisive and
guileful leader." This sets up a contradictory dynamic within
which a president is torn between toughness and tenderness:
the role of the "kindhearted son of a bitch" is difficult to pull off.
Likewise, "The common man who gives an uncommon
performance" is another paradox. It calls for a folksy leader who
can perform heroic deeds — the "uncommon common man."
Apparently Truman successfully handled this conflicting demand.
Carter surely could not. Finally, there is the traditional
constitutional paradox that confers on the president the dilemma

of being both "national unifier and national divider." As head of state and head of government, the president must at least try to create the impression of rising above politics while leading a decidedly political administration (and also serving as party chief). Again, the president is left in a difficult position—perched above the fray yet standing up to his neck in it.

Together these and the other paradoxes constitute an imposing challenge to presidential leadership. Asked to be all things to all people, the president has both too much and too little power to get the job done. When public expectations are not met by our elected "pseudomessiah," we react politically with "the wrath of our vengence." "It is almost ritual destruction," Cronin explains. "[W]e venerate the presidency, but we destroy our presidents."[75] Cronin overstates the fury of public retribution here, given the remarkable and troubling unwillingness of the media and political pundits to bury the corpse of the nation's most resilient presidential Lazarus, Richard Nixon, whose books and presence seem never to fade from the public eye. Yet Cronin's main point remains useful: the political system is geared toward the coronation of a person of superhuman qualities every four years. He locates the responsibility for this distortion of reason in the minds of the people, who constantly search for a "savior-hero." "The paradoxes of the presidency do not lie in the White House," he asserts, "but in the emotings, feelings, and expectations of us all."

One prime consequence of inflated public expectations is what Cronin refers to as "the textbook presidency." The textbook presidency is an interpretation of the office replete with myths about the "benevolent, omnipotent, omniscient, and high moral" chief executive. A product of post-FDR political science, this "romantic—benevolent father, Big Daddy" version was extolled in college textbooks of the 1950s and 60s. Cronin examines more than 30 such books to glean the common ingredients of this mythic scholarly model. He finds surprisingly little variation on the president-as-great-man theme.

> What resulted very often was a storybook view that whatever was good for our president must be the right thing. We were told the president is the embodiment of all that is good in America: courage, honesty, integrity, and compassion. We began to hail the power-maximizing president.[76]

Standard texts portray the president as the engine of national progress, leading the people as their teacher and preacher, and advocating a wide government presence to ensure prosperity and social justice. The vision presented is that "if Americans could only identify and elect the right person, their loftiest aspirations would be fulfilled." Rossiter and Neustadt both are grouped among the purveyors of the textbook conventions.[77] Summarizing this academic concoction, Cronin highlights two dimensions which together describe the textbook ideal type president. The "Omnipotent-competent dimension" holds that the president is *the* strategic catalyst for national progress, and that only the president can fashion public policy to meet the crises plaguing the republic. On the "moralistic-benevolent dimension" the president is viewed as the true personal and moral leader of the people, and if the right person is found for the job, all will be well.

In hindsight the textbook perspective seems woefully inadequate, even somewhat silly. And one would think that it would have foundered on the shoals of the Vietnam and Watergate debacles. But Cronin thinks this orientation is alive and well, if perhaps less assured. After a period of disillusionment within the public, "the prevailing view once again took hold that only the president can get things done, only the president can lead legislatively, only the president can negotiate effectively with other nations, and only the president can make the country governable."[78] Gerald Ford and Jimmy Carter tried a more austere presidency, Cronin thinks, but the voters repudiated their attempts. Public expectations just will not let the larger-than-life image of the president die, for

> Americans still long for dynamic, reassuring, and strong leadership. Watergate notwithstanding, we still celebrate the gutsy, aggressive presidents—even if many of them did violate the legal and constitutional niceties of our separation-of-powers ideal.[79]

Cronin attributes the persistence of the textbook model to a number of mutually-reinforcing factors.[60] These include the American sense of mission which grew out of our experience in World War II, resulting in the prevalent image of the president as "leader of the free world"—an image enhanced to an enormous degree by the solidification of nuclear weapons as an element in the calculation of U.S. foreign policy. A second factor is the enduring human tendency to believe in the ability of "great" people to guide a nation through difficult times. An important psychological role is played by the president as a "national symbol of reassurance," leading Americans to place certain chief executives "on a pedestal rather than under a microscope." The personal values of presidency scholars come into play as a third force. Predominantly beholden to liberal ideology, many authors trumpet the activist presidents, particularly FDR. Likewise, the modes of analysis employed by authors are another influence. Authors typically use some combination of the public record, biographies, prior texts, executive department staff memoirs and memos, interviews with Washington officials, and newspaper and magazine articles—sources which are likely to encourage a more positive picture of the president. Political insiders, when not steadfastly trying to protect their president, often will discuss mistakes and dirty laundry only if such information is off the record. And finally, television has magnified the president dramatically. It places in the president's hands tremendous powers "over reality, perception, and over the whole way in which issues are presented and discussed in America." Thus the textbook presidency has become a "prime-time presidency" as well, a fact that the Reagan presidency has verified many times over.

These sustaining aspects of textbook orthodoxy (and there are others) have consequences about which Cronin has serious reservations. One cost of such an exaggerated version of the office is the extent to which it cheapens the quality of citizen participation, or stifles it altogether. Many people come to regard the president as "the national chaplain," therefore above reproach. This inhibits the development of an active, involved citizenry, since the president should be able to handle whatever troubles arise. The flip side of such an attitude, of course, is that it sets up people for cynicism and despair when a president fails to measure up to our lofty expectations. And such reactions can weaken the legitimacy of political institutions. The textbook imagery also affects presidents, who may actually believe the mythology of presidential invincibility. Expecting reverence from the people, a president's perspective on the world can become distorted. And White House aides often reinforce this danger by shielding their boss from outside influences. Both the Johnson and Nixon administrations have been critiqued on the grounds that they eventually lost contact with reality.[81]

But of all the costs of the textbook phenomenon, Cronin is most troubled by the publicity imperative it engenders—"looking presidential" as he calls it. What follows from the need to look presidential is a public relations "script," which emphasizes style over substance, or "selling the appearance of leadership." The priorities of public relations often lead presidents "to 'act,' to fake and to mislead as they try to live up to the illusory notion that the right person in one job single-handedly can solve the nation's problems."[82] Moreover, when manipulation of images is elevated to a high art form, "telling the truth becomes dangerous," and hence a casualty.

Cronin concludes that the most fundamental question raised by the illusions surrounding public perceptions of the president— reinforced as they are by uncritical scholarship—is how the nation's political leadership and its citizenry can be brought back into a healthier relationship more closely approximating demo- cratic ideals. Sounding a bit like Schlesinger, he stresses the need for a strong but accountable president, with an informed, vigilant public an essential ingredient in any meaningful notion of accountability. As he asserts, "The presidency must not be allowed to become the only, or even the primary, instrument for the realization of government of, by, and for the people."[83] Social change occurs as often from the active commitment of "militant mobilizers" and "political prophets" as it does from "visionary presidents." The contributions of "extragovernmental pressures" such as movements for civil rights, women's rights, and consumer and environmental protection are valued for their consciousness- raising and their challenge to vested interests—interests to which presidents often are beholden. For in order to get elected, aspiring presidents must play by the rules of the game, a game they get locked in to.

One would like Cronin to explore the linkages between presidents and these dominant interests, as well as the problems faced by mass movements which hope to alter fundamentally some aspect of the status quo. Such an examination would situate the president and the public within a political, economic, and social context that clarifies the structural dimensions of life and explores the ways they inhibit change. But he offers only these sketchy impressions, almost as afterthoughts. His final point reiterates that he is in no way denying the importance of dynamic presidential leadership. On the contrary, presidential leadership remains at a premium:

> We shall, of course, need a strengthened and effective presidency. We shall, of course, need brilliant, talented presidents. But we need to deflate the notion that presidents can provide all or even the major amount of our national leadership.[84]

Hence, Cronin urges people to take the political initiative, looking less to Washington for solutions to problems. He proposes that a balance be struck between presidential leadership and citizen activity, lowering our expectations of the former and raising our faith in the latter.

The work of Theodore Lowi, the last restrictivist thinker I will discuss, has an affinity to the ideas of both Schlesinger and Cronin. Like Cronin, he fears that public expectations of the president have surpassed by far any reasonable chance of being met. And like Schlesinger, he senses that the entire political system is out of balance, weighted too heavily toward the president. Indeed, he argues that the combination of these factors actually has changed the very nature of the American political system, nearly creating as a general condition what Schlesinger saw as only a dangerous possibility under Nixon—a plebiscitary republic, led by a plebiscitary president. "Already we have a virtual cult of personality revolving around the White House," he observes darkly in the preface of his 1985 text *The Personal President*. The book traces the rise of the personal presidency, assesses its impact on political life, and offers a way to overcome the "inherent pathologies" it has created. And it provides an indication of where the restrictivist perspective might be heading as its proponents look to analyze the office in the 1980s and beyond.

Lowi contends that the dramatic expansion in the powers of the presidency since the New Deal cemented a connection between big government, strong presidents and democracy. The connection is tantamount to a "redefinition of democratic theory with the presidency at its core." President-centered politics created an entirely new social contract whereby the president provides services to the people while the people, in return, identify directly with their leader. "This is the personal presidency," Lowi explains, "an office of tremendous personal power drawn from the people—directly and through Congress and the Supreme Court—and based on the new democratic theory that the presidency with all powers is the necessary condition for governing a large, democratic nation."[85] But the personal presidency carries high costs, for its very nature breeds frustration. Unavoidable barriers prevent presidents from making good on all their promises to the electorate, yet to the extent that they fulfill any of them, expectations climb even higher. Presidents are left trying to fashion the appearance of success. The outcome is a no-win situation, much like what Cronin delineated. "The harder presidents try to please their mass constituency, the more alienated that constituency becomes," according to Lowi, and the situation arises regardless of who holds office.[86]

It was not always like this in American politics. Throughout what Lowi terms the "traditional system," from 1800 to 1933, Congress reigned as the dominant national institution. Patronage handed out by congressmen and committees was the glue that held everything together, as policies were framed to provide resources for distribution to clients. In this "patronage state" the president was of secondary importance. The patronage state went into decline by the late nineteenth century, though, as public pressure for government action mounted, first in the state capitals but eventually in Washington. It was moribund by the arrival of the New Deal. And since FDR's time "every president has been exceptional, as compared to presidents under the traditional system." Roosevelt did not give up the patronage state, however. Rather he added to it what Lowi calls the "regulatory state" and the "redistributive [welfare] state," whose new functions "finally brought the national government into a directly coercive relationship with the people." A new criterion for judging the success— even the legitimacy—of government was established as the ability to deliver services became a test of government effectiveness.[87] With the president supplanting Congress as the central institution of the ever-expanding federal government, a new sense emerged that "the president is the government."

Roosevelt's adept use of the available communication technologies of the time helped ossify this revolutionary attitude. Lowi sums up his legacy in the concept of the plebiscitary presidency, indicating that FDR achieved his goals through "direct mass political methods." It was not novel for presidents to assume such great power. Schlesinger, for example, amply documents the accretion of power to the chief executive in wartime. What was new was the combination of national security and economic security as a dual rationale for a sustained government presence. In the absence of vibrant political parties—manifested by the spread of split-ticket voting, the rise of the independent voter, and the like—the presidency seeks to carve out its own personal, independent constituency which further weakens the party structure. The public, for its part, vigilantly watches the executive branch to see that agencies come through with the promised services. Lowi offers this observation on what he terms the resulting "Republic of Service Delivery":

> [S]ince the president has become the embodiment of government, it seems perfectly normal for millions upon millions of Americans to concentrate their hopes and fears directly and personally upon him. It is no wonder that the United States has developed such a tremendous stake in the "personal president" and his personal capacity to govern.[88]

The proliferation of presidential primaries has augmented the focus of the political system on the chief executive. With party leaders a marginal player at best, candidates individually compete to amass delegates who really have nothing in common with either the candidate or each other, save for their pledge of support. The base of support that comes out of this process bears little resemblance to a genuine coalition. Lowi compares it to a "flux," a word used in physics to describe independent, unrelated particles revolving around a temporary center of gravity. The plebiscitary president is not actually "made," however, until after the primaries, during the campaign when television exposure magnifies the politician's persona and shapes the presidential mystique. Celebrity status and isolation (the candidates increasingly want to appear to be "above" party, managed by their personal campaign organizations) coalesce to form the presidential personality, which Lowi sees as "a combination of Jesus Christ and the Statue of Liberty: Bring *me* your burdens. Bring *me* your hopes and fears. Bring *me* your search for salvation."[89]

Once such demigods reach the White House Lowi finds they all behave essentially the same way. This is not to say that presidents all have the same psychological composition. Obviously their characters cannot be identical. But Lowi marvels at the surprising degree of continuity in their behavior despite character divergence. All presidents strive to keep the programmatic initiative, and further, to restrict it as much as possible to the White House proper, as opposed to the larger cabinet. Thus it is common to hear about "the president's program, the president's budget, the president's administrative initiative"— again, personalizing and centralizing the responsibility for government. Lowi posits that the resulting dynamic sets up job demands and public expectations which are "pathological, paranoid, and perverse." He adds:

> The president is the Wizard of Oz. Appearances become everything.... The more the president holds to the initiative and keeps it personal, the more he reinforces the mythology that there actually exists in the White House a "capacity to govern."[90]

It is precisely this capacity to govern that Lowi thinks has been drained from the political system by the onset of the plebiscitary presidency. The loss affects both domestic and foreign policy. Domestically, the presidency is based on the assumptions of liberalism. Liberal presidents want to expand the scope of government intervention. Increasingly, though, Lowi sees liberalism as an unrestrained set of values, a philosophy unable to establish priorities among competing claims for government programs and thus, unable to say no to any groups seeking support. Such indiscriminant expansion of government has influenced—captured, actually—the presidencies of avowed conservatives as well as liberals. Hence we have the example of Nixon, the hard-nosed Republican, presiding over the growth of a host of regulatory programs. Lowi places the even more conservative Reagan in the same category, calling his espoused desire to get the government off the backs of the people "completely phony." On this reading, all Reagan has done is shift the priorities of the government from social spending to defense expenditures, leaving "the liberal presidency" intact.

As for foreign policy, Lowi identifies several "syndromes" afflicting presidents regardless of their political stripe. The "star syndrome" compels the White House to resist most resolutely any sharing of foreign policy initiatives. Similarly, presidents

succumb to the "anti-diplomacy syndrome," relying heavily—
and in crisis situations almost exclusively—on the Secretary of
State, special assistants for national security or special envoys,
at the expense of developing an independent professional foreign
service trained in diplomacy. Most importantly, presidents face
"the oversell syndrome" (lying in state). They simplify and
dramatize appeals to international challenges they perceive,
overselling every threat and always finding "a commie in the
woodpile." The danger here is that if proclamations of threats
mount, the president may end up locked into a position where,
because "results" are expected, military escalation is the only
course of action.

When weighing the costs and benefits of the plebiscitary
presidency in foreign and domestic policy, Lowi turns up mainly
costs. The expectations placed on the president virtually guarantee
the cultivation of deceit. Moreover, since the presidency and the
state are viewed as essentially synonymous, any opposition to
the president's will can be construed as to some extent unpatriotic.
To remedy the situation, Lowi concludes with an appeal to restore
the balance between the president and other institutions—
particularly Congress and parties. Restoring the balance would
bring the presidency back down to earthly dimensions, an
absolute necessity as far as Lowi is concerned. Interestingly, Lowi
does not share Schlesinger's optimism that Watergate stimulated
a fundamental move toward this end. Watergate did not cleanse
the political system; it did not teach us lessons about the ultimate
workability of the Constitution. On the contrary,

> [N]o substantial direct lesson can be learned from Watergate except
> not to engage in illegal activities or be caught doing so.... In every
> respect other than the extent of illegal activities, there is a
> Watergate of some kind everyday in the life of a president.[91]

Lowi faults Schlesinger for emphasizing the personal
dimension of Watergate and the imperial presidency. He rejects
the view of Nixon as "aberrant, illogical, or psychopathological."
In fact he thinks Nixon was operating in a "consistent, logical,
and normal" manner under the plebiscitary assumptions of the
office. Those assumptions hold that the president is state
personified, that the powers of the office should match its
crushing responsibilities, that the president should not be bound

by normal legal restrictions when the state is at risk, and that
opponents of the president are disloyal. Acting on these
assumptions, Lowi writes, "then his [Nixon's] actions, including
his crimes, are entirely consistent and rational, quite possibly
motivated by the highest sense of public interest." Lowi is not
being soft on Nixonism. But he is trying to foster appreciation
of the fact that the modern plebiscitary presidency must routinely
cope with enormous, unrealistic pressures from many quarters,
including "the greatest source of everyday pressure on the
presidency—not the Soviet Union, not world leadership, but the
American people and their expectations."[92]

Dealing with these expectations requires reform and Lowi
proposes such measures. First, though, he dismisses as inadequate the War Powers Resolution of 1973, the Budget and
Impoundment Control Act of 1974, and several older plans such
as the proposal for one six-year term and a presidential cabinet.
Real reform, as he sees it, requires the establishment of a
responsible *multiparty* system. Enumerating nine myths about the
existing two-party system, he contends that "nothing about the
present American party system warrants the respect it receives."[93]
Enacting changes which would facilitate a multiparty system (he
thinks the most workable number would be three) would have
a number of advantages, most notably reviving parties as
meaningful institutions. His point, however, is not to lay out the
details of a new set of party rules but simply to argue that the
reinvigoration of parties would be a big step toward "building
down" the presidency. Multiple parties, Lowi says, would reduce
the need of parties to appear to be all things to all people. They
would be expected to have a more limited, hence more realistic
scope of coverage which would mean that "presidential candidates would no longer have to appear omnicompetent." Collective
political responsibility could be fostered if the president came
to be viewed on a more human scale. Restrictivist scholars share
a common desire to take some of the burden off the president's
shoulders by parceling a portion of it out to Congress, parties
and other institutions. It is hoped that this would tame the
tendency toward fixation on the president—whether currently
conceived of as "imperial," "textbook" or "personal."

Lowi's prescription for change seems provocative for its
commitment to creating the space for the institutional airing of

political alternatives ("Why, a couple of the parties might even be radical!" he exclaims at one point). He assumes, at least implicitly, that the policy alternatives currently available are in some way insufficient. But the value of his proposals depends upon a much closer examination of the *reasons* why presidents have so much difficulty getting things done. What structural forces inhibit the fulfillment of a president's objectives? How are those objectives decided upon? What *ends*, if any, are given policy priority and what does this tell us about the competing interest groups Lowi claims vie for government favor? It is to such questions—questions largely ignored by expansivist theorists and given only a surface treatment by restrictivists—that we now turn our attention.

CHAPTER TWO

The Structure of the Presidency

> The life of the nation has grown infinitely varied. It does not centre now upon questions of governmental structure or of the distribution of governmental powers. It centres upon questions of the very structure and operation of society itself, of which government is only the instrument.
> — Woodrow Wilson

The idea of structure

Woodrow Wilson's cogent 1912 observation belies his conventional intent in moving beyond governmental structure. This slice of campaign rhetoric—taken from his speeches and subsequently compiled in book form—introduces a critique of the rise of monopoly corporations in the American political economy around the turn of the century.[1] His attempt to redirect people's attention to the structure underlying the operation of governmental institutions involved, at times, very harsh words for the giants of U.S. capitalism, as this classic Progressive Era indictment of monopoly power shows:

> The masters of the government of the United States are the combined capitalists and manufacturers of the United States. It is written over every intimate page of the records of Congress, it is written all through the history of conferences at the White House, that the suggestions of economic policy in this country have come from one source, not from many sources. The benevolent guardians, the kindhearted trustees who have taken the troubles of government off our hands, have become so conspicuous that almost anybody can write out a list of them.[2]

But the venom Wilson reserved for big manufacturers, bankers, the great railroad combinations and other trusts shoud not, of course, be mistaken for a general rejection of the business ethos or the basic structural arrangements of the political economy. He sought to preserve all of that. What he opposed—what progressives opposed, in word if not deed, as a movement— was the pernicious effect of monopoly on market competition and business opportunities for smaller enterprises. "I am for big business, and I am against the trusts," he added, drawing a distinction which reveals the limits of his examination of "the very structure and operation of society itself." He elaborates on this distinction in a passage that fetishizes big business:

> Big business is no doubt to a large extent necessary and natural. The development of business upon a great scale of cooperation, is inevitable, and, is probably desirable. But that is a very different matter from the development of trusts, because the trusts have not grown. They have been artificially created; they have been put together, not by natural processes, but by the will, the deliberate planning will, of men who were more powerful than their neighbors in the business world.[3]

Big business is "natural," even organic; trusts are a contrived impediment to the "natural" forces of the market. With this understanding it becomes clear how Wilson could campaign on a platform calling for " the emancipation of business" which would usher in the "The New Freedom" of capital, of free enterprise, of individuals' human energies, and still often have the flavor of a progressive, or even a populist, politician.

For Wilson, then, his focus on the structure of society beneath the mere governmental structure entailed an essentially conservative reading of the political economy. He admits as much in an explanation of what it means to be a "progressive," stating that "if I did not believe that to be progressive was to preserve the essentials of our institutions, I for one could not be a progressive."[4] As a consequence it can be said that Wilson had a thin notion of structure, or better yet a shallow notion. Were trusts the *lone cause* of skewed economic policy in the halls of Congress and conferences in the White House? Or must politics in capitalist society necessarily favor the interests of capital over the interests of others? Would the elimination of monopoly and concomitant preservation of big business cure "the problem," or would this simply leave different, perhaps less self-conscious elites as " the masters of the government?" Did Wilson's version of progressivism really look forward, or was it actually a lapse into a supposedly pristine past when markets, and the government, were free of coercion from mammoth combinations of capital?

Obviously many other questions could be posed concerning Wilson's position. The point, though, is to draw attention to the idea of including an explicitly structural dimension in one's analysis of political, economic and social phenomena. And further, to note how muddled the concept of "structure" can become, even when correctly treated as something more than simply the way government institutions are arrayed, as with Wilson. Structural analysis, in short, has not received adequate attention in the discipline of political science as a whole, nor in the specific subfield devoted to study of the presidency. The latter area is notable for its blind spot when it comes to the structural relationship between the political economy and the chief executive.

James MacGregor Burns' writing on the presidency is a case in point. Burns' role as a leading exponent of the expansivist theory of the presidency has already been touched upon in Chapter One. His book *Presidential Government* is regarded as one of the very best treatments of the subject. For Burns, the problems confronting the presidency in its necessary (in his view) drive for expansion of its purview are mainly structural in nature. This point was forcefully argued in his well-known work, *The Deadlock of Democracy*, and has been renewed in his book, *The Power to Lead: The Crisis of the American Presidency*. The basic premise of the latter text is that presidential leadership (and leadership at other levels as well) today faces a severe crisis. "The roots of the crisis lie in structural problems that have been noted since the start of the system two hundred years ago," he contends. "The symptoms of the crisis take the long-observed form of political disarray, institutional stalemate, and governmental ineptitude and impotence."[5]

This is familiar turf for Burns. He is redeploying his argument that the constitutional system of divided powers inherited from the framers makes unified, programmatic government a rarity in the U.S., and that the solution to this dilemma requires consideration of a more parliamentary-style reshaping of power to render centripetal the forces that currently pull apart governmental authority. In particular, often-antagonistic relations

between the executive and legislative branches must be harmon-
ized, while concurrently reviving the role of political parties as
vital centers of debate and disciplined action. The problem for
the presidency thus is "structural" for Burns in the sense that
it is embedded in the very structure of institutions either erected
in the Constitution or flowing out of the founding period. He
refers to those advocating a wholesale adoption of a parliamentary
system in the U.S. as "structuralists." And he terms his own more
modest version of strengthened parties, collective leadership and
constitutional reform "gradual structuralist."[6]

To be sure, there is nothing wrong per se with probing the
institutional machinery of government for flaws and speculating
on how to remedy them. Burns has made a lifetime of valuable
contributions to our appreciation of the high price paid for the
fragmented allocation of constitutional powers. Whatever political
direction one would like the nation to take—and Burns clearly
favors Democratic presidents (supported by principled parties)
advancing a liberal agenda—an understanding of how and why
institutions function the way they do obviously enhances the
prospects of beginning the journey. Where Burns comes up short
is in his *preoccupation* with government structures. For him,
analysis of the president is confined to an understanding of
institutional structure and processes, and the constitutional theory
undergirding them. Such a focus is too exclusive, the examination
too shallow. The equation of structure with *political* institutions
leaves uncovered myriad issues of fundamental importance to
making sense of the presidency. It neglects the fact that the office
itself is situated within a deeper structure of power and privilege
which shapes and constrains those who occupy it, regardless of
whether or not the president operates in greater, or lesser,
cooperation with Congress. Questions addressed by the structure-
as-institutions perspective certainly are not unimportant. They
simply do not confront a host of alternative questions that shed
light of a different hue on the office.

Burns, it should be noted, is not alone in his treatment of
the presidency as comprehensible through an exploration of
government structures. Political science generally has not had an
easy time figuring out how to study the office, or how to theorize
about it.[7] When the discipline has thought in terms of structure
it has done so almost exclusively in terms consonant with those

of Burns. So, for instance, we get books devoted to the crisis in American politics that explore the "structural matters" and contemplate "structural change," with "structure" referring to the institutional division between the president and Congress.[8] Proposals for constitutional reforms to unify divided government typically flow from such studies. Similarly, we get surveys of research approaches which cite various perspectives on the office—empirical, legal-constitutional, psychological and institutional are common ones—with structural concerns discussed as a variant of the institutional orientation.[9] Or, we see responses to the growing cry to make presidency research more empirically grounded, which designate "structural variables" as elements describing the constitutional composition of different political systems (in the case of comparative studies), such as type of executive, party systems, power of dissolution, re-eligibility for office, and the like.[10]

Again, the importance of these issues is not in question. All of them can be useful in furthering our understanding of the office. However they stop short of locating it within a broader and deeper setting of the political economy and the social and ideological structures within which institutions operate. They tend, almost uniformly, to offer atheoretical, descriptive accounts of political mechanics. Such limitations are evident, as well, in the major works of those theorists discussed in Chapter One as representing expansivist and restrictivist schools of thought. This is the case even though some of them implicitly, and at times even explicitly, display a Wilsonian regard for the force of a structure beneath government institutions.

Harold Laski illustrates the problem nicely. As noted in the first chapter, Laski includes some elements of a broader structural analysis in his book on the presidency. He refers to the need of chief executives to maintain the confidence of the business community, and sees political parties as captured by propertied interests. Both of these insights suggest a structure of economic power more fundamental than the office itself. But the points remain on the level of suggestion. They are sprinkled throughout his work, never fused into anything approaching a coherent argument. His most critical insights thus trail off into obscurity, while the president appears as someone able to transcend whatever obstacles to effective action emerge. The potential for a more meaningful structural analysis is lost, curiously abandoned. For such potential to be realized, Laski would need to face squarely the implications of business power. The structural approach I am advocating would ask Laski whether the president is in fact compelled to value the interests of business above all others, how such compulsion actually manifests itself, and what this implies about the quality of democracy in the U.S.

Much the same may be said of Clinton Rossiter's work. An expansivist like Laski, Rossiter is most comfortable simply enumerating and celebrating the chief executive's diversity of roles, a job he does well. Even he alludes to real structural constraints. His repeated references to "private liberty and public morality" as restraining a president's course of action imply, but do not explore, substantive limits placed on the office by public opinion. Moreover, his famous metaphor of the president as "a kind of magnificent lion" also includes boundaries to presidential roaming, since the chief executive is warned against trying to "break loose from his broad reservation." The *nature* of this reservation, though, is left unexamined, perhaps because Rossiter assumes it as a given, an unassailable truth. But whatever the reason, precisely at the point where thin notions of structure draw away from inquiry—where cherished commitments to "free enterprise" or conventional defenses of America's national interests abroad are asserted—deeper structural analysis forges ahead.

Arthur Schlesinger's restrictivist critique of the imperial presidency runs into a similar problem of depth. One cannot help but be impressed with the scope of Schlesinger's genealogy of presidential-congressional relations in foreign affairs. His grasp of the constitutional issues involved in the changing cycles of executive and legislative balance of power is impressive. But for all the depth he incorporates into his account of presidential usurpation of power, he forecloses a host of other questions that penetrate more deeply into the dynamics of the office. The rationale behind American foreign policy, in general and specifically in Southeast Asia; the economic, political and ideological dimensions to traditional definitions of U.S. "national security" concerns; the authenticity of frequent postwar invocations of the threat of communism; the morality of U.S. behavior in Vietnam, and at home in defense of that behavior abroad—such issues are not addressed, and in some cases are dismissed, in Schlesinger's elucidation of the imperial presidency. All complex, deeply troubling questions are reduced to their singular effect on the central (for Schlesinger) issue at stake, the constitutional balance of power between the White House and Congress. The causes of the imperial president thus boil down to congressional timidity in the face of challenges to its institutional integrity, or are turned into accounts of Nixon's psychology. Such a theoretical strategy reinforces conventional foreign policy assumptions and doctrines by confining analysis to tactical, in this instance institutional, questions. And it assumes—wrongly, on a structural reading—that a more active, resistent Congress would have made national security judgments based on criteria different from those of the aberrant Nixon. Left unexamined, such an assumption is a particularly weak peg on which to hang a theory of the presidency.

The proclivity of expansivist and restrictivist theorists to either ignore outright, or mention in passing without investigating in depth, structural questions that implicate the office in an ensemble of political, economic and social relations should be clear at this point. We need only think of Thomas Cronin's observation near the end of his *The State of the Presidency*:

> The reality is that all too often on the long road to the White House our sometime-to-be-presidents become the servants of what is, rather than the visionary shapers of what could be. In the long process of working their way up and learning to operate within the system they become rewarded for playing along with the dominant interests and for playing within the traditional rules of the game.[11]

These pregnant sentences hold out the promise of, but do not in fact reflect, an analysis of the presidency that fully considers structural issues beyond governmental institutions, even though Cronin skillfully exposes many myths surrounding the office, and even though he does make mention of some "extragovernmental pressures" that influence the president's policy agenda. In sum, structural concerns are not wholly absent in mainstream theories of the presidency. They simply are so marginal, so underdeveloped, that they appear only as afterthoughts, not meriting close elaboration.

A brief example will help illuminate the difference between mainstream approaches to the presidency and an approach that

puts structural concerns at the forefront. Consider President
Ronald Reagan's decision to seek $100 million in lethal aid to the
contras attempting to overthrow the Sandinista government in
Nicaragua, part of his ceaseless two-term campaign to oust a
regime he views as a great menace to U.S. national security.
Spanning the spring and summer of 1986, this initiative received
considerable coverage in the media and involved Congress
actively as the body whose approval of the money was needed
to complete the program. What, if anything, can we learn about
the presidency from this one presidential initiative? Expansivist
and restrictivist theories probably would draw fairly similar
lessons.

Rossiter's orientation would direct our attention to Reagan's
role as chief legislator, guiding Congress in its lawmaking duties.
Or, he might point to the aid package as a manifestation of the
president's job as commander-in-chief, developing our military
strategy. Similarly, he might see Reagan wearing his "hat" as
world leader, warning the western world of the dangers of
communism encroaching into our territory and threatening our
freedom. His framework would be very congenial to the Reagan
program since its ostensible goal is to protect the liberty and assert
the morality of U.S. objectives. If he dissented at all it would be
because of the Reagan administration's decision to ignore the
World Court's ruling against the U.S. mining of Nicaraguan
harbors, thus flouting the rule of law which Rossiter cherishes
highly in his work. But this does not bear directly on the aid
question, and Rossiter might well support the administration
against the Court anyway, since its legitimacy has been denied
by U.S. officials.

Neustadt's expansivist analysis would focus on the tremendous persuasive ability of the president. As he did so often during
his first and second terms, Reagan deftly exercised his power to
persuade within the Washington community (though his success
in the public at large is more questionable), winning support for
the military funds, after much debate, in both the House and
the Senate. His victory reconfirmed his professional reputation
as "the great communicator." Neustadt might ponder why it is
that President Reagan usually wins his case on issues related to
Nicaragua (or Central America in general), and accordingly might
study his information-gathering systems within the executive

branch, his personal power drive, his mastery of television as a medium of communication, and the like. More generally, Neustadt certainly would wonder about Reagan's ability to use Rooseveltian means to achieve decidedly un-Rooseveltian ends, for instance in regard to social welfare policy. Overall, like Rossiter, Neustadt would see Reagan's victory on contra funding as at least a short-term triumph of the governmental bargaining process led by a powerful president, although since the ultimate outcome of the U.S.-sponsored fight against the Sandinistas is in doubt, the "viability" of administration policy cannot be determined.[12]

Restrictivists might consider the contra aid bill as an example of balanced executive-legislative interaction. Reagan did get his way on the measure. He did act powerfully to protect his version of the nations's security interests. But the bottom line for the restrictivists would be that the president worked his will *in concert with* the coordinate branch of government. Like the expansivists, restrictivists would have to concede that the process was sound. Certainly some degree of caution would creep into their analysis. Schlesinger and Lowi both might be concerned that President Reagan's method is highly personal, tending toward plebiscitary in style. Lowi especially would be likely to voice concern that Reagan had too much power to set the entire agenda for contra aid, linking approval or denial of aid to approval or denial of his administration's overall goals and, indeed, linking approval or denial to congressmen's sense of patriotism (an aspect of what Lowi calls the "oversell syndrome"). As an issue of the balance of power between Congress and the White House, though, restrictivists—regardless of their personal view of the contras—would have to agree that the process was reasonably balanced. Congressional opponents had ample opportunity to voice their vociferous opposition to the program. And supporters succeeded in making the case that contra aid would help preserve democracy in "our own backyard." A bipartisan commitment was affirmed.

Given the factors orthodox theories might explore, how would a truly structural view of the presidency handle this case? First of all, structural inquiry would put the issue of contra aid in the perspective of the history of U.S. relations with Nicaragua, noting repeated U.S. interventions there to assert our will in the name of preserving our concept of "democracy" and "freedom." It would assess those claims of preservation against the kind of political,

economic and social life Nicaraguans have had since our
involvement there, noting the generally abysmal level of political
freedom and material sustenance gained under the regimes
supported by the U.S. Next, a structural view would examine the
economic context of our historic interaction with Nicaragua, to
locate our relationship with this third world nation within the
overall U.S. strategy toward the world economy. A structural
orientation also would assess the nature and uses of anticommunist appeals to engender a domestic climate receptive to the
goals of U.S. policy, appeals invoked repeatedly and long before
the Sandinistas achieved their victory over Somoza's forces in 1979.
Relatedly, the geopolitical assumptions corresponding to such
appeals would receive attention, especially the premise of a zero-
sum superpower struggle which fuels assertions of the Soviet
threat in Central America. Finally, touching all these concerns
but in a sense rising above them, a structural analysis would open
to question the whole notion of "national security" as used to
defend the conduct of U.S. policy in relation to the contras.[13] This
is the policy foundation of President Reagan's approach to the
issue and, as such, merits closest scrutiny.

A full accounting of the structural view would, of course,
involve a lengthy development of all these points, contrasted with
the mode of analysis expected in the expansivist-restrictivist
debate. I am not pretending to undertake such an endeavor here;
the second part of this chapter goes into the structural interpretation in much more detail and Chapters Three and Four are
case studies intended to apply it. What I would suggest, though,
is that having combined these lines of inquiry, a structural position
would conclude that what is remarkable about President Reagan's
handling of the contra aid bill is not so much his mastery of
Congress, or his continued success at drawing from the well of
persuasion. The remarkable aspect is not that he could win
approval of $100 million for rebel forces regarded as murderers,
rapists and thugs—"freedom fighters" in Reagan's parlance of
persuasion—by virtually every respected international human
rights monitoring group and a sizable number of U.S. allies. What
is remarkable is the degree of *continuity* between the
interventionist policies pursued by the Reagan administration and
those pursued by every administration since the mid-nineteenth
century. Presidential consistency of purpose and strategy in regard

to Nicaragua would be the structural insight. And as for the orthodox concern for the balance of power between the president and Congress, the crucial point here is how Congress has accepted the values and assumptions that *all* presidents have had toward Nicaragua, regardless of whether any given president was more or less plebiscitary in character. In the case of contra aid, of particular note is the extent to which even the most forceful and articulate opponents of the president's position—Senator John Kerry, (D.-Mass.) is the best example—accepted his basic premises regarding the nature of the Sandinista regime, their alleged "betrayal" of the revolution and the geopolitical implications of further Sandinista leadership.[14] In sum, while a structural reading of contra aid would not dismiss the contributions of expansivist and restrictivist theories, it would give primacy to other factors and ask a host of different questions bearing upon the nature of U.S. aims and interests vis-a-vis Nicaragua.

From the preceding discussion we can distill the elements of a broader critique of conventional approaches. Specifically, there are *three interrelated deficiencies* in the expansivist-restrictivist debate. The first shortcoming of mainstream theories is hyper-institutionalism. The two variants seek to explain government institutions largely by studying their internal composition, their political-constitutional dynamic, and the balance of power between them. Often this leads to analyses that are mainly descriptive in nature, with too little regard for the importance of what I am calling structural dynamics.[15] Second, conventional accounts of the presidency stress means over, and almost to the exclusion of, ends. They view the office instrumentally, focusing on how to make it "work better,"instead of investigating the fundamental reasons why it works the way it does, and subjecting the goals of the presidency to rigorous inquiry. Such approaches at least implicitly assume the goals of presidential leadership to be, ipso facto, beyond question and reconsideration, thus ruling out the structural possibility that the pursuit of those very ends may produce, or contribute to, the profound troubles all analysts see plaguing the office. Ira Katznelson and Mark Kesselman's comment—aimed specifically at Neustadt's thesis on presidential power as the unifying ingredient of executive authority—thus seems generally applicable to the entire debate between expansivist and restrictivist positions:

In our view, Neustadt is correct in stressing the need to understand the overall coherence of presidential activity. Yet he does not specify what ends are served by the successful exercise of presidential power. Unless one can supply an answer, the exercise of presidential power appears meaningless, like a dog chasing its tail.[16]

Third, the expansivist-restrictivist spectrum offers an exceedingly narrow range of debate. A president is located, analytically and normatively, somewhere between the poles of relative activity and relative restraint. Such a cramped intellectual space provides little room for perspectives that question the assumptions upon which previous theories have rested. Some scholars have noted that the difference between the two schools is more apparent than real, a shift in emphasis rather than substance. They are, in fact, two sides of the same coin. As Bruce Miroff has argued concerning what some call "revisionist" theories of the presidency, "This supposedly 'revisionist' literature is soft at the core; despite their disillusionment, most presidential scholars cannot conceal the fact that they are still in love with the Presidency."[17] He adds that since such theories are rooted in an uncritical analysis of the office, and cling to the illusion of the president as an historic agent of progressive change, they "will survive no longer than the arrival of the next liberal in the White House."[18] Genuinely structural analysis avoids such pitfalls by broadening the scope of debate currently confining the conventional approaches.

Structure, the state and the presidency: The missing links

Mainstream political science has been reluctant to acknowledge the challenge posed to its theoretical enterprise by alternative views of the presidency. Theorists on occasion will briefly mention a structural approach. Sometimes such an approach receives a modicum of respect, albeit while being woefully underdeveloped and inadequately contrasted with the preponderant mainstream theories. At times a solid structural contribution is noted, but subsequently ignored in what should be its most salient capacity as a basic challenge to the reigning orthodoxy and, further, jettisoned as an avenue warranting future exploration.[19] But more common is intellectual invisibility. For instance, in his recent work

Lowi—while perhaps the widest ranging theorist still operating within the parameters of the debate between the two hegemonic schools of thought—employs what he terms an "institutionalist approach" to the presidency. This approach is in accord with the conventional structure-as-institutions position within the discipline. He makes his case for proceeding along institutionalist lines by asserting its superiority to the other available model, the "psychology/character approach."[20] The impression he leaves is that these two approaches exhaust the realm of the possible as far as studying the office is concerned. Elsewhere I have argued that the psychological approach, which gained a wide following among presidency scholars in the early 1970's, fits easily within the expansivist-restrictivist range of debate.[21] The point here, though, is simply that Lowi seems to bar the emergence of truly structural perspectives.

An ironic opening can be found, though, if one looks beyond Lowi's stated institutionalist framework. For while on the one hand, his work confirms the widespread, historic invisibility of critical orientations within the presidency literature, it also supplies some of the matter out of which a structural approach could materialize. In making his argument that the presidency has grown too personalized, untied from its traditional institutional moorings, Lowi contends that the American people have come to hold gargantuan expectations of the office. These expectations place enormous pressure on the president to solve the nations's problems. Recognizing this burden, modern presidents quite logically have sought to claim power commensurate with such awesome responsibility and in the process have assumed—regardless of their political party—that the office is "tantamount to the state."[22] This view of the president as "state personified" raises a number of vital questions. What is the state? What is the nature of the relationship between the state and the president? How does the state constrain the presidency? Can the president influence and shape the state as well?

One could come up with other queries. Interestingly enough, Lowi pursues none of them. The equation of state and presidential power evidently raises no important issues beyond those of the institutional balance of power between the president and Congress. The nexus between state power, private power and the president remains a dark area. A structural theory of the presidency throws open this dark area to the light of critical inquiry. It accepts Lowi's position on the state-presidency connection and draws the inference that if the president is the state personified, then it must embody the goals of the state. The presdidency must marshal *its* power to pursue ends consonant with state power. Therefore, theories of the state must be brought to bear on theories of the presidency. An encounter needs to take place. But herein lies a problem for conventional theories of the presidency.

Traditional theories of the presidency share a common foundation (whether acknowledged or not) in the pluralist theory of democracy.[23] In large part this accounts for the deficiencies of the works discussed in Chapter One. The ideological assumptions of the theorists predispose them against questioning the core assumptions of liberal democratic capitalism. Instead, in discussing the office they strongly tend to reinforce what is familiar to readers within an American context, making accounts often laden with apparently "mere" description of the office and its responsibilities seem unbiased, and giving their analyses the undeserved appearance of being neutral. But despite what is at least an implicit positivism in conventional theories, pluralism is hardly a non-ideological approach.[24]

Pluralism holds that the social order is best understood as a collection of multiple, voluntary interest groups competing over a variety of policy areas. Through these groups, or acting as individuals through the use of other democratic freedoms such as elections, representative institutions, civil liberties and the like, citizens can become involved in political life. The role of the state is to serve as an umpire, a neutral referee that sets the ground rules for group conflict and for the continued vitality of political rights. Beyond the maintenance of a relatively stable setting for bargaining and compromise, the state has no specific purpose, no interests of its own. Democratic government, by definition, serves the interests of the people. The policy process is thus viewed as a reasonable approximation of the "public interest." Power is diffuse so that no one group has an undue influence on the government. Therefore, pluralists detect no underlying pattern or class bias to state behavior.

For pluralists, then, the nature of the state has not been the focus of sustained analysis. To find such attention to the state as an object of inquiry, one must move beyond scholarship wedded to the concerns of liberal democracy and into the orbit of the Marxist and non-Marxist left.[25] It is here that we find the state situated in the framework of the larger social and economic order. The state is not viewed as a neutral judge presiding over the relatively fair, and immanently open democratic game of group competition. Rather, the state is intimately involved in making and protecting what Cronin referred to above (though vaguely, without any accompanying analysis) as the "rules of the game." Understanding these rules is analogous to understanding the operation of the political economy, understanding, in short, the articulation of democracy and capitalism. To have such an understanding, and to give it primacy in explaining the social order, is to bring a structural perspective to bear on whatever is being studied. In this case, the presidency is being explored. But with a structural analysis, the presidency can only be explained within the broader, more enduring interaction of the democratic state and the capitalist economy.

Joshua Cohen and Joel Rogers, for example, provide an excellent account of structural analysis in their book *On Democracy*.[26] For them, the workings of American politics cannot be seen as just the outcome of the exercise of constitutionally-granted political rights, whether by individuals or groups. Those rights and civil liberties, absolutely essential to any kind of genuine democracy, are severely limited by the capitalist context of our "capitalist democracy." As Cohen and Rogers point out, "the political rights granted to all citizens, workers among others, are formal or procedural, and not substantive. That is, they do not take into account in their own form and application the inequalities in the distribution of resources, characteristic of capitalism, which decisively affect the exercise of political rights and importantly limit their power of expression."[27] Such "resource constraints" give the owners of capital enormous structural advantages in the gathering of information about, and the coordination of, their shared interests, contributing to substantive political and economic inequality despite formal political equality of rights.

Moreover, the structure of capitalist democracy encourages people to seek fulfillment through the satisfaction of short-term material gain. Such "demand constraints" powerfully encourage calculations of economic rationality as the normal way of thinking, a logic that privileges, by necessity, the interests of capital before the interests of all other groups in society. Because of the inherent link between the control of investment decisions, production and employment, the accumulation of private profits must be the condition upon which the interests of all members of society rest. It is likewise the basis of capital's power over state policy—a kind of veto power over public policy that has come to be known as "capital strike."[28] The authors conclude, "Under capitalism, therefore, the welfare of workers remains structurally secondary to the welfare of capitalists, and the well-being of workers depends directly on the decisions of capitalists."[29] And this condition for national politics has ramifications for the world arena as well, since the accumulation of capital requires the state to pursue certain fundamental foreign policy goals. Within this milieu, then, citizens' motivations, their horizons, are structurally constrained to the pursuit of short-term material gain, rendering seemingly irrational the demand for longer-term political and economic struggle against capitalist democracy, or for a system based on other forms of human motivation. This is hardly a set of conditions conducive to the pluralist notion of democracy as the open competition between groups, involving free and equal citizens.

This digression into the work of Cohen and Rogers is intended to show how much deeper a notion of structure can be found in critical accounts of the political economy. The institution of the presidency only makes sense, on a truly structural reading, if located within the environment of capitalist democracy, an environment which the state defends and extends through the exercise of public authority and power. Theories of the state enrich our comprehension of this environment and, hence, further our knowledge of the presidency. Generally speaking there are three approaches to theories of the state that have vied for preeminence within left scholarship. These can be classified as *instrumentalist*, *structural-functionalist*, and *social struggle* theories.[30] Despite their important differences, these approaches do shade into one another at times. What follows is a brief discussion of these points of contact and diversion.

Instrumental theories of the state are most often associated with the work of Ralph Miliband and G. William Domhoff, although both are heavily indebted to the path-breaking career of C. Wright Mills and his studies of the "power elite."[31] The essence of the instrumentalist perspective can be found in its explosion of the pluralist paradigm through a careful detailing of the influence of members of the corporate capitalist class on the activities of government. Domhoff makes the case directly:

> Contrary to this pluralist view of power ... there is a social upper class by virtue of its dominant role in the economy and government ... [T]his ruling class is socially cohesive, has its basis in the large corporations and banks, plays a major role in shaping the social and political climate, and dominates the federal government through a variety of organizations and methods.[32]

Instrumentalism holds that the capitalist class dominates state policy in two ways. On the one hand, members of the ruling class have inside influence by virtue of the direct participation of class members in the state apparatus. Class participation hinges on a complex set of interlocking relationships between members of the corporate community, the banking sector and the government.[33] The state is, in this sense, the instrument of corporate capital. On the other hand, the dominant class has outside influence through a network of policy planning organizations that shape the range of acceptable thought on the leading issues of the day. This context of "reasonable" thought is reinforced by secondary aspect of outside control, the conferral of large sums of money to political candidates through the proliferation of business-related political action committees.[34] In this outside sense, capital expresses its will through the state.

Instrumentalists do not argue, however, that elite domination of the state is total. As Domhoff explains, corporate domination means "the ability of a class or group to set the terms under which other classes or groups within a social system must operate."[35] Within these terms, some social mobility occurs. Non-ruling class people do occasionally work their way up through the class system, but at the price of being assimilated into the norms and beliefs of the upper class along the way. Domination also does not negate the importance of interclass and intraclass conflict over state policy. But to the extent such conflicts exist, they "do not involve challenges to the rules that create privileges for the upper class and domination by its leadership group."[36] It is, in short, conflict within a shared consensus, a consensus to a significant extent manufactured through class power.

   Structural-functionalist theorists consciously defined themselves in opposition to instrumental theories. Within Marxian
thought, a classic debate occurred between Miliband and Nicos
Poulantzas.[37] Poulantzas contended that Miliband placed far too
much emphasis on the social background of state members and
the direct links between corporate and state officials. By contrast,
he argued, the relationship of the state to the capitalist class is
an objective one.

> The relation between the bourgeois class and the State is an
> *objective relation*. This means that if the *function* of the State in a
> determinate social formation and the *interests* of the dominant class
> in this formation *coincide*, it is by reason of the system itself."[38]

He went on to assert that the state serves as a "factor of cohesion"
in a social formation, reproducing the conditions necessary for
capital accumulation. This is the function of the state, a function
performed independent of whether members of corporate capital
actually have direct or indirect influence in government. And he
argued further that "the capitalist State best serves the interests
of the capitalist class only when the members of this class do
not participate directly in the State apparatus, that is to say when
the *ruling class* is not the *politically governing class*."[39] The state,
Poulantzas contended, is "relatively autonomous" from any class
or class fraction. It performs its function of maintaining capitalism
and its system of power because objective structural constraints
compel it.

   Other structual-functional theorists have tried to specify how
and why these structural constraints operate. Fred Block cites two
prime "structural mechanisms" that limit the options of state
managers. Both constraints rely on pressures other than the individual or collective designs of capitalists. One constraint is the need
to maintain a high level of "business confidence." Governments
must do everything in their power to ensure that businessmen
have confidence in the stability of the country's "general
political/economic climate." Investment decisions of firms, the level
of employment and inflation, tax rates and many other factors
are linked to the overall health of the economy. And it is that
health which is essential to the existence of any regime, since
economic decline could spark an accompanying decline in
business confidence and the withdrawal of productive investment.

Without such investment, no government can hope to function from a position of strength, or even remain in power, for long. Notice that this threat of "capital strike" does not assume a class conscious elite. "[T]he chain of events can unfold without any members of the ruling class consciously deciding to act 'politically' against the regime in power ... since decisions made by individual capitalists according to their own narrow economic rationality are sufficient to paralyze the regime ..."[40]

Samuel Bowles and Herbert Gintis concur with Block's position, stating the case for capital's "veto power over public policy" this way:

> The power of capital—its command over state policy—thus derives not so much from what it does but from what it might not do. As in many other situations, power resides with the party that can effectively (and without great cost) withdraw resources and thereby inflict large costs on an opponent.[41]

The mobility of capital is at the root of its power. The "freedom to move" wherever the business climate looks most promising gives capital a power which labor can approach only under extraordinary circumstances. Concerning the different nature of capital and labor, hence, their different kinds of power, Bowles and Gintis add:

> Capital is owned by people and alienable from them; it can be invested or withdrawn or sent around the world by nothing more than the touch of a computer keyboard. Labor is embodied in people. The withdrawal of labor services from an employer requires an alternative source of income, which workers generally lack. The withdrawal of labor from an entire economy requires the costly and often jarring and politically or culturally obstructed physical movement of the workers themselves.[42]

To return to the second, and secondary, structural constraint noted by Block, class struggle also impinges on the options of state managers. Concerted pressure from below can force state managers to expand the state's role into areas that reduce the hardships of the economy for various constituencies. Such reforms are most likely to occur in periods of economic crisis or postwar reconstruction. But as crisis conditions diminish, the impetus for further changes wanes and what reforms have been enacted serve, ultimately, to rationalize the system.

This dimension of Block's structural-functionalist argument shows an affinity with the third approach to state theory, the social struggle school. Social struggle theories recognize the importance of the state's need to secure and maintain business confidence, often referred to as the accumulation function (promoting the accumulation of capital).[43] But they also see this functional requirement conflicting with the need for state policies to be legitimate in the eyes of the public. If the state favors the interests of capital to the extent that people no longer can endorse the systemic bias toward business, causing widespread disaffection—whether overtly-articulated or more implicit—from the established order, citizen allegiance to state institutions and goals can weaken.[44] The state therefore walks a fine line. It must balance its capitalist accumulation function and democratic legitimation function. This opens up a space for social struggle to have an impact on the outcome of state decisions. The state at times may be forced to do things that are *dysfunctional* to the accumulation process, a point Bowles and Gintis make to critique the structural-functionalist tendency to assume the state always reproduces the conditions for capital accumulation. Bowles and Gintis contend that the relationship between the capitalist economy and liberal democratic state can best be understood as "a contradictory rather than a functional totality."[45]

The contradictory nature of this articulation of state and economy means that the state does more than just respond to crises generated by capitalism, as structural-functionalists assume. It "is integral to the production of a crisis as well as to its resolution."[46] Bowles and Gintis cite the success of social struggle on many fronts in the postwar period as forcing the state to make concessions to, among others, the labor movement—costly concessions that seriously limited the profitability of capital by increasing the "citizen wage" (socialized consumption) and reducing the negative impact of the reserve army effect on wages. In this way the state helped create the crisis of capitalism which was manifest in the early 1970s and whose effects are still with us today. Popular pressure thus must have a place alongside other factors in explaining the operation of the state. The state helps set, as well as protect, the "rules of the game" governing liberal democratic capitalism. Bowles and Gintis believe that both instrumental and structural-functionalist theories of the state do not appreciate the fact that those rules can change.

There are important differences in emphasis and particulars between instrumental, structural-functionalist and social struggle theories of the state, and I am in no way trying to resolve them here. But despite these differences, they share a common premise that the basic structure of capitalism profoundly and inseparably influences democratic political life. All the elements of these theories—the class background of state actors, the role of the policy planning network, the functional imperative of accumulation, social struggle and the tension between democracy and capitalism—are vital to what I am broadly calling structural analysis. Yet while the literature on theories of the state is large and growing, the number of analysts who have attempted to use such theories, or elements thereof, to uncover the dynamics of the presidency is modest by comparison.[47] Two efforts do stand out, though, as offering a promising structural blend of these scholarly areas. Both Miroff and Alan Wolfe explicitly examine the specifics of presidential policy-making to glean insight about the nature of the office. They ask what presidents have done and why. And in seeking answers they explore the relationship between the goals of the presidency and the goals of the state.

Miroff's study of the Kennedy administration, *Pragmatic Illusions*, debunks the myth of JFK as a progressive chief executive and the larger myth of the office as a progressive institution in the twentieth century. Focusing on foreign and domestic policies (the Berlin crisis, the Cuban missile crisis, the Alliance for Progress, Vietnam, the New Economics and civil rights), Miroff concludes that Kennedy's tenure was essentially conservative in character and substance:

> Kennedy's presidential record cannot ... sustain his reputation as a progressive. Behind the image of the popular hero lies the reality of service to established power and established values.[48]

Kennedy's leadership style was premised on the liberal belief in pragmatic, hard-headed adherence to objective facts, free from the taint of ideology. This illusion of pragmatism, of being above the fray—reinforced by the veneer of empirical social science so fashionable in the 1950s and 1960s, and highly touted by the corporate executives Kennedy brought into top administration positions—concealed the thoroughly conventional intent of Kennedy's policy objectives. These objectives, according to Miroff, in no way departed from the basic, and politically-laden, goals of liberal ideology, goals all presidents must endorse in their role as the "central figures in the maintenance of established socioeconomic arrangements."[49]

Despite JFK's lofty rhetoric, then, Miroff maintains he held to the earthly interests of the status quo. Those interests were supported by the economic and ideological context of the American political economy. Within that context, the principle domestic function of the Kennedy presidency—and, to extrapolate, all presidencies—was the "stabilization of corporate capitalism." Miroff elaborates:

> It has not mattered greatly that recent Chief Executives have been relatively unlearned in economics; the imperatives of giant corporations who dominate the American economy impose themselves on the Presidency with a force that cannot be misunderstood . . . . The complex partnership between the White House and the corporate community thus transcends personalities and party lines.[50]

Activity on the foreign policy front complements the stabilization of domestic corporate power by facilitating an accommodating climate for international capital. The expansion of U.S. military power and the concomitant perpetuation of cold war assumptions about the threat of communism are crucial features of this objective. Toward this end, Miroff contends that the president can be much more openly assertive in style than in the sphere of domestic policy, even though the chief executive is the most visible national voice on virtually all important public questions.

What Miroff leaves us with is a picture of the president (Kennedy, or any other) as the "chief stabilizer" of political and economic order in the U.S. He probes the structure of power in the U.S. and finds two major intertwined areas—the domestic economy and its international, defense-related equivalent—where the president serves as the dominant supporter of systemic maintenance.[51] In contrast to Miroff, Wolfe looks at successive administrations from FDR onward to discern the underlying imperatives they faced. His work is at once broader in the sense of covering more presidents, and broader in the sense of containing a more highly developed account of the phenomena he finds. But in his basic assertion that "there are only two issues at work in American politics most of the time: economic growth and military strength," he is in substantial agreement with Miroff.[52]

Wolfe arrives at this conclusion by tracing the development of American democracy and the relationship of the presidency to it. Late eighteenth and early nineteenth century debates about the nature of democratic society—crystalized in the competing visions of America held by Jefferson, who favored republican government, and Hamilton, who was an early advocate of modernist expansion and commerce—were settled at the turn of the twentieth century. Searching for a means to rationalize the unsteady growth of capitalism, Progressive Era presidents solidified the Hamiltonian conception. The impetus for the victory of nationalist economic expansion was the need to tame the uneven rhythm of the industrial economy. The chief tool for the job was a strengthened presidency at the helm of a state with its reach broadened to an unprecedented degree. Wolfe posits the presidency as "the major instrument by means of which modernizing elites have sought to overcome or remove obstacles to the expansion and revitalization of American capitalism."[53] People increasingly put their faith in the institution of the presidency as the surest available solution to the maladies facing them.

By the time of FDR and the exigencies of depression, a political bargain of sorts had been struck between the electorate and the chief executive. The people got reforms and a measure of security from uncertainty, while the president got political support for the increased purview of the state. "Implicit in the bargain that made the Rooseveltian formula possible were two conditions," according to Wolfe, "continuous economic growth at home and persistent U.S. hegemony abroad."[54] The conditions fed into each other. Out national security and economic security were indissolubly united—hence the welfare-warfare state.

Wolfe devotes an entire book to exploring the effect of these twin postwar imperatives on American political life. He develops the history of what he terms the "growth coalition," a collection of centrist liberals (pragmatic to the core) spanning the Truman years through the end of the Johnson administration. These recycled elites, and the policy planning organizations with which they were affiliated, fashioned a strategy whereby hard political choices could be avoided by spreading the benefits of solid

economic performance. Political challenges from social democrats
seeking to expand the welfare state, and free-market conservatives
trying to contract or eliminate it, could be circumvented. For as
Wolfe asserts, "instead of making a political choice, America opted
for an economic surrogate."[55] Wolfe exaggerates his case here, for
the pursuit of corporate expansion under the umbrella of a
worldwide military presence certainly *is* a choice. It is a choice
to endorse the priorities of business, which in turn had reached
an accommodation with the realities of state intervention into the
economy. But his major point, that growth and empire constituted
the primary policy objectives for all postwar presidents, is useful.
It is clear that such goals appeared to them as largely technical
issues, revolving around questions of means, not ends.

The price paid for this "Faustian pact" with growth politics
was high. And in Wolfe's account of how different administrations
dealt with various policy areas we get a sense of how the fixation
on growth as the basic end of politics subverted anything truly
resembling the public interest. Whether in the case of public
housing that essentially tore down buildings for urban renewal,
or health care policy that built hospitals without improving health
care delivery, or foreign aid for "development" which sacrificed
humanitarian concerns for the sake of economic indicators,
growth politics often undermined the very ends it was supposed
to achieve. And herein lies Wolfe's larger lesson. The fact that
real domestic economic growth did occur in the postwar period
served to obscure the fact that purported reforms, especially those
of liberal presidents, were conceived in a way that was bound
to expose them as woefully inadequate once growth abated.

Such a scenario did transpire, beginning with Nixon's
presidency. All the circumstances which contributed to the growth
of American power were subject to eventual diminishing returns.
In particular, as the long wave of economic expansion underlying
U.S. postwar hegemony came to an end in the late 1960s and early
1970s, the presidency faced mounting pressure. Presidents
accustomed to being a "cheerleader for economic growth"
domestically, and a "cheerleader for American power" internationally suddenly had very little to cheer about. As Wolfe
writes: "The American presidency requires economic growth to
work; when economic growth cannot be generated, the presidency cannot work."[56] State crisis and the crisis of the presidency

are bound together. And their collective fortunes are tied to the health of the political economy, whose basic needs shape the needs of government. Difficulties with the generation of growth, and challenges to hegemony, put the office, and the state, in a bind, leaving the nation at what Wolfe calls an "impasse."

Presidents Carter and Reagan both assumed an office under seige from the conditions sketched above. I now turn my attention to their presidencies, with the hope that an analytic approach informed by the work of Miroff, Wolfe and the theorists of the state can offer a richer account of the institution than that available within conventional frameworks. What follows are two case studies that probe the structural dynamics of the central imperatives of economic growth and national security, as reflected in the presidents' policy toward occupational safety and health, and the MX missile. Both issues are important in their own right, potentially affecting the quality of everyone's lives. But my foremost concern here is to see what these issue areas can teach us about the nature of the chief executive. Insight into the presidency, and the forces that constrain it, is what I am after. Hopefully this examination will extend, deepen and refine the tools of structural inquiry so as to provide a fuller explanation of the American presidency. And in so doing I will take seriously what Woodrow Wilson, at the outset of the chapter, called attention to—namely, "the very structure and operation of society itself, of which government is only the instrument."

—CHAPTER THREE—

The Presidency and Economic Growth: The Case of OSHA Under the Carter and Reagan Administrations

> I think OSHA can be a great program. The concept is good. I intend to enforce the law rigidly, but I also hope that we can have an acceptance of the OSHA program by the business community. But there would be no backing down on the concept or the purpose of the law concerning OSHA. I just want to make sure that it is administered with a maximum amount of support from labor and of industry.
>
> — Jimmy Carter
>
> My idea of an OSHA would be if government set up an agency that would do research and study how things could be improved, and industry could go to it and say, 'We have a problem here and we seem to lose more people by accident in this particular function. Would you come and look at our plant and then come back and give us a survey of what should be done?'
>
> — Ronald Reagan

On April 1, 1986 the Occupational Safety and Health Administration (OSHA) proposed what was then the stiffest penalty in its 16-year history. The fine of nearly $1.4 million was assessed against Union Carbide Corporation for "willful disregard for health and safety" at its Institute, West Virginia, plant.[1] The Labor Department accused the corporation of widespread "constant, willful, overt violations" of safety and health laws at the facility which manufactures highly toxic phosgene gas — violations including the customary practice of asking employees to detect

89

the presence of the potentially deadly gas by sniffing the air after
alarms indicate a leak.

At first glance, it might appear that the imposition of such
a large penalty indicates vigilant enforcement of the nation's safety
and health statute. However, such an appearance would be
deceiving. In reality, under the Reagan administration OSHA has
become an anemic regulatory agency, its feebleness perhaps
surpassed only by the soap-operatically embattled Environmental
Protection Agency (EPA).

In the case of fine levied against Union Carbide, for example,
the entire proceeding was handled not by the OSHA director
(officially called an Assistant Secretary of Labor for Occupational
Safety and Health), but by Labor Secretary Bill Brock, along with
an interim head of the agency. The reason: at the time, there was
no official administrator of OSHA, and there had been none for
almost a year. OSHA was awaiting Senate confirmation of its third
director in six years, John A. Pendergrass of the 3M company.[2]
His two predecessors had succeeded in substantially reducing the
scope of the agency's standard-setting and enforcement function,
immersing the already beleaguered agency into even deeper
controversy.

From the very beginning of his presidency, Ronald Reagan
made OSHA a primary recipient of administrative animus and
ridicule. His agenda had as one of its central tenets an assault
on social regulations as an impediment to economic growth. And
of all the social regulations he—and the business community—
depised, OSHA was singled out as the most intrusive, the worst
of the worst. As the editors of *Business Week* put it, OSHA
"touches more individual companies than does any other arm
of government except the Internal Revenue Service."[3] Business
resentment of that alleged intrusiveness helped elevate "regulatory reform" and "deregulation" to a privileged position within
the economic policy debates of the late 1970s and 1980s generally,
and to the status of an eternal verity within the Reagan camp.

Widespread counterattacks against the OSH Act and other
social regulations did not simply commence with the advent of
the Reagan years, however. There were many precursors. The
story of the rise of regulatory retrenchment and the overall
rightward shift in economic policy thus must include an account
of the relative positions of business and labor during the economic

tumult of the mid-1970s. Moreover, and of paramount importance for this project, the Carter administration's attempt to fight inflation and revive sagging economic growth and profits in a period of deepening economic crisis must be understood. How these goals influenced the Carter administration's policy toward occupational safety and health, the extent to which Carter's tenure laid the groundwork for the Reagan years, what all of this says about the office of the presidency — such issues are the concern of this chapter.

The picture that emerges is one of a contingent presidency constrained by the imperative of ecomonic growth, one of the twin imperatives of the office. The dynamic interplay of state power and the pursuit of a vital economy, as viewed through the lens of OSHA policy, will provide the substance out of which I will build my case for a structural approach to the study of the presidency, as discussed in the preceding chapter. It is my contention that neither of the conventional orientations to the presidency — the expansivist and restrictivist perspectives — offer as rich or as revealing an account of the office as does structural inquiry. Bearing in mind, then, that the structural approach operates at the intersection of the instrumental, structural-functional and social struggle components of theories of the state, I now will focus on the query: how would a structural approach to the presidency look at the imperative of economic growth as it affects the Carter and Reagan administrations?

A brief history of the Occupational Safety and Health Act[4]

The Occupational Safety and Health Act of 1970 was the child of political and social struggle. Born amid domestic turmoil over the Vietnam War, the "War on Poverty," and the nascent environmental movement, the OSH Act is most profitably viewed as an outgrowth of a general climate of enhanced receptivity to government reform. This climate produced not only OSHA, but a host of "new regulatory agencies," such as the EPA, the Consumer Product Safety Commission and the National Highway Transportation Safety Board. The mere existence of the law thus stands as a testament to the power of sustained public pressure to affect the actions of state actors, particularly the president.

The policy agenda of that era was shaped, in great measure, by the confluence of social forces advocating an aggressive federal role in the area of workplace safety and health. Chief among this coalition of forces were labor unions, rank-and-file agitation, the environmental movement, and public interest pressure (especially the work of Ralph Nader).[5] Together they kept awareness of a workplace safety and health crisis—soaring injury and death statistics from the mid-1960's onward, coupled with rising sensitivity to the incidence of health-related problems associated with the use of toxic substances—prominantly in the public eye.

The role of workers merits special note, for it was within a tradition of struggle that they, sometimes with union support and often without it, pressed for passage of the OSH Act from 1968–1970. The mine workers' effort bears greatest notice because it was their determination to enact basic health and safety reforms that helped galvanize the national health and safety movement. Their three-week wildcat strike in the West Virginia coal mines in February, 1969, including a march on the state capital, following as it did the tragic Farmington, West Virginia mine explosion which killed 78 miners, provided the impetus for not only the 1969 Coal Mine Health and Safety Act, but for the OSH Act as well. Most active among organized labor were the United Steelworkers of America, the Oil, Chemical and Atomic Workers Union and the United Mine Workers. The ensuing union lobbying and public information effort on behalf of the OSH Act was without precedent in U.S. history.

Within this milieu of ferment, a conservative president such as Richard Nixon could only hope to channel existing energies in a direction that might prove beneficial to his political fortunes. Preventing the passage of a health and safety law was simply out of the question when he assumed office in 1969. Such a law was, by then, high on the list of congressional priorities. And Nixon, it should be remembered, was the first new president in over a century to win office without his party controlling at least one house of Congress. His interest in maintaining his political legitimacy, then, dictated that he not oppose the inevitable. Moreover, Nixon was ambivalent about the legacy of New Deal and Great Society programs. While certainly conservative on many issues, he harbored animosity toward much of big business and what he considered the "Eastern establishment," and he also longed to be thought of as a "modern man."[6] As political scientist Charles Noble has argued, "Although President Nixon appeared to be an opponent of the welfare state at the time [of debate over the OSH Act], his administration oversaw what can only be perceived, in retrospect, as the second phase of the Great Society."[7]

Nixon's options were further limited by the general lack of a coherent business strategy to deal with the prospect of an OSH Act.[8] Rather than taking a leading role in crafting a piece of legislation to suit their needs, businesses of all sizes generally opposed the statute as unfairly weighted toward supplementing the power of organized labor. With capital unwilling to accept an expansive role for the Department of Labor in the health and safety area, they forfeited their chance to guide the outcome of legislative negotiations. In addition, here was no leading business organization to champion the cause of reform from the perspective of "enlightened" capitalists, as the corporate liberal variant of instrumental theories of the state would posit.[9] Thus, the task of articulating the prime capitalist response to the law was left to the U.S. Chamber of Commerce, whose shrill, reactionary laissez-faire rhetoric was out of step with the prevailing ethos of responsible public policy. Business disorganization left Nixon with no credible group of industry allies upon which to rest a case for an alternative approach to the issue.

For his part, President Nixon did propose three different versions of the bill which would have been much more favorable to the interests of employers than the version which ultimately passed. White House efforts centered on the strategy of dividing the authority over health and safety matters so that the Labor Department would not be unduly strengthened, and keeping provisions of workers' rights to a minimum. In this sense, the Nixon administration tried to mobilize the state to perform a coordinative function that business could not pull off collectively. But his attempts did not bear fruit. A strong version of the OSH Act finally passed, with the Labor Department obtaining the standard-setting and enforcement powers most conservatives had feared. Responding to what his Secretary of Labor termed "a new national passion, passion for environmental improvement," Nixon signed the landmark bill on December 29, 1970, hailing it as an example of "the American system at its best."[10]

The bill itself stands as the first comprehensive federal effort to deal with workplace safety and health. It is far-reaching, even potentially radical—depending on how it is interpreted and the vigor of its enforcement—in its provision of a universal right to a safe and healthful workplace.[11] Intended to "assure safe and healthful working conditions for working men and women," the act makes it the "general duty" of every employer to "furnish to each of his employees employment and a place of employment which are free from recognized hazards that are causing or are likely to cause death or serious physical harm to his employees."[12] In the bitterly contested health area, the law goes as far as saying that in setting health standards dealing with toxic materials or other harmful agents, OSHA "shall set the standard which most adequately assures, to the extent feasible, on the basis of the best available evidence, that no employee will suffer material impairment of health or functional capacity even if such employee has regular exposure to the hazard dealt with by such standard for the period of his working life."[13]

The law establishes a tripartite institutional apparatus to meet its goals. OSHA, located in the Labor Department, promulgates rules, sets safety and health standards, and oversees enforcement. It is the organization that has the most power and has drawn the most criticism. Its research arm is the National Institute for Occupational Safety and Health (NIOSH), located in the Department of Health, Education, and Welfare (now called Health and Human Services). The third body, the independent Occupational Safety and Health Review Commission (OSHRC), adjudicates all disputed enforcement actions. The law also provides for a vast expansion of employee rights, including the right to participate in workplace inspections and standard setting, and the right to have access to information about potential safety and health dangers.

Writing more than a dozen years removed from the heady days of regulatory explosion, Herbert Stein, chairman of Nixon's Council of Economic Advisers from 1972–74, views the passage of the act as an example of governmental excess. He attributes the administration's inability to moderate the scope and expense of such social regulations to the momentum of "a tide of Congressional demagoguery and sentimentality plus bureaucratic zeal," contending that "the juggernaut of environmental regulation proved not to be controllable by the Nixon administration."[14] His words implicitly attest to the power of social movements to pressure the state for concessions on important issues. Nixon surely was constrained in many ways. But he also used passage of the act to help his chances of siphoning off the support of labor unions and workers from its traditional home in the Democratic party. This blue-collar affiliation with the Democrats was viewed by some analysts at the time as soft, and Nixon quite consciously set out to include workers, considered to be conservative on many social issues, within his "silent majority." Therefore, the OSH Act had a positive political side for the president; it was not simply a grudging concession to popular pressure.

Moreover, few observers, least of all Richard Nixon, foresaw the economic crisis of 1973–75 on the horizon. In 1970, concern for the overall health of the U.S. economy was not as salient as other social and foreign policy issues. The public and politicians generally assumed the economy could support additional regulatory measures. The argument that social regulation constitutes a substantial impediment to economic growth did not serve as a major organizing tool of OSHA opponents. All of this changed, of course, as the economy experienced sustained downturn, the recession of 1974–75, and the onset of the previously unheard of phenomenon of stagflation.[15] As the unprecedented long wave of postwar expansion came to a rather abrupt halt—dramatized by the oil price shock, but manifested in numerous other developments of lesser visibility—government and corporate leaders began to rethink the issue of social regulation. The perspective that emerged reflected the roughly mid-decade shift to the right in the balance of political forces.[16] Corporate capital and policy planning organizations initiated a campaign to fight excessive social regulation as a costly, burdensome, irrational way to achieve public policy goals. Calls for "deregulation" have proliferated during the last decade. Economic decline thus afforded big business the opportunity to mount the kind of coherent attack on social regulation that it lacked from 1968–70.

Here a digression is needed to note the important distinction between two kinds of activities that are often placed together in the category "government regulation:" economic and social regulations.[17] *Economic* regulation involves an attempt by the state to stabilize market conditions within a given industry. Most such efforts to rationalize market behavior—through regulation of prices, rationalization of competition between firms, reduction of risk and the creation of a more predictable market environment—occured before the 1970s. The Interstate Commerce Commission of 1887, the first such agency, was a regulatory program aimed at the railroad industry. The Civil Aeronautics Board, the Federal Communications Commission and regulation of the airline and banking industries are all examples of economic regulation. Often such market-smoothing measures were welcomed by, if not substantially written by, businessmen. In the context of economic regulation, then, the call for *deregulation* means either partial reduction, complete withdrawal, or rewriting of government regulatory activity.[18] Often the "regulated" industry will oppose deregulation because it will hurt the market position of its leading firms by increasing competition.

Social regulation, by comparison, seeks to alter the non-market behavior of corporations, notably to correct for market failures or "externalities" of production, such as air or water pollution, or unsafe working conditions. Unlike economic regulations, social regulations cut across industry lines, restricting the freedom of large numbers of different businesses to injure third parties (workers and consumers, for example). They grew out of a sense of fairness and justice, to achieve social objectives. Here government is involved in the production process itself, affecting a firm's production and investment decisions. Such regulations invade the terrain of the capitalist firm and are widely seen by companies as an unwarranted invasion of privacy. In the context of social regulation, although the call for "deregulation" is heard, the more common charge is regulatory excess or *overregulation*. Virtually no one would publicly advocate the elimination of EPA or OSHA. But the claim that government has overregulated in these areas is common, to both political parties and to both liberals and conservatives. And strategies for reducing the alleged inflationary impact of social regulations— which could be termed "social deregulation" or, more humorously "de-overregulation"—are now routinely received with favor by businessmen and politicians.[19]

Within the overregulation thesis, the cost of social regulations has become a convenient scapegoat for the overall decline in the performance of the economy. The cost of regulation as a major obstacle to economic growth is, at best, a spurious claim, which will be examined in greater detail later. A more likely cause of the intense hostility of business toward social regulations—and especially toward OSHA—lies in their nature as intrusions into property rights, their violation of the inner sanctum of business.[20] Economic crisis provided the condition for corporate capital to make OSHA a lightning rod for opposition to the whole array of social regulations enacted in the early 1970s. OSHA unified corporate thinking on this issue, helping to undermine, within changed economic circumstances, the basis of its support from the state. And because so much else had changed by mid-decade—organized labor, for example, has not won a significant legislative victory in the U.S. since the OSH Act—OSHA policy retrenchment became the order of the day. The constraints on the state had shifted over time from being primarily generated by the need to respond to social struggle, to being preoccupied with the functional provision of business profitability and confidence. Into this radically altered climate of economic uncertainty, corporate mobilization and labor defensiveness stepped Jimmy Carter.

The Carter presidency:
The internal tension

From the beginning of his presidency, Carter was of two minds on the issue of occupational safety and health regulations. On the one hand, he carried with him a desire to retain some degree of the traditional Democratic attachment to the concerns of organized labor. This included a commitment to enforcing the OSHA statute. As he remarked to a gathering of Labor Department employees in the first weeks of his administration:

> I think that of all the beneficial legislation that has been passed by the Congress in recent years, the one that has the best prospect of improving the lives of American workers and the one that had the most adverse acceptance has been the OSHA program.[21]

He went on to praise OSHA as "a great program."

On the other hand, having inherited an economy in trouble from a long-term growth standpoint, he wanted to please the business community and, in particular, allay their fears about the threat of inflation. In the early months of his term, Carter's remarks also reveal his ambivalence toward OSHA. "We need to have, though, some sensitive approach at the delivery end of the OSHA program," he continued in his talk cited above, stressing the need for "a minimum number of regulations" and a "maximum amount of common sense."[22] A few months later he decried as "unnecessary and burdensome" OSHA safety regulations implemented over the preceding seven years, saying that the agency would now "develop and enforce effective standards for occupational health without repeating the exesses of the past."[23] Controlling OSHA's regulatory excesses surfaced again as a theme in July of 1977 at a public meeting in Yazoo City, Mississippi, where he assured small businessmen that while the OSH Act is "a good piece of legislation," enforcement has at times gotten too fiesty. "It's important that in the working places we protect the health and safety of employees," he asserted, "but the OSHA program is going to extremes."[24] He illustrated the extremes with a story about overly detailed OSHA safety regulations for ladders and stools, concluding that the federal government ought to withdraw from such details and focus on the provision of occupational health. The president's early ambivalence toward OSHA would only increase as his presidency encountered mounting economic pressures.

In his attempt to reconcile these competing concerns Carter pursued a strategy of centralizing the regulatory process within the executive branch, where his economic advisers heavily influenced the regulatory process. This approach led to the formation of two distinct camps within the White House on questions of OSHA regulations. And these camps periodically warred over occupational safety and health policy decisions.[25] The internal administrative tension was played out between what I will call the *economic technocrats* and the *OSHA supporters*. Briefly put, the economic technocrats included members of such groups as the Council of Economic Advisers (CEA), the Council on Wage and Price Stability (CWPS), and the Office of Management and Budget (OMB), along with their informal working group known as the Regulatory Analysis Review Group (RARG). Greater regulatory cost-effectiveness was the goal of these agencies charged with assisting in the White House review process of regulatory oversight. In order to rationalize health and safety regulations, emphasis was placed on economic incentives for safety regulations, and increasing use of cost-benefit analysis as a general guide for health standard-setting.

OSHA supporters within the administration, on the other hand, included Secretary of Labor Ray Marshall and Carter's OSHA director, Eula Bingham. This alliance contended that the OSH Act does not call for cost-benefit analysis of any type and resolutely defended OSHA regulations, existing and proposed, against its use. Bingham, in particular, pushed for stronger standards, especially for occupational health, her field of expertise. As for safety, OSHA supported vigorous enforcement practices through such measures as more accident inspections of workplaces (both initial as well as follow-up inspections), greater fines for violations, and the like. However, in a concession to the economic technocrats, and to common sense, OSHA did eliminate about a thousand of the nitpicking safety standards for which it had been chided by business groups since its inception.

The internal discord between these two camps commenced in the spring of 1977 and continued throughout Carter's term. Before examining this tension in detail, though, some background on the debate over OSHA safety standards will help put the issue in perspective. The crux of the debate over occupational safety issues is a disagreement between those who favor the enforcement of safety standards and those stressing the use of an injury tax approach to economic rationality. This disagreement turns on the question of whether safety regulations or the unfettered market is best able to prevent disabling or deadly accidents.

In 1971 OSHA adopted en masse some 4,400 existing "national consensus standards" set by the American National Standards Institute. Previously viewed as merely a nuisance, incorporation into the OSH Act as "the word" on safety gave the ANSI standards enhanced visibility and importance. OSHA's critics did not hesitate to make an issue of the frivolous nature of some of these safety rules.[26] It is, after all, tempting to ridicule the 140-odd regulations pertaining to wood step ladders or specifications for the shape of toilet seats as needless government nitpicking. In defense of OSHA it can be said that the ANSI standards appeared to be an efficient, quick way for the agency to make its mark. Unnecessary standards could be weeded out later and more relevant safety rules could be promulgated as needed. Perhaps more important, though, was the political mileage OSHA derived from meeting organized labor's desire to actively involve safety inspectors to get tough with companies that fail to comply with baseline regulations.

The problem with the enforcement of safety standards has been that this approach has failed to significantly affect the industrial injury and death rate. Indeed, in OSHA's first few years of operation, the national job injury and death statistics actually rose, and it is difficult to find a correlation between OSHA's enforcement activities and changes in the injury statistics.[27] Labor's evaluation of OSHA's impact centered on the agency's lack of adequate numbers of inspectors and the low level of fines levied. This interpretation has some plausibility given that through 1975 OSHA had so few inspectors that the average employer could expect to see one every 66 years, and the average fine was only $25 per violation.[28] The deterrent effect of such meager efforts would appear minimal, and both the probability of inspection and size of fines has not risen appreciably. Recognizing such limits on OSHA's resources, supporters of safety standards have either pushed for higher budgets to finance more inspectors issuing stiffer penalties or, more commonly, advocated that the agency target its efforts on accident inspections and on "general schedule" (i.e. routine) inspections in high injury rate workplaces. This strategy is not without problems, however, for it still must ensure that fines are high enough to deter dangerous workplace organization and practices. Likewise, provision must be made to prevent employers from understating their injury statistics when OSHA devises its targeting scheme, since employer self-reporting is the basis for injury data.

Opponents of safety standards have noted the failure of injury and death trends to decline with a predictable "I told you so" attitude. They propose instead a system of injury taxes to provide incentives for firms to bear all the costs of accidents resulting from the production process. This is the familiar cry of the market approach to economic management—"internalize the externalities"—raising the marginal benefits of injury prevention by raising the costs of accidents.[29] American Enterprise Institute (AEI) economist Robert Smith, a leading critic of OSHA, advocates such an approach, viewing it as a way to achieve economic rationality, especially efficient resource allocation, while minimizing (if not obviating altogether) the weight of moral issues, trade-offs among policy objectives and distributional questions.[30]

However "natural" the injury tax appears, though, (natural, in the sense of being more market-like) it has several political drawbacks which underscore the tension between economic rationality and political feasibility. Organized labor has vehemently opposed injury taxes for fear that they would not supply enough incentive to prevent injuries, hence by implication some injuries will be allowed to occur. Labor leaders characterize such taxes as "a license to maim." Injury taxes might also replace a union's power to call in safety inspectors, and in nonunion plants they might lead employers to replace workers with bad accident records. In addition, unions see any weakening of mandatory standards and enforcement procedures as an encouragement to favor risk-taking workers over risk-averse workers, an ethically questionable practice. Ironically, many businessmen also are wary of injury taxes, noting that once established tax rates could be subject to politically-motivated fluctuation, perhaps becoming a source of general revenue rather than a method internalizing social costs. One final argument against tax plans highlights the potential they have for engendering a layer of government bureaucracy to monitor corporate compliance with injury reporting requirements. While such monitoring would be necessary for any serious tax plan —given the motivation to fudge occupational accident reporting, inherent in the microeconomic "free-rider" problem—it also defeats one of the purposes of such market measures, namely getting the government "off the backs" of business.[31]

The stakes involved in the dispute within the Carter White House over these kinds of occupational safety issues were evident in the first internal flare-up, which occurred as a result of a May 27, 1977 memorandum to the president on OSHA reform. Signed by Charles Schultze, chairman of the CEA, Stuart Eizenstat, director of Carter's Domestic Policy Staff, and OMB director Bert Lance, the memo calls for "major changes" in OSHA, arguing that "serious consideration should be given to totally eliminating most *safety* regulations and replacing them with some form of economic incentives."[32] While the ostensible reason for the elimination of safety standards was to free OSHA resources for use in tackling health problems, an OMB issue paper attached to the memo made it clear that the economic advisers were calling for retrenchment in that area as well, of which more below.

The memo, which Carter accepted in its entirety, provides clearer reasons why the technocrats saw OSHA reform as a top priority for the new administration, the primary one being the link between OSHA reform and the broader effort to apply economic incentives to all social regulatory agencies. This link meant that OSHA reform would not be confined to the purview of the Labor Department. "Social regulations have pervasive impact on the economy," the memo continues, "and those concerned with economic policy and your anti-inflation program should be involved."[33] Noting that OSHA supporters would be concerned, if not outraged, by the proposed "reform" measure— which included a recommendation to establish an interagency taskforce on OSHA reform—Schultze and others stressed the importance of keeping foremost in mind the growing perception of the agency as an economic burden.

> OSHA is, as you know, the leading national symbol of over-regulation; not to act decisively would be perceived outside the labor movement as a retreat from your commitment to major regulatory reform.[34]

Ironically, for the economic technocrats the *perception* of OSHA was as crucial as the agency's actual impact on the economy. The credibility of Carter's reform program as a major component of his strategy for economic growth was at stake. OSHA had, in short, enormous symbolic value. It was a symbol aimed at securing business confidence—a symbol of the administration's determination to fight inflation and create prosperity.

This frontal challenge to one of OSHA's principle areas of interest as not presented as an attack on the agency. Rather it was couched in terms of making the agency more cost efficient. Nonetheless, it generated immense internal conflict, which eventually became public when someone in the Labor Department leaked the memo to the press. The administration devoted considerable time and energy to damage control in the ensuing months.[35] The primary objection to the "reform" campaign of the economic technocrats was its suggestion that OSHA rely in large part on stiffening payment of compensation to injured workers as a means of motivating employers to provide safe workplaces. Such incentive plans place the active prevention of injuries in a secondary position, and have all the afore-mentioned problems associated with injury taxes as well.

It was, of course, coincidental that while the Carter administration was taking its lumps (mainly in July) over the OSHA reform strategy, the American Enterprise Institute was busy preparing the premier issue (July-August, 1977) of its bimonthly journal *Regulation*, a publication which would provide a forum for the very ideas that Carter was finding so controversial. The AEI was a leading conservative policy planning organization in the coordination of the business case against OSHA, helping to create a climate receptive to the corporate perspective on the relationship between government and economy.[36] *Regulation* was one of AEI's carefully conceived tools for use in this ideological offensive against social regulations, an offensive fought within industry, government, academia and the mass media in the name of liberating market capitalism. Given its ideology, the journal more appropriately might have been titled *Deregulation*. As we will see, President Reagan selected many of his top economic advisers from the ranks of the AEI and *Regulation's* staff.

It is revealing to point out that Carter's economic technocrats—above all Schultze—supported much of AEI's overregulation argument. The organization even excerpted in *Regulation* Schultze's paean to the free-market, his Brookings Institution study *The Public Use of Private Interest*, in which he opines that "Market-like arrangements not only minimize the need for coercion as a means of organizing society; they also reduce the need for compassion, patriotism, brotherly love, and cultural solidarity as motivating forces behind social improvement."[37] This happy thought accords well with the economic ethics of the Reagan administration, whose views the Carter economic advisers foreshadowed. While there were important differences between the two administrations, there were substantial and fundamental areas of agreement. The major difference was the existence of genuine supporters of OSHA within the Carter White House to counterbalance the views of the technocrats.

Reaction to the May 27 memo eventually subsided and few concrete results ever came from it. The Interagency Task Force on Workplace Safety and Health that it recommended—approved by Carter and co-chaired by Labor Secretary Marshall and OMB director James T. McIntyre—produced recommendations (released in the summer of 1978) that had little real impact on OSHA.[38] For the remainder of the year, relative calm prevailed on the OSHA front. The agency did propose its comprehensive carcinogens policy in the fall, but the major criticism of it from the Council on Wage and Price Stability and the Regulatory Analysis and Review Group came in 1978. By the end of 1977 a relaxed Carter thus could stand before a meeting of the Business Council and joke: "I understand this is where I was supposed to come to restore business confidence."[39] Peppered with deferential, almost fawning, remarks to the leaders of corporate America, Carter's address focused on conveying his personal sense of confidence in the course of the nation, and especially the economy. He stressed the "remarkable harmony" within the various departments of the government, singling out Charles Schultze as a trusted private voice on economic affairs. And as if to underscore the theme of harmony and confidence, the president brought along OSHA director Eula Bingham to make the point that his administration was reducing "unnecessary paperwork and regulations and intrusion into the business lives by Government." The president added that "Dr. Bingham has brought forward revisions in those administrative procedures that have helped to remove this burden on your shoulders."[40] OSHA and other regulations were being pared back, the administration was in harmony on its basic goals, the economy was experiencing "no serious or major imbalances or distortions"—all in all it was, officially, a rosy picture for the president's first year in office.

If the president seemed to forget the contentious internal debate over OSHA reform, he would not be afforded that luxury in 1978. In March of that year he signed Executive Order 12044, codifying the shift toward emphasizing increased use of cost-benefit analysis as a general guide for regulatory standard-setting—most importantly, for this study, in the area of occupational health.[41] Entitled "Improving Government Regulations," the order required an assessment of the economic impact of regulations because, as Carter put it, "we want to be sure that they don't contribute to inflationary costs." Specifically, E.O. 12044 mandated that all new "significant regulations" be proposed only after assurance could be given to White House reviewers that alternative approaches had been carefully considered and the "least burdensome" of the acceptable alternatives had been selected. Moreover, regulatory analysis was required for all regulations projected to have "an annual effect on the economy of $100 million or more."

The intent of this regulatory centralization was to ensure that new regulations be cost-effective. The administration did not explicitly call for cost-benefit tests as the method of regulatory analysis until one year later in proposing its Regulation Reform Act of 1979.[42] But cost-benefit criteria were used as standard operating procedure. As Kitty Bernick, Assistant Director of the Domestic Policy Staff, described the use of such analysis:

> The idea is that the agency [OSHA] should be informed of the costs and benefits of its actions but not that the substantive statute should be overruled by such analysis. Our point is that cost-benefit analysis is a useful tool, but it is not the only factor the decisionmaker can consider.[43]

The OMB was nominally in charge of overseeing the White House review process, but in practice the agency delegated responsibility for the program to a rather loose coalition of CWPS, RARG and the CEA, with OMB providing input on occasion. This group, it should be noted, had no veto power over proposed regulations. But the implementation of its oversight activity did spur the internal administration battle once again, this time extending the debate over economic incentives and the appropriateness of cost-benefit techniques to the health area, a much more heated arena of conflict than that of job safety. While this conflict arose over health standards for benzene, arsenic, DBCP, acrylonitrile and lead, it was the controversy surrounding the proposed revision of the cotton dust standard that received the most attention.

The dispute over cotton dust generally was indicative of the others, except for the *intensity* of hard feelings it invoked. Its inclusion here draws attention to the level of in-fighting and bureaucratic maneuvering within the institutional confines of the executive branch—involving conflict which eventually worked its way up to President Carter himself. Conventional accounts of the presidency would be likely to focus exclusively on this intra-institutional discord, drawing lessons about the personal and political impediments to the smooth implementation of the president's program. The need for better management of the policy process is the kind of insight we could expect to be derived from such a mainstream inquiry. While there may be some value in such institutional, process-oriented insights from the cotton dust story, conventional accounts omit the more important *structural* point that, as we will see, the imperative of economic growth eventually consumes other domestic policy agenda items, in this case OSHA policy, relegating the administrative give-and-take to a secondary (though not unimportant) status.

The cotton dust case revolved around OSHA's plan to release its final standard on permissible levels of exposure to cotton dust, which causes a respiratory disease kown as byssinosis or "brown lung." First proposed in 1976, OSHA's standard was subject to a lengthy period of public comment and written opinions on how best to achieve reductions of cotton dust concentration in workplaces in all segments of the industry—ginning, milling, yarn and fabric manufacturing, and waste processing.[44] OSHA's final standard was to be a revised version of this original standard. In the late May memorandum to the president, Eizenstat and his Domestic Policy Staff aide Simon Lazarus warned him rather starkly of the consequences of endorsing a revised cotton dust standard. If a version suitable to the economists was endorsed, organized labor and other OSHA advocates "will explode." Mentioning Labor Department rumors of Bingham's "vague resignation threats," Eizenstat and Lazarus asserted that in the event of the promulgation of a more cost-effective option, "the resulting propaganda—alleging that you care more about cotton industry profits than workers' health—could be ugly."[45] Yet the alternative, from the economic technocrats' perspective, was worse: "On the other hand, permitting OSHA to promulgate could damage the credibility of your anti-inflation commitment and of Charlie's [Schultze] Review Group process."[46] This type of linkage would surface repeatedly on this issue.

By June of 1978 the disagreement between the OSHA supporters and the economic technocrats had narrowed to one over the cost of reducing cotton dust concentration in the ambient air of workplaces in just the yarn-producing segment of the industry. In brief, Labor Secretary Marshall and Bingham favored mandating plant-wide *engineering controls* (such as ventilation equipment), while Schultze and Eizenstat argued for *performance standards* that set target goals for dust reduction to be met in any way the industry saw fit. In practice, Schultze admitted, performance standards would allow heavy reliance on personal protective equipment, namely respirators worn by employees. The lone virtue of respirators is their low cost. Indeed, virtually everyone agrees that they are the most cost-effective way to reduce exposure to airborne pollutants. The problem is, as Marshall and Bingham contended, an enormous body of evidence exists to show that, for a variety of reasons, respirators are demonstrably ineffective in keeping harmful substances out of workers' lungs.[47] The technocrats' response was a very vague "that can be worked out." For them the bottom line was that the proposed standard's reliance on engineering controls confronted industry with excessive costs, placing a "major burden of uncertainty on the industry." And perhaps most important for Schultze, as head of both the CEA and RARG, "the credibility of our anti-inflation and regulatory reform effort requires some modification—even if only a modest one—in the draft OSHA [cotton dust] regulations."[48]

Once again sensing the *symbolic* value of OSHA regulations to Carter's larger economic program, Schultze decided to challenge the agency's new cotton dust standard. It was, to him, a matter of preserving the mettle of the administration's anti-inflation commitment. Unable to convince Marshall to modify the OSHA regulation in a direction favorable to the position of those engaged in the regulatory review process, a meeting was called for June 7 to take the issue directly to Carter. In attendance were the president, Vice President Mondale, Schultze, Eizenstat, Bingham and Marshall.

An exhaustive accounting of this important meeting is not necessary. The upshot is that after hearing Bingham deliver what Eizenstat describes as an "impassioned discussion" of engineering standards, President Carter "much to our surprise ... seemed to embrace this alternative and to push Charlie [Schultze] to accept it."[49] The exact degree of warmth of Carter's embrace immediately became an issue, however. Participants seem to agree that the president suggested a compromise plan that would have phased in a new cotton dust standard in two stages over a four-year period. But after that, disagreement and misunderstanding abounded. Schultze interpreted the meeting as resulting in a compromise regulation which, while requiring engineering controls to be installed on an industry-wide basis at the end of the four-year period, would have allowed firms to receive an extension beyond four years for economic reasons. More importantly, he thought there had been consensus on allowing firms to develop performance standards using alternate means of protecting workers (eg. respirators) if they could demonstrate their plan was at least as effective as more costly engineering controls. This would, of course, be a vindication of Schultze's orientation toward health regulations.

Bingham and Marshall, by contrast, interpreted the meeting as vindication for their position. They judged Carter's reaction to their proposals as a "reversal" of his earlier stand and a "victory" for them—and said so publicly at a post-meeting press briefing. The newspapers played the story as a major Labor Department victory and a "turnabout" on the president's part, with him "apparently reversing an earlier decision." One account of the affair, appearing in the *New York Times*, carried this passage that particularly upset the White House staff:

> As for the inflationary impact of regulations, Dr. Bingham commented that "my ignorance of economics is comparable to the ignorance of the Council of [sic] Wage and Price Stability and the Council of Economic Advisers of industrial safety and health." She added that the Occupational Health and Safety Law mandated the protection of workers and said nothing about inflation.[50]

Acting on her understanding of the June 7 meeting, Bingham two days later signed an new cotton dust regulation which Schultze and Eizenstat viewed as in "flat contradiction" of the principles agreed to. They were angry at provisions for OSHA to cite firms for noncompliance before the four years had expired, the difficulty of firms obtaining a waiver under the rules, and the lack of a provision for firms to show they have an equally effective alternative to engineering standards. They informed the president that they "consider this a flagrant and deliberate attempt by OSHA to frustrate an express agreement reached directly with you."[51]

From the perspective of the White House review team, the cotton dust decision was an absolute disaster. As Eizenstat expressed it to Carter's chief administrative assistant Hamilton Jordan:

> The way in which this has now come out makes it look like the Administration is not serious about fighting inflationary regulations .... Barry Bosworth [CWPS director] is depressed about what this means for the regulatory process—as is Charlie. It will make everyone less likely to tackle these tough regulatory issues in light of the results of this debacle.[52]

Surveying the damage done, Lazarus wrote to Eizenstat of the importance of "modifying the perception that the President reversed himself," and of "re-establishing CEA's and the White House's authorization to review this and other regulations." Clearly for these advisers, the legitimacy of the White House review effort was on the line. And the first step toward regaining that legitimacy was to dispell "the notion of discord within the administration that OSHA has generated."[53] This notion proved difficult to dispell.

In fact, in December of 1978, Bingham was still something of a loose cannon on the Carter ship, this time in regard to OSHA's lead standard. Speaking before a United Steelworkers' conference on lead regulations, the OSHA director reemphasized her personal commitment to stringent workplace health rules. Executive branch insiders were upset about her remark that "Marshall and I have been through the palace guard once to see him [Carter] about a standard [for cotton dust] and we are ready to do it again."[54] She was especially critical of economists—the strong implication is administration economists—who argue that health and safety regulations are inflationary. Suggesting that the lead standard was being delayed within the administration, she commented, "These economists never look at the working men and women I look at." "I prize men and women more highly than the GNP," she added, charging that many industrial leaders and economists "are complacent about cancer in the workplace." Bingham concluded by urging the unionists to lobby Washington and the administration to "free the lead standard." Roughly one year after Carter spoke to the Business Council about the harmony within his staff, discord reigned over the relationship between OSHA regulations and economic vitality.

Despite Bingham's convictions, the end of 1978 marked a major domestic policy shift for Carter's presidency. As structural analysis highlights, his presidency henceforth was held hostage to the unsuccessful quest to promote economic vitality and restore business confidence. Therefore, while OSHA did successfully fend off the economic technocrats' challenge to the cotton dust standard, the agency actually issued no *new* health standards after January of 1978 and existing proposals continued to be subject to the scrutiny of economic cost-effectiveness tests, often with more success than in the cotton dust case. In effect, Bingham and OSHA won the battle but lost the war, a war whose importance eclipses the specifics of administrative turf battles.

OMB and CEA tightened up regulatory review considerably after 1978, seriously blunting OSHA's earlier activism. As Charles Noble has pointed out:

> Particularly after 1978, OSHA found it difficult to set new health rules or intensify enforcement. But the shift in agency strategy is clear in standard setting and, to a somewhat lesser extent, in enforcement.[55]

The shift toward greater use of White House reivew of regulations and overall retrenchment in OSHA activity was not prompted so much by the power of the technocrats' arguments, as by rising fear over economic downturn. Specifically, by 1979 Carter's concern over economic growth, especially as threatened by rising inflation, became a major domestic policy preoccupation, lasting the duration of the second half of his term. Noble points out that there is a strong correlation between changes in the business cycle and changes in White House regulatory policy. As the economy worsens, regulatory initiatives become harder to justify. This relationship is confirmed by the Carter experience. Business leaders were making the case that regulation was hampering economic growth. In the new economic context of the 1970s businessmen considered it a cost of production no longer affordable.

Restoring economic growth and fighting inflation are ubiquitous objectives in administration documents and public pronouncements of the period. The level of administration anxiety over the economy is clear in the words of Treasury Secretary Michael Blumenthal, who wrote to the president in late May of

1979 that attention needed to be focused on "how best to sell publicly a policy of long-term economic austerity."[56] He attached to his presidential memorandum another memo he wrote for the Economic Policy Group Steering Group, in which he outlined his thoughts on how to accomplish this task. Basically, Blumenthal saw Carter's entire presidency, and his re-election chances, hinging on convincing the public to accept "continuation of tough and austere macroeconomic policies, requiring sacrifices by many." He strongly believed that Americans would swallow the bitter pill of deferring liberal spending programs, deferring expensive environmental and health and safety regulations, and other (eight in all) painful executive economic decisions if a program of economic austerity was infused with a spirit and an exciting theme "that engages the imagination and deep convictions of the people." And he offered the idea of America's economic preeminance in the world as such a theme. America could be number one again, he reasoned, if a "frank appeal to national pride" was carefully crafted, "creating genuine excitement and commitment for economic policies that would otherwise cause him [Carter] great political problems." He elaborated on his plan to put Carter on the political offensive "as a responsible visionary":

> This new approach attempts to lend shape, color, and excitement to the general interest—by associating it with widespread anxieties about our economic position in the world and about our productivity and economic discipline at home. A "strong economy" has, I believe, the same political potential as a "strong defense."[57]

Blumenthal was dismissed as Treasury Secretary only a few months after writing these words—in the wake of Carter's July retreat to Camp David and subsequent fabled "crisis of confidence" television address.[58] But his thoughts on the psychology of damage control—getting the body politic enthused about austerity—perfectly capture the domestic dilemmas confronting Carter as the economy headed into a tailspin. Public confidence, as well as business confidence, was waning. Eizenstat echoed Blumenthal's strong economy/strong defense theme in a confidential memorandum to President Carter in March of 1980, at a time when, coincidently, the Labor Department and organized labor were reduced to trying to defend OSHA against a series

of bills in Congress that would have made the most dramatic cuts
ever in the agency's jurisdication.

In his memo, Eizenstat warns that "we truly are on the verge
of an economic crisis which is as severe for the country as the
foreign policy crises you have been dealing with over the last
several months."[59] Citing a "growing national sense that things
are out of control," he urges Carter to "get out and let people
know *you* are the general in personal charge of this war"—the war
being the war against inflation and general economic malaise.
Like Blumenthal, Eizenstat believed the psychological dimension
to economic decline was crucial. If people expected routine rises
in the inflation rate, they would get them. Carter, it seems, needed
to break the psychic grip of hard times through judicious exercise
of presidential leadership.

As we know, the results of the 1980 election, held in the midst
of a recession, in part attest to his failure on this score. The nation's
economic indicators by election day were predominantly ominous,
continuing the trend of the previous year and a half.[60] Inflation
was hovering around 10 percent, driven in part by the second
oil price shock of the decade which saw OPEC double petroleum
prices in 1979. Moreover, unemployment had risen to more than
7.5 percent, real wages had dropped almost 3 percent from a year
earlier, and interest rates, fueled by the Federal Reserve's vacil-
lating tight money policy, were gyrating upward. Within this
overall context it is no wonder that OSHA initiatives of all kinds,
for the most part, languished in Carter's latter years. They were
overwhelmed by the force of the structural imperative to maintain
economic growth in the face of conditions mitigating against it.

The Reagan administration: Unity in opposition

President Carter established the centralization of regulatory policy
as the administrative norm. This effort was not a smooth one;
there was a certain contradictory nature to it as different wings
of the administration worked at cross-purposes. Yet while not
given the legal authority to single-handedly squelch new
regulations, the White House reviewers were able to have a
substantial impact on the regulatory environment. When coupled
with the overriding problem of economic crisis, the impact was

nothing short of chilling. It should come as no surprise, then, that things got tougher for OSHA after 1981, since Ronald Reagan was welcomed to Washington by an economy in even worse shape than the one Carter had inherited. As a candidate for president, Reagan had expressed his relaxed concept of OSHA—quoted at the outset of the chapter but worth repeating—in these terms:

> My idea of an OSHA would be if government set up an agency that would do research and study how things could be improved, and industry could go to it and say, 'We have a problem here and we seem to lose more people by accident in this particular function. Would you come and look at our plant and then come back and give us a survey of what should be done?[61]

Notice here the omission of any notion of workers or organized labor actively using OSHA as a resource to protect their interests, although the law expressly establishes workers' right to "safe and healthful" workplaces. Notice also the passive role for the nation's primary guardian of workplace safety and health. On this reading of OSHA's purpose, industry assumes the active role, going to the agency when it suits the needs of business. This is part of what came to be known as Reagan's "voluntary" approach to OSHA. There is a peculiarly uneven quality to his notion of voluntarism, though, as one safety specialist has pointed out:

> No one in the Reagan administration has ever proposed a "voluntary" approach when it comes to food stamp fraud or illegal immigration. "Law and order" in these areas is a brisk, menacing enterprise that has thousands of federal enforcers vigilantly patrolling their turf for violations of the law.[62]

To understand why the situation is so radically different when it comes to OSHA enforcement, we can begin by looking at Reagan's very first address to a joint session of Congress. There he outlined the basic components of his economic program that remained relatively unchanged throughout his presidency.

In his February 18, 1981 speech outlining his economic recovery program, President Reagan attempted to sum up the nation's dire economic predicament. High on his list of culprits was overregulation, "a mass of regulations imposed on the shopkeeper, the farmer, the craftsman, professionals and major industry that is estimated to add $100 billion to the price of things we buy and it reduces our ability to produce."[63] The result of this "virtual explosion in Government regulation during the past decade," has been "higher prices, higher unemployment, and lower productivity growth." It was quite a damning indictment. He went on to make "a far-reaching program of regulatory relief" one of the four pillars of his recovery package.

Reagan's speech is instructive for at least two reasons. First, he prominently cited the figure of $100 billion for the costs of regulations and has done so on numerous occasions. This figure—sometimes increased to upwards of $115 billion, or even $126 billion—is the handiwork of Murray Weidenbaum, a leading AEI economist and the first chairman of the CEA under Reagan, who calculated the number from a 1976 study. Weidenbaum's purpose was to charge that regulations in general are too costly, and that social regulations in particular make up the lion's share (roughly four-fifths) of the excessive cost. Neither charge has stood the test of close scrutiny. Many subsequent analyses have exposed these calculations as deeply flawed, for reasons which include the double counting of costs, failure to distinguish between different types of regulations, and the use of a constant multiplier to estimate costs into future years.[64] His work on regulatory costs is of dubious real value, beyond its reflection of his ideology. More telling, his figure is derived without any regard for the benefits of social regulations, as even *Business Week*—a publication hardly unsympathetic to Weidenbaum's ideas—had to concede. All costs and no benefits—that is the view of social regulations espoused by Weidenbaum and President Reagan. And that the facts speak otherwise has not deterred them from continuing to use this fabricated claim. Given Weidenbaum's penchant for less than rigorous economic analysis, perhaps this should be expected. After all, it was his "visceral computer" that concocted the mendacious "rosy scenario" economic forecast in 1981, exposed as a fraud by one of its principle perpetrators, former OMB director David Stockman.[66]

The second important element of Reagan's talk was its insistence that rampant regulation was responsible for a host of macroeconomic ills. This claim is an outgrowth of the mid-decade mobilization of business against social regulations. It reflects a strategy shift on the part of corporations and many think tanks, such as AEI.

As mentioned earlier, the OSH Act and related statutes originally were justified by the *micro*economic principle that the market failed to hold individual firms accountable for all the costs of production, such as the "external" costs of pollution or hazardous work conditions. Regulation was viewed as a vehicle for inducing companies to bear all the costs of doing business, and disputes revolved around different methods of providing such inducement. In other words, some regulation could help make the market fairer.

Increasingly, however, OSHA opponents deployed the *macro*economic argument that the law fueled a greater kind of market failure—that it inhibited the operation of the market *system* as a whole. Thus, OSHA threatened the general interest of society, not just the narrow interests of a given firm, or industry.[67] The Carter administration made this kind of argument in its insistence on the connection between OSHA regulations and rising inflation. But the Reagan economists associated the law with a much wider variety of maladies, the list being almost limitless. And it did so with dizzying frequency, with the assertion of regulations as manifestations of the evils of "Big Government" appearing in seemingly every domestic speech the president delivered. But as with Weidenbaum's cost figure, the connection between OSHA and broader economic decline is substantially overdrawn.[68] This is why it is essential to point out the *symbolic* value of White House regulatory reforms, as I did with the Carter administration. As a symbol of overregulation, OSHA's impact is enormous; as a substantive, quantifiable drain on economic growth, its impact is considerably more modest. Yet again, this has not stopped OSHA's detractors from making their case against the agency. Some presidency scholars also have accepted the Reagan position uncritically.[69]

With regard specifically to OSHA, President Reagan's attempt to remedy the problem of overregulation with his "voluntary" approach has taken shape in the form of the pursuit of a "cooperative" regulatory strategy. His first, and longest-standing (of the three), OSHA director Thorne Auchter proclaimed the advent of this new attitude to the New York Chamber of Commerce and Industry in September of 1981:

> OSHA has always been in an adversarial position. This adversarial spirit has hampered the effective functioning of the agency long enough. . . . The OSHA of today is a cooperative regulator.[70]

Raymond Donovan, Reagan's first Secretary of Labor, underscored
this ongoing change of attitude at the agency in his submission
of *The President's Report on Occupational Safety and Health for 1982*,
stating that OSHA had "continued its campaign to change the
focus of the Agency from one of adversarial enforcement to one
of cooperative assistance."[71] In practice this orientation has been
"cooperative" in a double sense: OSHA has been cooperative
internally, in its relations with the economic technocrats of Reagan's
regulatory review team, while at the same time being cooperative
externally with the business community it seeks to unfetter from
government intrusions. Understanding the two dimensions of
OSHA's cooperativeness is the key to grasping the relationship
between Reagan and OSHA.

Reagan resolved the *internal* tension that plagued the Carter
administration by appointing an OSHA director who was openly
hostile to the program. This point cannot be overemphasized. As
head of the agency, Auchter's credentials as a small businessman,
whose company reportedly had many OSHA violations, were
a far cry from those of Eula Bingham, an eminent industrial
toxicologist. Whereas Bingham made clear from the outset her
desire to have OSHA and its research arm at NIOSH deeply probe
the dangers of occupational health hazards, Auchter began his
tenure at the agency by challenging its previous efforts in this
regard. Two of his initial acts upon assuming his post serve as
stark illustrations; both involve the health issue which proved
so contentious in the Carter administration—cotton dust.

First, he shocked organized labor by ordering the destruction
of 100,000 booklets pertaining to cotton dust because he found
the cover, showing a gravely ill textile worker, "offensive" and
"obviously favorable" to labor.[72] He justified his act of censorship
(which later included withholding distribution of several films
and slide shows pertaining to workers' health and safety rights)
by referring to his oft-stated desire to keep OSHA "neutral" with
regard to business and labor. For him, that meant espousing
market-oriented, laissez-faire ideology as the best way to provide
protection for the nation's workforce. It was the manifest failure
of this type of approach, of course, which led to the need for
an OSH Act in the first place. Nevertheless, such market
"neutrality" meshed well with the aims of the technocratic side
of the administration at OMB and the CEA, agencies which now

worked in relative harmony with their OSHA-Labor Department counterparts to promote deregulation.

Auchter's second major act complemented this attempt to reverse the "adversarial spirit" at OSHA. He threw the Supreme Court into disarray by issuing a "notice of proposed rulemaking" announcing that OSHA was disavowing its position against cost-benefit analysis in the cotton dust case—the textile industry's legal appeal of the Carter administration's 1978 cotton dust standard. In a highly unusual move, the OSHA chief pulled the government's lawyers off the case as they had argued it (along with union lawyers) two months earlier and instructed them to re-examine the cotton dust standard to "evaluate the feasibility and utility of relying on cost-benefit analysis in setting occupational health standards."[73] Auchter, in effect, asked the High Court not to decide the case and instead allow the Labor Department to reconsider it in light of President Reagan's new cost-benefit policy, thus switching the government's stance on cotton dust rules in the middle of the judicial proceeding. And while the court eventually ruled against the textile industry-Reagan administration position in June of 1981, upholding the Carter administration's OSHA standard, this specific decision has not prevented OSHA, OMB and other regulatory reviewers from embracing cost-benefit criteria generally as a major component of their campaign against overregulation.[74]

The Reagan administration's endorsement of cost-benefit analysis in the cotton dust case is symptomatic of its larger purpose in promoting economic analysis of regulations. Reagan fostered internal administrative cooperation most markedly by further centralizing executive oversight of OSHA and other social regulations, putting OMB in charge of White House review via Executive Order 12291 in February of 1981.[75] This measure went far beyond Carter's centralization effort, giving the OMB the power to rewrite or veto rules as they are being formulated. E.O. 12291 has as a general requirement the stipulation that "regulatory action shall not be undertaken unless the potential benefits to society for the regulation outweigh the potential costs to society." Only regulations "involving the least net cost to society" can be promulgated. The order also established a Task Force on Regulatory Relief, headed by Vice President George Bush, to assist OMB in weeding out "burdensome" regulations, monitor industry

views on regulatory matters, and urge executive agencies to cut
back certain regulations by requesting OMB to undertake regulatory reviews. In practice, though, OMB wielded much more
influence on OSHA matters, and the Task Force was eventually
disbanded.

Above all, the major outcome of the executive order was to
mandate strict cost-benefit analysis as an explicit *rule* for regulatory
decisions. This represented an important shift in emphasis: while
President Carter's executive order encouraged cost-benefit criteria
as a *guide* to analysis, President Reagan enshrined them as a rule
of operation.[76] CEA chairman Weidenbaum made the case for the
widespread use of cost-benefit analysis this way:

> Benefit-cost analysis is inherently a neutral concept, giving equal
> weight to a dollar of benefits as to a dollar of costs. Those who
> quiver at the thought of subjecting their favorite program to such
> analysis may know more than we do. Do they inherently fear that
> the regulatory activity would flunk the most elementary benefit-
> cost test?[77]

For some, Weidenbaum's words might have an air of reason-
ableness at first blush. After all, who could oppose a "neutral"
concept. And if one does oppose the technique, perhaps they
are trying to hide something. On closer inspection, however, his
words can be seen as transparent ideology, pure and simple.

There are a host of problems associated with cost-benefit
analysis generally, and most of them belie the claim that it is
merely a neutral technique. One major area of uncertainty
involves the problem of how to quantify the benefits of alternative
regulatory strategies. In the case of OSHA, this entails placing
a dollar value on human life or various lifesaving programs, in
order to determine of a level of "socially acceptable risk."
Economists have devised analytic techniques for determining
levels of socially acceptable risk, all of which use cost-benefit
calculation to impute dollar values to non-marketed things such
as human life. Perhaps the most widely accepted of such
measurements is the "willingness-to-pay" criterion, which seeks
to gauge how much money a worker would be willing to pay for
marginal decreases in his or her exposure to a health hazard on
the job. However, this economic device is fraught with technical
and ethical ambiguity.[78]

In the first place, people typically are not fully informed about all the risks involved in such decisions. Secondly, the workers in question may not have alternative job prospects, throwing off any true measurement of their willingness. Third, willingness-to-pay assumes there is no difference between how people value certain things in private individual transactions and how they might value those same things in decisions for the larger public. Fourth, some people believe that to put a value on something cheapens its worth, and thus might claim that life has an intrinsic value that is priceless. Finally, to the extent that occupational health is viewed as a *right*, it may not be deemed socially acceptable to put a price on it, even if the costs outweigh the benefits. This point was driven home succinctly by a steelworker who commented at an OSHA hearing that the Emancipation Proclamation was not subjected to an inflationary impact statement.[79] For these reasons and others, the ambiguity surrounding efforts to determine acceptable risk cannot be clarified simply by the use of economic calculations.

Indeed, the uncertainties in the area of benefit calculation are so great that when the Congressional Office of Technology Assessment (OTA) studied various estimates for the implied value of a life, they found no fewer than a dozen. And they varied so widely that the choice of one over the others would itself be a highly political act, dramatically altering the outcome on the benefit side of the equation. Estimates are based on no greater certainty on the cost side of the equation either. Industry estimates of the cost of compliance with OSHA health regulations are notoriously exaggerated—the classic case being the chemical manufacturers' dire predictions of the imminent collapse of the industry if OSHA's standard for vinyl chloride was implemented in the early 1970s. Ultimately the regulation was adopted and the industry has since flourished, its predictions of economic ruin and technological infeasibility enormously overstated.[80]

All this is to say that cost-benefit analysis, far from being a neutral tool, easily can serve as a weapon with which corporations combat the often glaring need to clean up health hazards in the nation's workplaces. The Reagan administration aided this effort internally with its emphasis on the use of respirators as the cost-effective alternative to plant-wide engineering controls. The aforementioned inadequacies of respirators notwithstanding, they

remain the preferred method of compliance with OSHA health
standards for big business. James C. Miller III, co-director of the
AEI's Center for the Study of Government Regulations, a member
and subsequent chair of Reagan's OMB, and executive director
of the administration's Task Force on Regulatory Relief, expressed
his view of prevalent worker complaints about the inconvenience
and discomfort of respirators (among the *many* drawbacks of
them), this way: "Perhaps we should rename the agency the
Occupational Safety, Health and Comfort Administration."[81]
Auchter responded with similar disregard for the concerns of
workers: "Well, employers are asked to do things under the
government's safety and health act and under OSHA regulations
that are not always comfortable for them."[82] The equation of
monetary discomfort on the part of business with the physical
discomfort of workers displays a particularly callous attitude on
the part of Reagan technocrats and regulators. This is especially
true when, as was the case with the cotton dust standard, the
lives of an estimated 74,000 textile workers, at risk of contracting
brown-lung disease, are at stake.

In the final analysis, then, the cost-benefit criteria so beloved
by both the OSHA-Labor Department side and the economic
technocratic side of the Reagan administration served to augment
their conservative political agenda. As an economic tool of the
Reagan presidency, cost-benefit analysis was used to conceal
political ends behind reams of seemingly objective data. But the
objective appearance is an illusion. And the illusion has a cynical
hue when we consider that the Reagan technocrats at OMB saw
to it that the budget for NIOSH—as OSHA's research arm, the
one government agency capable of generating reliable, non-
corporate data for cost-benefit studies—was dramatically reduced
between 1981 and 1985.[83] This forces OSHA to rely even more
heavily in industry-dominated economic analysis at precisely the
time when a premium is being placed on cost-benefit analysis.
The conclusion reached by the OTA after an exhaustive review
of the literature on cost-benefit criteria and economic analysis in
regard to OSHA policy decisions thus seems especially salient
here:

> [W]here moral, political, and cultural values—not simply economic
> ones—are at stake, we need to make moral, political, and aesthetic
> judgments. Cost-benefit analysis does not replace these

"subjective" judgments with "objective" or "neutral" ones. Rather, it distorts or ignores the noneconomic values it cannot handle.[84]

Or as Mark Green bluntly put it during the Carter years, in words even more appropriate today, "Given the current state of economic art, mathematical cost-benefit analyses are about as neutral as voter literacy tests in the Old South."[85]

By increasing the use of cost-benefit analysis while tightening the centralization of OSHA policy in the executive branch, the president further insulated the policy process from outside pressures. As one analyst—who served as both Deputy Director of CWPS under Carter, and as a consultant to OSHA for Reagan—has favorably commented, "By reviewing regulations before they are formally proposed, [Reagan's] OMB can limit the role of external political actors." Along these lines he added, "the criteria being applied to new regulations will be less transparent and the possibilities of informed public participation more limited."[86] This essentially anti-democratic impulse—"negotiations between the White House and the [regulatory] agencies have gone underground"—jibes well with the president's larger strategy of isolating organized labor as a political force. Labor obviously has far less access to personnel and processes in OMB than it does in the Labor Department. Moreover, by subjecting OSHA regulations to greater economic rationality, the hope is that the introduction of new regulations will be inhibited.

The inhibition of new regulations was but one part of President Reagan's strategy for promoting *external* cooperation on the OSHA front, the second dimension of his cooperative approach. During his presidency, OSHA dramatically reduced its ability to do the job it was empowered to do, leaving business feeling good about cooperation, while labor feels concern for workers has been drastically slighted. As a leading agency on Reagan's oft-noted regulatory "hit list," OSHA has cut back in a variety of ways on the number of general schedule health and safety inspections, the number of follow-up inspections, the frequency and amount of fines levied for violations, and workers' right-to-know about information on occupational hazards.[87]

For instance, under Auchter the agency began exempting companies from inspections on the basis of their lost workday injury rate (called an LWDI—basically the injuries that result in days away from work and/or days of restricted work activity). If a company's LWDI falls below the national average for manufacturing industries, they are in effect guaranteed inspectors will not set foot inside. This is justified as a targeting program that rewards "safe" workplaces, even though "OSHA has never published any statistical study showing that an adequate relationship exists between lost workday injury rates and the hazardous conditions at a workplace."[88] Such "paper inspections," as they are called (they rely on examination of company injury logs), are fraught with pitfalls, not the least of which is their reliance on businesses to faithfully and truthfully record injury data. The incentive (and means) to fudge on these numbers has been noted earlier. But with a cooperative approach, such problems are not seriously considered.

Auchter also has championed the use of "informal conferences" during which OSHA area directors can reduce the severity of fines and citations and receive extensions on hazard abatement deadlines. While both inspection targeting and informal conferences were used with greater caution in Bingham's OSHA, under Reagan they have become mechanisms for avoiding the teeth of the agency. And attempts by Reagan's OSHA to claim credit for the decline in injury statistics during the first few years of the administration are overdrawn, if not cynical, given that slowdowns in economic growth are a well-established causal factor in injury rate declines, and the U.S. economy experienced a sustained drop in the business cycle from 1979 through 1983.[89]

Of a perhaps more serious nature in the area of external cooperation with the business community, OSHA has cut back on the promulagation of new health standards. Only two new major OSHA rules—covering ethylene oxide and farmworker field sanitation—were issued in Reagan's first term, and both of them occurred only after intense wrangling and court pressure. OSHA likes to boast that it will propose a host of health regulations within its own regulatory timetable. But to date, virtually all proposed standards would *weaken* existing regulations, not develop tough new standards. Often the delay in issuing regulations has been a function of the agency's own insistance on the use of regulatory review and cost-benefit analysis—an approach promoting "paralysis by analysis." OSHA now pursues health regulations at a glacial pace. While there are less than two dozen

OSHA exposure limits for hazardous and toxic substances, there remain more than 2,000 known and suspected carcinogens used in the workplace. If President Reagan's ideological orientation toward social regulation endures, the outlook for the welfare of the nation's workforce, on this score, is not bright.

We now can better understand how, as discussed at the outset of the chapter, the Reagan administration could reach a juncture whereby in 1986 it could issue a record penalty against Union Carbide Corporation, yet still not have such an action be indicative of the vigor of a healthy agency. Auchter gave OSHA a directon, albeit a negative one. Since his departure in 1984, the agency has been adrift. And while Pendergrass, Reagan's third OSHA director, may have begun "rekindling OSHA" as one publication speculated, it will not soon return to even the level of activity under Bingham because of federal budgetary constraints."[90] The agency certainly will not, in its current configuration, escape the fluctuation of presidential expansion and contraction of its activity, a fluctuation most dependent on the executive branch's assessment of the prevailing economic climate and, especially, the prospects for economic growth.

Conclusion: The triumph of economic structure

After examining the policies of Carter and Reagan, the picture we are left with is one of both divergence and continuity between their strategies toward OSHA. The divergence lies in the genuine commitment to workplace safety and health on the part of Carter's OSHA apparatus. The agency certainly was relatively more active, and in some respects arguably more effective, during his term. But it also was in deep conflict with another part of the administration, and eventually the concerns of that economic-technocratic side took precedence over the concerns of the other side. Indeed after 1978, the Carter approach begins to look like it is paving the way for Reaganism, as worried attention to the generation of economic growth virtually overwhelms all other domestic priorities. Alan Wolfe's structural insight into Carter's macroeconomic policy is applicable here to his OSHA policy as well: "In pursuing a centrist strategy, Carter learned that in an age of austerity the center shifts to the right."[91]

The solidification of centralized and insulated OSHA policy stands as a chief *continuity* between the two presidencies. In a sense, President Reagan simply sustained and deepened this weakening of OSHA with his vocal advocacy of deregulating the workplace. During his presidency the structural imperative of economic growth was nearly the only issue on the domestic agenda. With his business-dominated approach to OSHA, the concerns of workers were minimalized and, at times, trivialized. OSHA has not disappeared, although that might be a goal in President Reagan's heart of hearts. More effective is a strategy that keeps the agency on the books, but renders it essentially impotent. This allows OSHA to be figuratively invisible, while not having literally vanished.

The desire to promote economic growth and satisfy the business community thus has effectively torpedoed the pursuit of vigorous safety and health enforcement for the foreseeable future. OSHA appears caught in a cycle of liberal presidents—who want to retain some health and safety regulatory programs, but who also need economic growth for political survival—and conservative presidents, who focus almost exclusively on the growth side of the equation. Such a cycle will always tend to subordinate the need for safe and healthful workplaces to the needs of the economy, ensuring that commitment to OSHA will only be as strong as the priorities of business will allow. For as Noble has correctly observed:

> [T]he relationship between the development of the White House review program and changes in the economy suggests a clear relationship between presidential concern for business confidence and the subordination of social regulation to White House review.[92]

Having been burned in the early 1970s, corporate capital is not likely again to fall into a state of disorganization over social regulations.

As for the presidency as an institution, the fundamental point seems to be the *contingent* nature of the office, dependent as it is on the dynamic interaction of state power and economic vitality. The extent of the dependency becomes clearer when the structural constraints on the state shift from accommodating social struggle to the generation of economic growth, as they had by the time Carter assumed office. His roughly mid-term rightward shift attests to this fact. President Reagan happily moved with the tide, all the while helping to quicken its speed. This, then, is the *overriding domestic continuity* of the Carter and Reagan years—a continuity which reminds us that the liberal democratic state is in the bind of being publicly accountable for the performance of a private economy over which it has only a very limited set of tools for achieving public purposes.[93] In the case of OSHA policy, if those purposes hang in the balance, the lives of workers quite literally may as well. This is the structural bind of the presidency. Political science—above all, presidency scholars—would do well to devote greater attention to the exploration of this bind as it envelops the chief executive.

National Security/National Insecurity: The MX Missile Confronts Two Presidencies

> I discussed my disappointment with the weekly
> memorandum on MX mobile basing. It was a
> nauseating prospect to confront, with the gross
> waste of money going into nuclear weapons of all
> kinds.
> —Jimmy Carter

> I do know that the debates that are going on about
> the MX, I think they're a lot of wasted rhetoric and
> we ought to get on with it.... We need it.
> —Ronald Reagan

The attitudes of Presidents Carter and Reagan seemingly move in opposite directions. Jimmy Carter longs to be thought of as a man of peace and global cooperation. A cursory glance at the record of the first two years of his presidency lends credence to such a judgment. Among the achievements of his administration during that period were the signing of the Panama Canal treaties, the Camp David summit on Middle East peace which culminated in the Camp David accords, and the announcement of normalization of relations with the People's Republic of China. Specifically concerning the nuclear threat, he can claim credit for halting production of the B-1 bomber, deferring production of the neutron bomb, and reaching an agreement on a framework for the SALT II Treaty. Particularly in this latter area of nuclear weaponry, President Carter prided himself on thinking the sobering thoughts and feeling the human fear of the nuclear threat. The "shadow over the earth," as he calls it in his memoirs—"That horror was constantly on my mind."[1]

Historian Gaddis Smith thus is generally on the mark with his assertion that "President Carter and some of his advisers were readier than any of their predecessors to stare directly at the reality of nuclear weapons," to "think deeply" about the implications of national security in the nuclear age.[2] A reasonable case can be made that on some level President Carter was considerably more thoughtful about and knowledgeable of nuclear weapons issues than his successor as well. As the quotes which frame this chapter suggest, Carter did give sustained consideration to the moral and human dimensions of the multifaceted nuclear dilemma, even staffing his administration at the highest levels with advisers whose own views on the issue varied substantially. Moreover he refrained from engaging in the kind of cold war fantasies evident in President Reagan's famous (for a day) quip: "I've signed legislation which outlaws the Soviet Union. The bombing starts in 5 minutes."[3]

For his part, Ronald Reagan has shown much less care than Carter, often adopting his familiar bull-in-a-China-shop attitude toward this most vital issue. He staffed his various national security-related agencies uniformly with well-travelled cold warriors. And as a barometer of the depth of his own ignorance of the technical side of strategic weaponry, he admitted having occupied the presidency for more than two-and-a-half years before realizing that roughly three quarters of the Soviet's entire strategic nuclear arsenal is concentrated in land-based missiles—an elemental fact whose importance cannot be overemphasized when analyzing national security policy and arms control in general, and the MX missile in particular.[4]

The difference between the two presidents, then, can be construed as marked on such basic issues as nuclear weaponry and national security. President Carter began his tenure with an inaugural address pledging "perseverance and wisdom in our efforts to limit the world's armaments to those necessary for each nation's own domestic safety," and movement "this year a step toward our ultimate goal—the elimination of all nuclear weapons from this Earth."[5] He also early on urged a commitment to "replace balance-of-power with world order politics," and advocated the need to jettison our "inordinate fear of Communism" in thinking about foreign policy.[6] For such views he often is popularly portrayed as a relatively dovish chief executive, compassionate, morally committed, and yet ultimately weak. By contrast, Reagan is viewed as an exemplar of the tough, power-conscious, defense-minded president, a hawk in hawk's clothes. His firm, denunciatory approach to the Soviet Union, which colors all of his administration's national security policies, was articulated in his frist presidential press conference:

> Now, as long as they do that [promote world revolution] and as long as they at the same time have openly and publicly declared that the only morality they recognize is what will further their cause, meaning they reserve unto themselves the right to commit any crime, to lie, to cheat, in order to attain that, and that is moral, not immoral, and we operate on a different set of standards, I think when you do business with them, even as a detente, you keep that in mind.[7]

Only in the wake of the revelations of the Iran-contra scandal are the American people coming to see how accurately much of Reagan's glib characterization of Soviet conduct describes *U.S.* behavior in the world.

Such facile "weak" v. "strong" comparisons of the two presidents gloss over or ignore outright the absurd quality of ideas of "weakness" and "strength" when applied to presidents who have at their finger tips the capability to destroy life as we know it on this planet in a matter of hours, if that long. As Alan Wolfe has written, the U.S. is a superpower, having literally accumulated super amounts of power.[8] In the nuclear age, no president is militarily "weak." More importantly for this chapter, though, charges of relative weakness or strength obscure the most fundamental point that President Carter underwent a pronounced shift to the right on national security issues as his tenure wore on. Roughly comparable to his growing conservatism in domestic policy, as evidenced in his OSHA policies, his increasingly militarized foreign policy agenda was even more dramatic, since the foundation of whatever liberal reformist ideas he harbored was most securely rooted in this arena. As in the domestic sphere, the Democratic president laid the basis for the international dimension of Reaganism which followed.

Particularly from mid-1979 onward, Carter repudiated anything resembling his earlier embrace of the cooperative, world management policies espoused by his brethren of the Trilateral

Commission.[9] This perspective, which had supplied the elite establishment's analytic rationale for his initial moralistic orientation to world issues, was a distinct casuality of Carter's hardened stance. As Smith points out, "The character of the Carter Administration's foreign policy changed radically during 1979, continuing and completing a shift which had begun in 1978."[10] Indeed it had. For when all was said and done, his professed nausea over nuclear weaponry notwithstanding, the erstwhile detente-minded Carter had—in the name of preserving "national security"—presided over the greatest buildup of offensive nuclear weaponry in the nation's history, of which the MX stands as a prime example.

President Carter's shifting foreign policy perspective had had its analogue in President Reagan's apparent eleventh-hour abandonment of his "evil empire" rhetoric about the Soviets. When asked at the 1988 Moscow summit to reconcile his positive assessment of the Soviet Union and arms control with his 1983 speech in which he characterized the Soviet Union as "an evil empire" and "the focus of evil in the modern world," Reagan responded, "That was another time, another era." Despite these shifts, neither Carter's cold war transformation nor Reagan's born-again arms control posture fundamentally exhausts the enduring vigor—and danger—of conventional notions of national security. Indeed, their ideological convergence toward the center of mainstream foreign policy debate serves to reinforce established national security norms. The president is both prisoner of and benefactor of these accepted ways of thinking, rallying the public behind the office when perceived threats to national security arise, yet unable to actually provide anything like real security in the nuclear age. Simultaneously trapped by and sustained by such notions—it is this dual bind that the structural view of the presidency wants to explore and challenge. My intent here is to undertake this kind of analysis by examining the policies of Presidents Carter and Reagan toward the MX missile, a weapons system that captures well the dilemmas faced by presidents in their pursuit of national security.

The secluded history of the MX missile

The genesis of the MX missile (for "Missile-Experimental") stands in sharp contrast to the origins of OSHA discussed in the previous chapter. Whereas OSHA emerged from the sometimes acrimonious interplay among public officials, private industry and citizens, both organized and unorganized, the MX missile system was conceived in relative obscurity. Like all major weapons systems, the MX was insulated from public scrutiny until its development and deployment effectively were a foregone conclusion. As one group of analysts has observed concerning the vital issue of the function fulfilled by the nation's strategic nuclear forces, such as the MX:

> On a question of such fundamental importance to the security of the United States and the world, one might expect to find either general agreement among scientists and policy makers, based on a coherent body of doctrine and analysis, or alternatively an informed, sustained public debate. Unfortunately, this is not so.[11]

What is true in this case for overall U.S. nuclear policy, also is true in the particular instance of the MX program.

Certainly the need for some amount of secrecy dictates that military planners not indiscriminately broadcast every technical feature of proposed weapons systems. Yet one result of the nearly total insulation and lack of broad debate is that both strategic theories and actual weapons systems growing out them—which obviously carry with them important implications for the security of all of us—can become virtually unalterable facts of life in the military world before being subject to legitimate outside critique. A good example is the notion of a *strategic triad*, a cornerstone of nuclear policy.

The triad concept simply means that U.S. (and Soviet) weapons are distributed over three modes of delivery: air-based, sea-based and land-based. Presidents and their military planners routinely treat the triad as sacrosanct. This results in the apparently ironclad need to always have ongoing modernization plans for each leg of the triad, guaranteeing the quantitative and qualitative proliferation of nuclear hardware. Yet such fetishization of the triad is completely unwarranted.

Far from being primarily the outgrowth of a conscious, well-conceived plan, the triad actually resulted from bitter interservice rivalry and the peculiarities of the defense budgeting process in Congress.[12] The only logical necessity for strategic planners is the requirement that the nation's forces be diverse enough to ensure

reliability and survivability. This might be achieved by strengthening only one type of delivery system, say our invulnerable submarine fleet. In theory, there is no reason why a monad or a dyad
could not adequately meet U.S. defense needs as a deterrent, and
be both less costly and less destabilizing than a system that
includes relatively vulnerable land-based intercontinental ballistic
missiles (ICBMs). As Herbert Scoville, former Deputy Director
of the CIA and Past-President of the Arms Control Association,
has concluded, "there is nothing sacred about our triad of strategic
weapons . . . . The important factor is to have a diversification
of strategic forces."[13] Air Force, Army and Navy turf battles, more
than the requirements of military ones, have created the triad.
The concept does not deserve the respect it is given.

The triad stands as an example of how little serious thinking
at times goes into the determination of the nation's "strategic
thought." As I will subsequently contend, the MX missile system
itself, especially in its current scaled down deployment mode,
cannot withstand serious, thoughtful scrutiny. Another seemingly
intractable feature of the way nuclear weapons are developed,
very important for understanding the MX, is the tremendous lead
time they require. Of his experience with this phenomenon,
Carter has noted:

> New weapons systems are always being conceived; they pass
> through research, design, and testing, and then perhaps go on
> to deployment. This process can take as long as ten years, and
> once it gains momentum, it is almost impossible to stop.[14]

Having said this, he does not use this insight to draw much in
the way of conclusions about U.S. weapons systems, their impact
on the nuclear arms race and related perceptions of Soviet nuclear
capabilities and intentions, or the ability of a president to interrupt
or resist this momentum. This is unfortunate, since he opted to
confront the momentum of two such nuclear weapons projects
in decisions on the B-1 bomber and the neutron bomb[15].
Perhaps it is an understandable omission, however, given that
the *reasons* for these decisions would seem to preclude any
insights that fundamentally question the standard weapons
development process. In the case of the B-1, cancellation was
ordered because newer, deadlier technologies (cruise missiles and
the stealth bomber) had obviated the need for this new bomber

(and still, Reagan revived it). And with the neutron bomb, deferral was ordered because of insufficient public support from our European allies, on whose soil the weapon would have been based.

In any event, the inertia of the process usually is taken as a fait accompli. Weapons are dreamed up by researchers and then some threat is concocted to rationalize the development and deployment of the now-"vital" weapon. Research money has been procurred; to waste it would be almost unthinkable. This is the pattern followed by the erratic trajectory of the MX missile "debate."

Planning for an MX-style mobile ICBM began in the late 1950s.[16] At the time, the Air Force was searching for possible ways to address the alleged possibility of U.S. vulnerability to a Soviet missile attack. Fueled by the hysteria over the infamous "missile gap"—one of the most spectacular deceptions ever perpetrated in the cause of whipping up support for national defense—the Air Force searched in vain for a secure basing scheme for a new mobile missile. Before discussing this search, however, it is absolutely critical to underscore the MX's origins in this period of military mendacity. For it has never been possible to separate the missile from a continual stream of official exaggeration and outright falsehood, up to and including President Reagan's latest MX designs. Indeed, the history of the MX is inextricably interwoven with the history of a major development in U.S. strategic nuclear doctrine—the advent and refinement of *counterforce* policy—the reality of which has been obscured, when not completely hidden, from the public.

The public face of nuclear doctrine, like the public face of the MX, usually has been presented as a product of the need to maintain deterrence.[17] To digress briefly, the doctrine of deterrence maintains that the policy of the U.S. is to amass nuclear weapons for defensive purposes, to respond to Soviet attack. Deterrence results in the nuclear stalemate often popularly known as MAD (for mutual assured destruction): neither the U.S. nor the Soviets would launch its weapons first because each could be certain the other would respond with massive retaliation against a host of targets, including cities and industrial centers, bringing widespread ruin if not complete societal devastation. Under the scenario of deterrence, nuclear weapons are intended for second strike only, that is, in response to the first strike of an opponent. It is not primarily a war-fighting doctrine.

The MX, by contrast, is an example of a weapon designed with another doctrine in mind, that of counterforce. A counterforce policy has definite offensive implications. It targets an opponent's weapons (such as missile silos) and military command, control and communications structures, with the idea that they could be destroyed before they are used, thus providing the aggressor with a decisive military advantage. Such a counterforce capability potentially provides the nation that initiates a nuclear attack the ability to achieve a *first strike.* While in a literal sense of the term, a nation that launches its weapons first is said to have undertaken a "first strike," the more precise and germane sense of the word entails a strategic first strike—a sudden, preemptive, disarming first strike rendering an opponent unable to respond.[18] Counterforce policy thus has war-fighting connotations. It requires weapons with particular characteristics, foremost of which is accuracy. Destroying cities calls for no special precision, since a variance of a few hundred feet would not affect the outcome of the mission. But to hit a silo or a bomber base, accuracy is essential.

Counterforce doctrine is unsettling because its premise is that nuclear war is something more than a MAD option promising to obliterate civilization as we know it. This option, while horrifying, is so to such a degree that nuclear confrontation may appear a relatively remote possibility. Yet by counterforce logic, nuclear war is something fightable and winnable, much like war with conventional technologies. Given that counterforce makes nuclear war *theoretically* "limited" in scope (limited to military/political targets), and hence *more likely,* it is understandable why U.S. military planners did not rush to extol its virtues to the public.[19] In fact, successive administrations developed strategic policies along two tracks, one essentially for public consumption and one for private military calculations. Publicly, national security posture has held that our nuclear forces aim to deter war and are strictly for "national defense." If the truth be known, however, counterforce has been at the center of U.S. strategic policy since the 1950s.[20] The top secret Pentagon document that assigns a specific target for each of the nation's nuclear warheads—known as the SIOP, for Single Integrated Operational Plan—has, since its completion in 1960, accorded counterforce policy a predominant place in U.S. strategy.

The disjuncture between the national security establishment's public and private plans rests on the psychological effects the steadfast pursuit of counterforce, first strike policy might have on the American people. As Paul Nitze—decades-long Defense Department adviser and Reagan's chief arms control negotiator— explained in 1956, there are two separate though related meanings to the word "policy":

> In one sense, the *action sense,* it refers to the general guidelines which we believe should and will in fact govern our actions in various contingencies. In the other sense, the *declaratory sense,* it refers to policy statements which have as their aim political and psychological effect (my emhasis)[21]

Presumably, it would be difficult to sell publicly the benevolent belief that our nation's nuclear forces are for "national defense" above all else, if at the same time the maturation of counterforce doctrine was the common public rationale for the evolution and expansion of our strategic forces. Defense is more palatable than offensive capability.

The existence of this longstanding public/private split in nuclear doctrine does not, however, mean that counterforce options literally have never been mentioned outside the back rooms of Foggy Bottom. Robert McNamara, President Kennedy's Secretary of Defense, alluded to the development of a counterforce posture in both 1962 and 1967. McNamara conceived of counterforce as a method of "damage limitation," to deter the potential annhilation of cities by striking at the enemies' forces. Presented this way, counterforce strategy *sounds* more humane; people allegedly are not held hostage to nuclear terror. A substantial gap existed, though, between the theory and practice of counterforce war-planning. It was a hardware gap of sorts. And *this* gap was an authentic one.

When President Nixon's Defense Secretary James Schlesinger again made public overtures toward counterforce policy in 1974, he also did so in the name of offering a more humane alternative to full-scale nuclear devastation. Nixon had stated publicly how troubled he was that his hands were tied by nuclear weapons, since the only response he had to a nuclear attack was the massive retaliation against enemy cities. "Should the President in the event of nuclear attack be left with the single option of ordering the mass destruction of enemy civilians in the face of the certainty that it would be followed by the mass slaughter of Americans?" he opined philosophically.[22] Nixon, of course, was formulating a straw problem; the Pentagon's SIOP had always included a major component of non-city-busting counterforce options.[23] But Nixon and Schlesinger together were playing a moral trump card, asserting the need for "flexible nuclear options" to obtain the necessary hardware to close the gap between counterforce theory and practice. This ploy was buttressed by the oft-used mythical scenario projecting that the Soviet Union would soon have the ability to threaten a large portion (usually set at about 90 percent) of our Minuteman ICBM force. Schlesinger removed the velvet gloves in 1975, though, asserting publicly for the first time the U.S. need for the ability to launch a first strike against the Soviets if the contingency arose.[24] He hoped for a "super missile," specifically designed to achieve preemptive hard silo kill capability. The MX missile, placed into advanced development in 1974, was to be a vital part of this overall plan.

The development of MX technology traverses this history of doctrinal refinement.[25] In response to the Navy's highly touted "virtually invulnerable" Polaris submarine, the Air Force in 1960 had been working feverishly on its Project Big Star, which resulted in the first major proposal for a new mobile ICBM. The Air Force came up with a rail-based system consisting of 60 missile trains, each with five missiles, rolling randomly on the nation's commercial rail network. Phase one of this project was approved by the outgoing Secretary of Defense. But the new Defense Secretary, McNamara, was dubious of the entire railway plan, and put the project on hold. Among his objections was a "public interface" problem, by which we can assume he meant that train passengers might feel somewhat squeamish about riding the rails along with weapons that could destroy the world as we know it. These kinds of problems with the basing of the missile would plague the MX concept throughout its years.[26] As we will see, they remain as formidable as ever today.

Many other mobile ICBM schemes have been considered by the Air Force since 1960, along with proposals for sophisticated missile characteristics. In 1967 it announced another land-based proposal. This was the first of many "shell game" configurations, which attempted to achieve invulnerability and deception by shifting the missiles among multiple silos (many more silos than missiles) hardened to withstand the impact of nuclear explosions. A year earlier, McNamara had ordered the Pentagon's Institute for Defense Analyses to undertake a study of follow-on generations of strategic weapons from all the armed services. Known as the Strat-X Study (for Strategic Exercise Study), this analysis shot down the Air Forces' elaborate shell game system. Strat-X had concluded that the Soviets eventually would be able to detect the silos actually housing the missiles. The study was enthusiastic about the Navy's proposed underwater long-range missile system (ULMS), though, and advocated further development of this project, which eventually became the Trident submarine system being deployed today.

Licking its wounds from Strat-X, but still undaunted, the Air Force commenced with research on a number of basing modes for its ICBM, which by 1969 included missiles that could be silo-based, rail-based, truck-based, and deeply underwater-based (in silos). In 1970 it added a version of an air-mobile ICBM, launched from a Lockheed C–5A transport plane. The point here is that the Air Force was searching for some way to credibly base its new ICBM, eventually considering more than 40 different basing options.[27] The motivation for this investigation came as much from interservice rivalry as it did from any outside threat to Minuteman missiles. According to *Aviation Week* of July 1970, the Navy's nascent Trident program "poses a potential threat to the Air Force's present monopoly on the ICBM arsenal, a fact of which USAF is well aware."[28] Thus, as one study recalls:

> In the early seventies . . . Minuteman vulnerability was still regarded as a relatively long-term threat. A more immediate threat to the land-based ICBM came not from the Russians but from the grand designs of the U.S. Navy.[29]

In 1975, with the MX officially in advanced development stage (development, that is, of missile design, independent of its basing), Defense Secretary Schlesinger rejected the Air Force's air-mobile concept in favor of further research into land-based modes. Decisions on how to base the MX, in other words, were still very much up in the air. What was certain by the end of the

Ford administration, however, was that despite conflicts over MX basing plans, the missile would be brought to fruition. Moreover, of special importance for the remainder of this analysis, the MX would proceed regardless of the veracity of claims that the system was needed to counter a Soviet nuclear threat to our Minuteman missiles. Soviet strategic capabilities were not the primary driving force behind the MX. Changes in U.S. nuclear doctrine toward a counterforce posture played the leading role. As is so often the case with new weapons systems, though, the *public* face of the MX decision would most often be painted in Soviet red. The situation by 1976 thus could be summarized as follows:

> Publicly, the decision to proceed with the MX was tied to Soviet restraint in building up its new ICBM forces. Within the Pentagon, however, the MX missile was non-negotiable.[30]

By 1977, then, President Carter was inheriting a full-fledged MX program in desperate search of a land-based deployment mode. The preferred Air Force basing mode at the time was a buried trench version although, as always, others were under consideration. But Carter inherited something else besides a missile without a home. He faced a shifting domestic climate on issues of national security, a climate in flux partly due to a well-orchestrated rightwing offensive. This ideological offensive provided the foreign policy analog to the AEI-type campaign against OSHA and other regulatory programs in the domestic sphere.

Leading the cause of resurgent militarism in the U.S. was the Committee on the Present Danger (CPD), an organization of both old (Nitze and Eugene Rostow) and relatively new (Jeane Kirkpatrick) conservatives who sought to help the nation regain its position of unchallenged world leadership and military superiority lost in the wake of defeat in Vietnam.[31] Ronald Reagan was a member himself and as president would select a number of his advisers from the Committee. The CPD counseled a revival of cold war containment of alleged Soviet global expansion to overcome the "Vietnam syndrome" and reassert U.S. military strength. Apart from Vietnam, the CPD was reacting to the multicausal erosion of clear, unbridled U.S. military superiority by the Soviets over the previous two decades. Although a U.S. margin of supremacy in overall conventional and nuclear power actually still existed, "the very fact of Soviet approximation has detonated the alarmist response in the USA . . . ."[32] The CPD goal was to relentlessly package the "Soviet threat" as virtually the singular cause of the country's ills, and by so doing pave the way for increased expenditures in all areas of the defense budget. More generally, the CPD functioned to move the terms of political debate rightward on a host of national security issues.

Among the many issues on which the CPD wielded considerable influence during the Carter years were opposition to the nomination of Paul Warnke as head of both the Arms Control and Disarmament Agency and the SALT negotiations, fierce opposition in the ratification debate on the SALT II treaty, and support for the MX missile decision. On the MX issue, the CPD essentially invented the most widely-cited rationale for deployment of the MX, the chimerical "window of vulnerability," about which more later. In terms of setting the context for the newly-elected President Carter, though, no issue was more telling than CPD dominance of the infamous Team B report.[33]

Under mounting pressure from hard-liners during the 1976 campaign, President Ford authorized Central Intelligence Agency Director George Bush to reassess intelligence estimates of Soviet military capabilities and doctrine. The group of outside analysts, unflinching hawks all, included several CPD members, with one of them, Richard Pipes, serving as chair. While the Team B analysis was never made fully public, its dire view of Soviet military power, notably its very dubious assessment of burgeoning Soviet military spending, was deliberately leaked to the press at the end of December. Although many well-respected national security establishment figures openly took issue with the Team B findings—particularly the alarmist and easily-refutable claim that the Soviets definitely had achieved overall strategic superiority—the CPD agenda had been furthered. It had made its stridently anti-detente position a force to be reckoned with. Its views had been prominent in the press as the Carter administration prepared to take power. It had, in short, presaged the cold war revival to come.

President Carter: In like a lamb, out like a lion

The metaphor of March actually overstates President Carter's shift on matters of national security. The incoming Carter foreign policy team in 1977 was not 100% pure lamb to begin with. In fact, it had at its core some tense internal divisions, which reflected the deep fissures within the national security establishment. Carter ignored CPD members when choosing his top advisers. But he did draw heavily from the ranks of the rival Trilateral Commission, the group responsible for opening his eyes to the larger world of national and international politics beyond the Atlanta corporate elite in 1973. Carter selected some 25 Trilateralists to serve in high level foreign policy posts, among them Cyrus Vance, Harold Brown, Paul Warnke, Andrew Young and the commission's co-founder Zbigniew Brzezinski.

Even within this group, however, competing policy tendencies existed. Most notable was the policy split between Vance, as Secretary of State, and Brzezinski, as National Security Adviser. Vance was seen as a strong supporter of arms control with the Soviet Union, searching for ways to forge cooperation between the superpowers. Trilateral world order politics fit well with his overall geopolitical outlook. As a fiercely anticommunist Polish emigre, Brzezinski took a tougher stance toward the Soviet Union, linking a host of issues (SALT negotiations being a major example) to their behavior in certain areas of the world. He was inclined to view world events through the lens of east-west rivalry, and would support arms control measures only if they codified U.S. advantages, as did SALT II with its allowance for the expansion of our counterforce capabilities which he so cherished. His attitude was decidedly more militarist than Vance's on issues of the arms race and U.S.-Soviet relations in general, although he shared Vance's Trilateral perspective on other important issues, such as the pressing need for greater collaboration among the major capitalist powers.

For perspective, it is useful to bear in mind that whatever the policy differences between these two tendencies, they represented conflict within a shared consensus on the baisc need for U.S. military prowess and the general benevolence of multinational corporate capital. But the cleavage was real, resulting in some heated internal debates over the specifics of policy, even if the ends were agreed upon. And it helped define the character of the Carter administration as it struggled to balance the disequilibrium. Smith describes the fundamental world order v. militarism split embodied in Vance and Brzezinski as a division that "ran like a fault line through the Carter Administration and all discussion of the wisdom or folly of its particular decisions."[34] He added that the tension contributed to Carter's downfall, commenting that "He knew they represented different viewpoints but did not appreciate how deep the incompatibility lay."[35] Carter's memoirs confirm his cognizance of this difference between Vance, who would become his close personal friend, and Brzezinski:

> Zbigniew Brzezinski was perhaps the most controversial member of my team.
> Dr. Brzezinski might not be adequately deferential to a secretary of state.
> There were some inherent differences in the character of the White House National Security Council staff and the State Department. I attempted to tap the strongest elements in each as changing circumstances demanded.[36]

Apparently the president thought he could handle whatever policy contradictions arose by selecting ideas from one or the other adviser when it suited his needs, perhaps because he ultimately believed Vance and Brzezinski accorded each other mutual respect. As Carter remembers: "(In looking at my old notes, I find it interesting that Vance recommended Brzezinski for this job, and Zbig recommended Cy for Secretary of State. Both were good suggestions.)"[37] Yet Vance claims that despite agreements to the contrary, and despite repeated directions from Carter, Brzezinski would not abandon his attempt to assume the role of chief foreign policy spokesman. In his memoirs, Vance writes of his growing rift with Brzezinski:

> Eventually, as divergences grew wider between my public statements and his policy utterances, Brzezinski's practice became a serious impediment to the conduct of our foreign policy. It also became a political liability, leaving the Congress and foreign governments with the impression that the administration did not know its own mind.[38]

What foreign policy analyst Fred Halliday refers to as the "studied ambivalence" of the Carter administration's national security policies (its mixture of conciliation and belligerency) simply could not be maintained.[39] In 1979 and 1980, the ambivalence was resolved in favor of cold war belligerency, punctuated by the departures of Warnke, Young and, eventually, Vance. By the end of the Carter years, the lions roamed freely.

In the beginning, though, it was Jimmy Carter, lamb and moralist, that brought a squeaky clean view of the world before the Joint Chiefs of Staff (JCS). There in January 1977 he proposed that the U.S. reduce its stockpile of some 30,000 nuclear warheads down to 200, a supply adequate to deter any potential adversary.[40] This was not a crazy idea. If deterrence is the lone goal of U.S. nuclear strategy, 200 warheads are sufficient to destroy the Soviet Union as anything resembling a modern society. Defense planners had known this at least since the mid-1960s, when McNamara's Pentagon "whiz kids" perfected their computer projections on nuclear war-fighting. But what neophyte Carter learned was the stark reality that deterrence was not the only objective of the nation's nuclear forces. In fact, the rhetoric of deterring nuclear war was, and is, largely for public consumption, as I've argued. The real JCS strategy was to "prevail" in a nuclear war, and to prevail required counterforce capabilities. This made it much more difficult to conceive of the arms race having an end point.

Undeterred himself, Carter did make some overtures toward reducing the threat of the arms race, a sincere desire on his part, including some early talk of banning all mobile ICBMs, such as the MX. Twice in 1977 the new president substantially cut funding requests for the MX. In January, faced with the outgoing Ford administration request for $294 million for full-scale development of the MX in fiscal year 1978, he postponed such development for at least a year and cut the request in half.[41] Again in December, Carter cut funds for full-scale MX development in fiscal year 1979. This time it was his own Defense Secretary's approval of an Air Force $245 million plan that was denied, largely because of uncertainty over how to base the missile, and because it was thought that approval at this time could adversely affect the ongoing SALT negotiations.

More telling than Carter's initial stopgap funding cuts specifically for MX development was his overall view of the way to address development and deployment of nuclear weapons as an issue in arms limitation talks with the Soviet Union. As the administration's SALT II strategy unfolded it became clear that a SALT-MX linkage was being forged, a linkage ensuring that—lofty rhetoric about ending the nuclear threat notwithstanding—the MX was non-negotiable.

With the SALT I Interim Agreement due to expire in October 1977, Carter wanted to reach a new agreement with the Soviets early in his term. Toward this end he sent Vance and Warnke off to Moscow in late March to begin laying the groundwork for a SALT II accord.[42] There they put forward, and the Soviets emphatically rejected, a proposal calling for "deep cuts" in nuclear weapons. Vance actually went with two alternative bargaining proposals. A modest option simply built on the agreement reached between President Ford and Soviet President Leonid Brezhnev at Vladivostok in November 1974. Vance and Warnke both favored this more cautious approach, figuring it offered the quickest route to a SALT II agreement, with "deep cuts" negotiable in what they hoped would be future SALT III discussions. But the decision was made to press ahead with more substantial reductions.

It is now widely acknowledged the Soviets had good reason to vehemently denounce the "deep cuts" tactic. Although there are a number of factors explaining why they did so with such fervor, the most reasonable and obvious was that the proposed "deep cuts" would have to come almost exclusively from the Soviet's heavy land-based ICBMs. Since roughly 75 percent of their strategic nuclear forces are land-based, this plan was transparently one-sided. Predictably, though, Soviet rejection was seized by anti-SALT forces, especially the CPD, as evidence of Soviet intransigence. With a homey flourish, Carter notes in his memoirs that about a week before Vance went to Moscow, "Henry and Nancy Kissinger came by for supper." With Vance and Brzezinski present, Kissinger (presumably Henry) endorsed the "deep cuts" idea, Carter recalls, saying it "had a good chance to be accepted by the Soviets if they are sincere and want to make progress on disarmament."[43] So the stage was set. The Soviets did indeed reject the biased offer, thus *they* are insincere, do *not* want progress in arms talks, and, relatedly, we therefore (to protect ourselves from these calculating Russians) should proceed at once with plans to add the MX, the Trident submarine, cruise missiles, and a stealth bomber to our nuclear arsenal. This kind of self-fulfilling prophecy—used by some in the administration to justify the need for the MX—is the stuff of the arms race.

The "deep cuts" gambit also revealed that President Carter considered the issue of land-based ICBMs particularly crucial to the larger issue of nuclear arms. Specifically, he bought into the

key argument that Soviet "superiority" in land-based missiles put
our entire Minuteman system at risk. This ICBM vulnerability
argument—later sloganized into a prime ideological debating tool
in Reagan's "window of vulnerability"—was a major rationale for
deploying the MX. Yet as we will see, given the speciousness of
the vulnerability argument and the vexing, if not insurmountable,
dilemma of MX basing, the more basic reason for the MX was
its war-fighting capability, its first strike accuracy. For although
there is a relationship between the design and characteristics of
a missile, on the one hand, and its basing mode, on the other,
it should be kept in mind that there is no logical connection
between a missile's accuracy and its pre-launch vulnerability. The
MX is no less vulnerable a target if it is super accurate, as planned,
or if its acuracy is just that of existing Minuteman III missiles.
Only mobility is a germane response to alleged vulnerability
problems.[44]

At times, administration officials admitted that the vulnera-
bility argument was much less than compelling. Defense Secretary
Brown's own words on this issue have been mercurial. In 1978
he openly ridiculed the idea of a Soviet attack against vulnerable
U.S. missile silos in his annual report for fiscal year 1979, saying
the Soviets would not risk such a "cosmic throw of the dice." The
U.S. would have a wide range of lethal options remaining if the
Soviets took such an unlikely risk, Brown contended, adding:

> In short, the [theoretical] vulnerability of MINUTEMAN is a
> problem, but even if we did nothing about it, it would not be
> synonymous with the vulnerability of the United States, or even
> of the strategic deterrent. It would not mean that we could not
> satisfy our strategic objectives.[45]

Brown would change his tone, though, as the prospects for a
SALT II treaty appeared to hinge on the U.S. going ahead with
new weapons systems, and as the 1980 election approached. In
1979 and 1980 he often warned of "the growing vulnerability"
of our land-based missile force, while adding the proviso that
this threat not only was more imminent than previously believed,
but also could eventually imperil our *entire* nuclear arsenal.[46]

Not surprisingly, Brzezinski saw a U.S. first strike threat posed
by the MX as "extremely, extremely threatening" to the Soviet
Union, but ultimately necessary to maintain a "strategic balance"

between the superpowers, given his endorsement of the view that the Soviets had achieved such a capability. First strike ability, and the modernization and expansion of U.S. nuclear forces, were unwavering necessities within his worldview. For his part, Carter generally was more cautious about assertions of U.S. vulnerability to a theoretical Soviet attack, and about U.S. first strike effort. In his June 1978 Arms Control Impact Statement for fiscal year 1979, he voiced his understanding of the MX as a potentially destabilizing factor in the arms race:

> With the MX deployed in substantial numbers, in addition to Minuteman, the U.S. would have acquired a capability to destroy most of the Soviet silo-based ICBM force in a first strike . . . . under extreme crisis conditions, Soviet leaders . . . . might perceive pressures to strike first themselves. Such a situation, of course, would be unstable.[47]

By 1979, with his MX plan in place, he would abandon altogether the notion of it as a destabilizing influence, repeatedly calling it vital to the maintenance of "essential equivalence" with the Soviets.

By and large, 1978 brought with it mounting pressure for President Carter to appear tougher on the Soviets, particularly as the superpowers worked to pare down their differences in the ongoing SALT II meetings. One indicator of Carter's readiness to do so was his commencement address at the Naval Academy on June 7. The president devoted the major part of his speech to a harsh denunciation of the Soviet record on human rights. Contending that the Soviets are engaged in an "aggressive struggle" for political advantage and are guilty of a military buildup "excessive far beyond any legitimate requirements," he flatly asserted that "the abuse of basic human rights in their own country—has earned them the condemnation of people everywhere who love freedom."[48] Carter pieced together this important address out of two drafts, a conciliatory one from Vance and a more confrontational one from Brzezinski. Vance interpreted the final product as an expression of the administration's inability to shed its image of inconsistency and uncertainty, but Carter believed the main impression it left was clearly hard-line.[49] This impression would grow in 1979, somewhat ironically, as the SALT II negotiations wound down.

Carter made the two major MX decisions of his presidency in 1979. On June 8, 1979 the White House announced its long-awaited decision to proceed with building a full-scale mobile MX missile.[50] While the details of the basing plan were to be revealed later, Carter had decided to build the largest version of the MX permissible under the SALT II treaty being negotiated. He authorized construction of a ten-warhead missile with a 92-inch diameter,instead of a smaller 82-inch version. This seemingly minor difference actually carried some import. It reflected at least two sets of pressures. First, the smaller version would have made the MX launchable from the new Trident class submarines, as well as from a ground-based mobile launcher. The "common missile" option was scrapped, though, when it became clear that the Air Force and the Navy could not come to grips with the idea of sharing any control over these new technologies, and the Navy additionally feared a common missile might decrease the need for its new deadly accurate Trident II missile. Second, the larger missile was appealing to those, like Brzezinski, who felt it was necessary to send the strongest possible signal to the Soviets about American intentions to "get tough." Warnke explains that Brzezinski pressed Carter to go with the bigger missile, summing up the NSC director's philosophy as, "The bigger, the uglier, the nastier the weapon—the better." The message to the Russians was to be: "Shape up, buster. We've got the ability to do you in. We're probably not going to do it—but it's an act of grace on our part."[51] Supposedly such breast-beating would scare them and, even better, appease the growing number of critics of a SALT II agreement.

The timing of the MX announcement accentuated Carter's mixed motives. Coming only a week before he left for Vienna to sign the SALT II accords, the MX decision was schizophrenic. The "man of peace" authorizes the largest new nuclear weapons program since the hydrogen bomb project, and then toasts the goal of world peace and reconciliation with Brezhnev. This contradictory juxtaposition fits well with what later would become President Reagan's "peace through strength" credo. Both Carter and Reagan have claimed on occasion that the MX is not a "bargaining chip." This is true, in a sense. MX was not, and is not, a bargaining chip to be used at the table with the Soviets. But is *was* a bargaining chip to be used with the U.S. Congress, with the intent of buying Senate votes for ratification of the treaty, opposition to which had become a kind of cause celebre to conservatives of both parties opposing detente. The treaty simply could not have been ratified without Carter agreeing to strongly endorse the MX, and to significantly increase defense spending, both of which he did. The irony, of course, is that for all his concessions to conservatives, the ratifying votes were never cast.

In reality, though, the SALT II accord signed by Carter and Brezhnev would not have made much difference anyway, in terms of abating the arms race. As the administration explained on several occasions, the treaty allowed the U.S. to move forward with plans to deploy not only the MX, but the Trident submarine system; air-, sea-, and ground-launched cruise missiles; cruise missile carrier aircraft; cruise and Pershing II missiles in Europe; and a new long-range bomber. These are all counterforce-enhancing weapons—hardly cause for celebrating an outbreak of peace. Vance writes of the "deep sense of satisfaction" felt by the Carter negotiating team as the president signed the SALT II Treaty on June 18. The satisfaction is understandable, if codifying substantial U.S. advantages over the Soviets was the goal. Of the final agreement, Vance asserts:

> I was confident that the treaty could stand up well in an objective debate. It was a balanced, carefully wrought set of agreements that left us with virtually full freedom of action to modernize our strategic forces in every area of interest, while requiring a significant reduction in Soviet strategic forces.[52]

The treaty was so "balanced" and "carefully wrought" that Brzezinski actually could support it.

After the Vienna summit, and as the administration was parading witness after witness before the Senate Foreign Relations committee to advocate the virtues of combining its military buildup with approval of the treaty, Carter announced the second half of his MX decision—his preferred basing mode. (For a sense of the tenor of the times, recall that this announcement came on the same day as the president went on television to quell the uproar over the monumentally ridiculous, Democratically-baited red herring of Soviet combat troops in Cuba.) Justifying the move on the grounds that it would strengthen deterrence and meet the threat of Minuteman vulnerability, the president sketched

basing plans for a mobile MX ICBM system on September 7.
"[T]his system will enhance our Nation's security," he assured,
saying it "is not a bargaining chip. It's a system that America needs
and will have for its security."[53]

The basic details of the plan have been well publicized and
do not need close scrutiny here.[54] Suffice to say, the plan employed
multiple protective shelters (MPS) configured in a "racetrack"
pattern.[55] Spread out across the Great Basin desert in Nevada and
Utah, the plan entailed 200 missiles (each with ten nuclear
warheads) to be shuttled among 4,600 missile shelters (23 per
site) on oval roadways, one roadway system per missile. The
elaborate shell game was thought necessary to achieve the degree
of deception and mobility requisite with some notion of
invulnerability. It carried a stated price tag of 33 billion in 1980
dollars, but virtually no one took that figure seriously. Pentagon
cost figures are legendary for being understated and unreliable.
Indeed, more disinterested assessments placed the cost of the
MX project in the range of 55 billion to well over 100 billion
dollars.[56] As the Air Force Brigadier General in charge of selling
the MX plan to residents of Nevada conceded under questioning,
"This is man's largest project."[57] It was common to hear that the
scope of the project would dwarf the pyramids of Egypt. Yet even
with such Rube Goldberg complexity, massive cost, and
environmental upheaval, the MPS scheme was no more certain
to ensure the deception necessary to achieve (in theory)
invulnerability than any of the other 40-odd basing plans the Air
Force has come up with over the years. A sense of the poverty
of the system's logic can be gotten by considering that in the
absence of a suitable arms control agreement, plans existed for
building thousands of additional missile shelters if the Soviets
responded by expanding their number of warheads to target all
the original 4,600 shelters.[58] National security, it seems, was a
spiraling, endless proposition.

President Carter provided a hint of the deeper logic of the
MX, though, in an interview with a group of editors after his
September 7 announcement. Responding to a question about the
wisdom of the U.S. always maintaining its "defensive posture"
in the face of Soviet "aggressiveness," Carter claimed the MX
"gives our country a better defense or attack capability."[59] This
attack capability is not often raised publicly, for reasons mentioned

earlier. But as the Center For Defense Information—a well-respected (because it is staffed by retired admirals and generals) Washington-based organization opposed to excessive military spending—argues, disapprovingly:

> Simple logic leads to the conclusion that the MX is a first strike weapon. There is no other logical mission for a system which is designed with the power and accuracy to destroy ICBM launchers.[60]

The MX makes no sense as anything but an instrument of first strike. Its pinpoint accuracy is not necessary except to preemptively attack hardened missiles. As a second strike, retaliatory weapon, it is useless. It would be aimed at empty missile silos, not exactly high priority targets. As the saying goes, with counterforce missiles, you either "use em, or lose em."

The fleeting candor of Carter's "attack" comment was offset by countless standard invocations of the national security goal of goals: deterrence. However, administration documents illustrate how confused attempts to justify this goal can become. In a fall 1979 letter responding to congressional inquiry, William J. Perry, Carter's Deputy Assistant for National Security Affairs, made the following argument:

> In regard to the first strike capability of MX, I should emphasize that we have not changed our basic strategy, which is and remains to deter war. Deploying MX will not give us a disarming first-strike capability against the Soviet Union, since the Soviets would still have large and powerful strategic forces remaining after an MX strike.[61]

Perry's case here is absolutely correct. As we will see later, a first strike, though we pursue it, is probably unattainable. But if one reverses his logic, it also absolutely refutes the Minuteman missile vulnerability argument used by all administrations, Republican and Democratic, since the problem surfaced in the 1960s. If the Soviets would have "large and powerful" forces left after a U.S. first strike attempt, the U.S. also certainly would have such forces remaining if the Soviets struck first. In fact, the U.S. forces remaining would be *larger* and *more powerful* because a proportionally *smaller* number of U.S. missiles (roughly 25 percent, to the Soviet's 75 percent) are land-based, the most vulnerable leg of the triad.

Carter's MPS race track system generated rising public concern in late-1979 and 1980. While some groups opposed the system and its justification outright—reacting negatively to the idea of turning such a large chunk of the west into a "warhead sponge," as the target of a saturation attack—the most frequent opposition centered on the environmental impact of the project, particularly its potentially devastating effect on the region's water supply. In July 1979, polls showed that 63 percent of the people in the Nevada-Utah area supported the MPS system in their states; by February 1980, support had plummeted to 39 percent.[62] The governors of the two states opposed the basing mode selected by the administration. But as the public posture of Utah Governor Scott Matheson indicates, much of the "opposition" to the MX plan wholeheartedly supported the ICBM vulnerability argument and also supported the need for an MX system.[63] Often this resulted in alternate proposals to involve other states in the project so as to minimize the impact to any one region or state, or plans to base the MX in the air or on the sea.

Reacting to these concerns, the Carter administration in May 1980 announced revisions of its MPS system. Most importantly, the new variation would array the missile's protective shelters in a linear fashion, abandoning the racetrack oval for a "drag strip." Defense Secretary Brown contended that this modification would save considerable amounts of land and would be less costly. Other basic characteristics of the system remained unchanged (eg. the number of missiles and shelters), although a new shelter design was contemplated.

Technical aspects were not the most crucial development of the MX system in 1980, however. Changes in the nation's political climate were paramount, although it is essential to keep in mind that the president's two major 1979 MX decisions *preceded* these climatic alterations.[64] In the wake of the Soviet invasion of Afghanistan in December 1979, Carter requested the SALT II treaty be withdrawn from Senate consideration. Although there was little or no chance of the agreement being ratified under *any* circumstances, pre- or post-invasion, the Soviet incursion obviated the need for this eventuality. Coupled with the seizing of American hostages in Iran, and the impending presidential election, U.S. policy toward the Soviet Union turned increasingly hostile. As former U.S. Ambassador to Moscow and historian George Kennan reflected, with proper establishment anxiety, in February of 1980: "Never since World War II has there been so far-reaching a militarization of thought and discourse in the capital."[65] A heightened cold war atmosphere pervaded as Congress authorized the Pentagon to proceed with full-scale development of the final Carter MX plan on August 1, calling the system "vital to the security of the United States." But the event most boldly confirming the central status of the MX in U.S. strategic thinking was the revelation of Presidental Directive 59 (PD–59).

Leaked to the press only a few days after the MX action in Congress, and only a few days before the Democratic convention, PD–59 provided the first public articulation of the administration's nuclear war-fighting strategy. The directive followed some earlier secret directives (notably PD–18 of mid-1977) that had called for thorough review of strategic targeting options. Brzezinski's aide Major General William Odom drafted the plan, which called for preparation to fight limited nuclear war, and to carry out decapitating strikes against Soviet political and military command structures. Counterforce targeting options had emerged from the shadows once again. A spate of articles and columns appeared decrying the fact that the U.S. was now "thinking the unthinkable." Of course, such thoughts were far from novel; their emergence now simply confirmed a trend underway for well over a decade. This time, however, the maturation of the doctrine was apparent, including military objectives easily interpreted as moving beyond even "limited" nuclear conflict.[66] Moreover, the strategy meshed with several new technologies coming on line to make a U.S. first strke technically feasible.

Such war-fighting plans verfied the triumph of Brzezinski's view of east-west relations. He had outlasted the primary detente-minded advisers in the administration. With protracted nuclear conflict on the agenda of options, Brzezinski had convinced Carter of the potential intimidatory value a nation might accrue by virtue of commanding the military resources and philosophy of counterforce. The stance created by PD–59 fit the president's precarious political situation as he struggled to project himself as a tough, even nationalistic, candidate for reelection. What had eluded both McNamara, during the Kennedy-Johnson years, and Schlesinger, during Nixon's second term, Carter was on the brink of achieving. With PD–59, he forged the synthesis of counterforce theory and practice.

President Reagan: The lion roams

Whereas President Carter's embrace of counterforce doctrine signified the final leg of his relatively measured journey rightward in foreign policy, punctuated as it was by exogenous factors, President Reagan did not need to learn any stark lessons of Realpolitik. He naturally thrived in a milieu of cold war militarism. Yet he brought to issues of nuclear war a kind of offhandedness— something akin to Dr. Strangelove—that was unsettling. A danger of PD–59 was that it would encourage and legitimize a sanguine attitude toward nuclear war on the part of the national security bureaucracy and future presidents. This danger received confirmation within the Reagan White House, a fact to which the casual story told by Reagan adviser Edwin Meese attests:

> Cap Weinberger came in to see the President, and he said, "Mr. President, you know, the press has been giving us a hard time on the MX missile. I suggest that we rename it the Hallmark missile . . . I hope we never have to do it. But if we do, I want the Russians to know that we cared enough to send the very best."[67]

This kind of a cavalier attitude toward such a cataclysmic possibility surfaced repeatedly during the Reagan years, though more frequently in his first term. It stems, in part, from the prevalence within Reagan's national security apparatus of nuclear strategists openly dedicated to the war-fighting proposition that nuclear conflict is in some sense "winnable."

Colin Gray is an exemplar of this war-fighting school. In 1980 Gray co-authored an article entitled "Victory Is Possible" in which he argued that nuclear war not only is winnable, but the president needs the strategic capability in *initiate* such action:

> The West needs to devise ways in which it can employ strategic nuclear forces coercively . . . . American strategic forces do not exist solely for the purpose of deterring a Soviet nuclear threat or attack against the United States itself. Instead, they are intended to support U.S. foreign policy, as reflected, for example, in the commitment to preserve Western Europe against aggression. Such a function requires American strategic forces that would enable a president to initiate strategic nuclear use for coercive, though politically defensive, purposes . . . . If American nuclear power is to support U.S. foreign policy objectives, the United States must possess the ability to wage nuclear war rationally.[68]

Reagan appointed Gray, a staff member of the Hudson Institute, to the advisory board of the Arms Control and Disarmament Agency and also named him consultant to the State Department. Arguing that "victory or defeat in nuclear war is possible," Gray clearly endorses the first outcome of prevailing. Elsewhere he has written favorably of the MX missile's war-fighting potential to help the U.S. prevail, contending that "survivable MX ICBM deployment is the key to victory-denial for the Soviets . . . . MX cannot guarantee success to American arms, but it should ensure failure for the Soviet Union."[69]

Other Reagan defense advisers made similarly provocative pronouncements, some laced with biblical references to Armageddon ushered in by nuclear conflict. And then there is T.K. Jones, named Deputy Under Secretary of Defense for Research and Engineering, Strategic and Theater Nuclear Forces. A staunch believer in the survivability of nuclear war, with the proper civil defense precautions, Jones created a stir by recommending that would-be nuclear war survivors "Dig a hole, cover it with a couple of doors and then throw three feet of dirt on top . . . . If there are enough shovels to go around, everybody's going to make it. It's the dirt that does it."[70] My claim here is not that Jones' extremism is typical of Reagan and his national security team. But his ideas grew out of the widely-shared administration belief in the efficacy and necessity of civil defense measures, and—central to Reagan's military policy—the unanimous assertion of U.S. ICBM vulnerability to Soviet attack.

The unreal nature of the military side of Reaganism can best be capsulized in two fundamental myths, both directly connected to the president's actions on behalf of the MX: the "decade of neglect," and the "window of vulnerability." Reagan employed the "decade of neglect" thesis to justify his crusade to "rearm" America. According to the accusation of neglect, the U.S. uni-laterally disarmed during the 1970s, leaving the new president no choice but to "repair" the country's "broken" military machine. The familiar Reagan charge goes like this:

> When we took office in 1981, the Soviet Union had been engaged for 20 years in the most massive military buildup in history. Clearly, their goal was not to catch up but to surpass us. Yet the United States remained a virtual spectator in the 1970s, a decade of neglect that took a severe toll on our defense capabilities.[71]

There is superficial plausibility to the charge: following the peak years of spending for the Vietnam War, U.S. military expenditures were down throughout much of the decade, bottoming out in fiscal year 1975.[72] This decline was due primarily to U.S. disengagement from Vietnam and the aftermath of the war, which included congressional reticence toward military spending and persistently high rates of inflation. Notice that these factors are independent of any "Soviet threat." The concomitant Reagan charge—borrowed from the aforementioned Team B fiction—was that the Soviets had undertaken a massive increase in military spending during these years of a relative U.S. ebb in expenditures and, relatedly, had overtaken the U.S. in expenditures. But both charges are false, except if grounded in the discredited accounting methods generated, in large part, by CPD members working with the CIA's Team B.[73] Soviet military outlays actually were gradual but steady throughout the period in question, rarely rising above two percent per year.[74] And if NATO and Warsaw Pact figures are included in the overall spending balance, the scale is tipped even more toward the west.

While bogus in general, the "decade of neglect" thesis becomes utterly ludicrous when applied to the Carter years. Actual defense outlays rose more than 12 percent during Carter's four years, and would have been higher if not for inflation. Increases in his last two budgets were particularly precipitous. While this does not measure up to Reagan's almost 30 percent increase in outlays during his first term—at approximately $1.1 trillion, the largest sustained peacetime military buildup in U.S. history—it hardly constitutes "neglect." Moreover, Carter was responsible for major additions in the area of strategic nuclear forces, including the MX missile, Trident submarine (with the new Trident II missile), stealth bomber, and cruise missile programs, as well as other military areas—a point Brzezinski has made in defense of his former boss against charges that he was "soft" on the Soviet Union.[75] As one careful analyst of the Carter military program has observed, "the Reagan rhetoric [of the 'decade of neglect'] tended to obscure the fact that Reagan's program was mostly an acceleration of the buildup already begun under Carter."[76] In light of the real military affinity between the two presidents, Carter understandably was upset by Reagan's repeated attempts to pin the "neglect" charge on him.

In a front page story on March 2, 1986, the *New York Times* carried an interview (arranged at Carter's request) to respond to Reagan's assertion the week before that he had not increased military spending or modernized strategic forces. The former president was "irate," saying Reagan "habitually" misrepresents the record of U.S. military programs with contentions "he knows are not true and which he personally promised me not to repeat."[77] Carter pointed with pride to his contribution to defense spending and strategic upgrading, saying that he and Presidents Ford and Nixon had initiated almost all strategic nuclear weapons programs. (Ignoring contrary evidence, Reagan repeatedly made demonstrably misleading claims, such as his assertion, in the middle of congressional debate over MX funding, that after taking office "we began immediately to make up for the irresponsibility of the seventies and to revitalize the three legs of our nuclear triad.")[78] "This is the first time I have gone public," Carter lamented, "but some of his statements are almost more than a human being can bear."[79]

Although as we will see, circumstances rendered President Reagan unable to use the slogan "window of vulnerability" any longer, the principle thesis of this second myth was still deployed. The Carter administration, of course, also had subscribed to a version of the idea that Minuteman missiles were becoming vulnerable to attack from Soviet ICBMs. But this threat remained more explicitly theoretical for most of Carter's term. It was only as the 1980 presidential election approached within an atmosphere of renewed cold war politics that administration officials claimed a more immediate ICBM threat, and extended it to include a threat to all U.S. forces, not just missile silos. For Reagan, however, vulnerability always was played as more imminent, a direct threat to our ability to deter. The comparative level of alarmism trumpeting the alleged danger was much higher. Of particular value during the 1980 election, the frightening window metaphor conjures up images of thousands of Soviet missiles flying into our national home, while we sit idly by with no recourse. Or, knowing of these awesome Soviet capabilities, U.S. leaders soon would have no choice but to succumb to nuclear blackmail, as candidate Reagan meant when he told an interviewer that the window soon would be open so wide "the Russians could just take us with a phone call."[80]

The beauty of the "window of vulnerability" thesis for the Reagan administration was its amorphous nature. Although the CPD-inspired scenario consistently proclaimed a Soviet ability to knock out 90 percent of our land-based missiles, the time frame has varied—early, mid, and late 1980s projections have been common—as has speculation of just how far open the window is at any one time.[81] And arguments have ensued over how to best close the window. Given the fluidity of the concept, its potential for ideological manipulation, it is useful to keep in mind what the Federation of American Scientists had to say in 1974 about the Nixon-Schlesinger version of a surprise Soviet counterforce attack scenario against U.S. ICBMs: "The entire scenario is bizarre—enormous risk for no point . . . . One can only imagine that the Joint Chiefs have been smoking pot."[82] Today such scenarios still offer an impaired perspective.

"Window of vulnerability" claims are deficient in a number of respects, some of which have been touched upon earlier. Briefly put, the argument about the vulnerability of land-based ICBMs requires one to suddenly become blind to the retaliatory capacity of the other two legs of the U.S. strategic triad. Fifty percent of all U.S. strategic nuclear warheads are in submarines which are virtually invulnerable to attack. And a full 25 percent of our warheads are aboard long-range bombers. Even *if* the Soviets could take out 90 percent of our silos, we still would retain the vast majority of our strategic weapons. It is implausible in the extreme to assume any adversary would harbor the intention of a first strike against such a force structure. Moreover, in the event the Soviets *intended* such a suicidal venture, the likelihood of them being technically *capable* of doing it is equally fantastic, given the enormous problems of accuracy and operational reliability of missiles under actual war conditions.

The details of the massive uncertainties of a first strike are well known.[83] Without delving too deeply here into this somewhat arcane (but actually comprehensible) world of technical nuclear calculus, they include problems of missile bias, the amount a missile drifts from its flight path due to uncorrected gravitational field anomalies. Testing to overcome bias never establishes anything approaching certainty, or even high probability, since neither country test fires its missiles over the north pole, the path they actually would travel in a nuclear exchange. The general accuracy of a missile is influenced by other factors as well, such as fratricide, which is the lingering effect of debris, wind currents and shock waves from earlier warhead detonations on incoming warheads. Warheads are extremely sensitive to such environmental phenomena, and since pinpoint accuracy is necessary to destroy a missile silo, even small decreases in precision can render a warhead useless for its intended job. Reliability and readiness also enter into calculations of vulnerability. Neither the Soviets nor the U.S. can be sure what percentage of their total force would fail to launch, or fail at other phases of its flight, although significant failure is virtually certain. And in the area of general readiness, the U.S. for a number of reasons is conceded to have a higher percentage of its nuclear forces at an advanced state of readiness necessary for a first strike.

Missile accuracy is measured by circular error probable (CEP), defined as the radius of a circle centered on a target within which half the warheads are expected to fall. The smaller the CEP, the greater the accuracy. The MX has an estimated CEP of 300 feet, meaning in theory it should be able to deliver five of its ten warheads to within 300 feet of their target. With the deployment of the Navstar global positioning satellite system, midcourse corrections for ICBMs (MX, Trident I and II, and others) could bring the CEP for the MX to less than 100 feet. The most accurate Soviet ICBM has an estimated CEP in the neighborhood of 600 feet, but they too are working to improve accuracy. Even a modicum of evenhandedness, and knowledge of history, would grant the U.S. a wide technological edge over the Soviets. Yet proponents of the "window" thesis exaggerate claims about the pace and quality of Soviet advances in accuracy, since in the absence of such improvements the window thesis is transparently false. As Federation of American Scientists, arms control analyst Christopher Paine points out:

> Crediting the Soviets *now*, or in the future, with "worst-case" capabilities which they *might* obtain 10 years hence . . . is one of the defense establishment's primary techniques for selling new weapons programs to Congress and the public. In the case of the 1980–85 "window of vulnerability," the available evidence points to a distortion and exaggeration of Soviet capabilities . . . . (his emphasis)[84]

Although Paine's assertion is valid, what needs to be added is acknowledgment that the *Soviets* are, by far, more vulnerable to a first strike threat because of their previously-mentioned *force structure*, top-heavy as it is with relatively vulnerable land-based ICBMs. Whatever the vulnerability of Minuteman missiles—and the evidence above suggests it is greatly overstated—the Soviets are saddled with three-quarters of their strategic forces on the ground. Farfetched as they are, vulnerability scenarios must be seen as a greater possibility—hence, danger—to the Soviets than to the U.S.[85]

Lest we be distracted by the details of the above discussion of the implausibility of vulnerability to a first strike, it bears reiteration that the MX is irrelevant to such scenarios. A new *missile* does not make American forces any less vulnerable. Equally irrelevant to vulnerability is the MX's characteristic degree of *precision*. New missiles with sophisticated capabilities have no impact on Minuteman vulnerability. Only a different *basing* mode for older land-based forces—or abandoning them altogether while enhancing our submarine force, thus eliminating them as first strike targets—genuinely would address concerns about their vulnerability. Nevertheless, armed with his two myths, which together instilled in him the belief that the Soviets had achieved a "margin of superiority" over the U.S. in strategic nuclear weaponry, President Reagan joined the MX fight.

Needless to say, Reagan viewed the missile system as a key variable in the quest to close the window of vulnerability. However, that rationale was becoming increasingly untenable. The first administration action on the MX came in March 1981, when Secretary of Defense Caspar Weinberger established a committee to explore alternative basing modes.[86] Opposition to the system had been gaining strength in Nevada and Utah, and the administration had doubts about the complexity and survivability of the Carter multiple shelter scheme. The committee, chaired by Nobel prize-winning physicist Charles Townes, was to report July 1, 1981, but in fact a summary of its findings was not made public until March 1982. Townes' panel found "no practical mode" of basing ICBMs on land that would ensure survivability, a finding that jibed with a major basing study released by the Office of Technology Assessment in March 1981. When two of Reagan's Senate allies, Jake Garn (R.-Utah) and close friend Paul Laxalt (R.-Nevada) announced their opoosition to the Carter plan envisioned for their states, the president realized the accumulated weight of opinion left little choice but to search for an alternative MX route.

On October 2, 1981 Reagan formally scrapped the multiple shelter basing system and, hoping to make the MX more saleable, reduced the requested number of missiles to 100. With an obligatory reference to the need to forestall the opening of a "window of vulnerability," he said that up to 40 missiles would be housed temporarily in existing but hardened Titan and Minuteman silos, the very silos under the gun from the alleged Soviet threat. In the meantime, he outlined plans to search for alternative permanent basing schemes, including air mobility, deep underground basing and silos protected by ballistic missile defense systems. All of these plans were mired in long-standing problems, though, and testified to the fact the president was clutching at straws in an effort to rationalize a fundamentally flawed missile. Even a Congress by and large supportive of the idea of strengthening the ground-based leg of the triad, and generally deferential to Pentagon strategies of all types, was finding it hard to square the new plan (and early 1982 revisions) with its stated aim of promoting invulnerability. Whatever misgivings Congress had, however, they did not prevent legislators from continuing to authorize money for MX development, although deadlines were set for final administration selection of a secure basing mode.

The next major administration push for the MX came November 22, 1982, as a congressional basing mode selection deadline neared. That evening the president went on national television to unveil his latest MX plan. Earlier in the day, in an Orwellian move, he had announced that henceforth the MX, a war-fighter's weapon if there ever was one, officially would be called "Peacekeeper." The president pulled out all the stops in his effort to introduce the waiting public to the ways of peace, augmenting his address with multi-colored charts portraying a dynamic and relentless Soviet arms buildup, along side a pathetic, weak-kneed U.S. stasis.

> You often hear that the United States and the Soviet Union are in an arms race. Well, the truth is that while the Soviet Union has raced, we have not. As can see from this blue line ...[87]

Ah yes, the blue line. A relationship of direct proportionality seems to exist between the magnitude of the deception and the need to embellish it with the trappings of objectivity. The president assured his listeners, "I could show you chart after chart where there's a great deal of red and a much lesser amount of U.S. blue." Indeed. The point of Reagan's theatrics was to support his contention that "the MX is the right missile at the right time." As for the big decision, the MX was to be based in 100 closely spaced superhardened silos in Wyoming. Also known as a "dense pack" mode, the plan hoped to maximize invulnerability by using the effects of fratricide to throw off incoming Soviet ICBMs. True, the Soviets would know exactly where all 100 missiles are, but they would be spaced in such close proximity that to destroy some of them would ensure that others survived because some attacking missiles would be thrown of course. One obvious problem, unaddressed by the president, is that the fratricide effect can be expected to throw off whatever surviving U.S. missiles were launched in immediate retaliation.

Despite the charts with blue and red lines, "dense pack" did not even make it through the Christmas holiday. The plan proved too hard for Congress to swallow, and in late December the president's request for roughly $1 billion for MX procurement was denied. Congress did, however, approve funds for research and development on the missile and basing, asking the president once again to reexamine basing modes and report back after March 1, 1983. Ushering in the new year, President Reagan established on January 3 his second MX commission, this time headed by retired General Brent Scowcroft, former national security adviser to President Ford. The president's Commission on Strategic Forces (usually referred to as the Scowcroft Commission) issued its final report in April.[88] The report made a straightforward argument for the further development of U.S. counterforce capability, saying that in order to "frustrate Soviet efforts at [nuclear] blackmail," and the accompanying advantages of political coercion, the U.S.

> must be able to put at risk those types of Soviet targets—including hardened ones such as military bunkers and facilities, missile silos, nuclear weapons and other storage, and the rest—which the Soviet leaders have given every indication by their actions they value most, and which constitute their tools of control and power. We cannot afford the delusion that Soviet leaders—human though

they are and cautious though we hope they will be—are going to be deterred by exactly the same concerns that would dissuade us.[89]

The commission found a place for the MX within this counterforce strategy, namely providing military planners the "ability to destroy Soviet military targets, hardened or otherwise." Accordingly, the panel recommended immediate deployment of 100 MX missiles in existing silos of older Minuteman and Titan II missiles scheduled to be decommissioned.

In order to justify this basing method in vulnerable, unhardened silos, the commission had to drop a bomb of its own—it slammed shut the "window of vulnerability." In essence, the commission said the window never existed. There was enormous irony in Reagan's own group of MX devotees putting the lie to his favorite slogan of fear, but the dubious nature of the administration's claim proved too much. With measured words, the commission report insists that "the different components of our strategic forces should be assessed collectively and not in isolation," for:

> whereas it is highly desirable that a component of the strategic forces be survivable when it is viewed separately, it makes a major contribution to deterrence even it its survivability depends in substantial measure on the existence of one of the other components of the force.[90]

In the language of establishment admonition, the commission gently chided those who "miscast" the issue of ICBM vulnerability by viewing them in isolation, thus pushing for the quick deployment of an almost totally survivable new ICBM. This haste and sense of immediate vulnerability is unwarranted if U.S. strategic forces are viewed in terms of their "mutual survivability."

Members of Congress were upset that MX survivability no longer mattered very much, particularly when their memories told them that ICBM vulnerability, in the words of Senator Gary Hart (D.-Colorado), "was precisely what we were talking about."[91] But in the view of the Scowcroft report, weapons programs sorely needed a "greater degree of national consensus," so a little historical rearranging seemed in order. The commission offered other recommendations as well, notably the development of a small, single-warhead ICBM (since dubbed "Midgetman") to augment the MX; research aimed at resolving the uncertainties regarding silo hardness, to apply to the MX, a small ICBM, and other future ICBMs; and accelerated research, development and testing of an antiballistic missile system.

The Scowcroft Commission's findings effectively have framed the MX debate over the last few years. And despite the fact that it censured the "window" thesis and its proponents, both the now-explicitly-vulnerable MX, and President Reagan's credibility on military issues, did not lose their appeal. Yet the deterrence argument stands exposed. The Scowcroft Commission said deterrence "requires us to determine, as best we can, what would deter them [the Soviets] from considering aggression, even in a crisis. . . ." The MX represents the most tempting target in the U.S. strategic nuclear arsenal. In Minuteman silos, it serves as the prime object of a preemptive Soviet attack. Indeed, to Soviet military planners, it must invite attack, since its principle utility can only be to facilitate a U.S. first strike.

In the wake of Reagan's endorsement of the Scowcroft findings, the MX was successfully test flown, and Congress authorized the production of the first 21 missiles. Since then, the most significant controversy over the project occurred in the spring of 1985 when, after considerable debate about the specific number, Congress placed a limit of 50 on the number of missiles that can be housed in Minuteman silos. Debate was acutely influenced by Reagan's skillful lobbying. In a radio address on March 15, he described the Minuteman missiles as "aging." "It's sort of like a 1963 jalopy with some new parts," he explained.[92] He failed to mention that Minuteman missiles have been upgraded continually right through the early 1980s, and that "some new parts" on the Minuteman III missiles include an improved guidance system giving them (theoretical) accuracy in excess of the Soviet's most accurate ICBMs, and higher explosive yield. To the "jalopy" gambit he added manipulation of the arms negotiations gambit. With U.S. negotiators engaging the Soviets in strategic arms reduction talks (known as START) in Geneva, he made the case that "The rug shouldn't be pulled out from under them." This is a variation on an old theme; as we have seen, the MX was linked to arms negotiations in the Carter administration as well, when the SALT II treaty was on the line.

The spring 1985 compromise stipulated that the president obtain approval of a new, more secure basing mode before this limit can be lifted. Following the Reykjavik Summit in October 1986, his second with Soviet leader Mikhail Gorbachev, Reagan began the process of complying with this requirement. In his address to the nation upon his return, the president had stressed the importance for arms control of the distinction between words and deeds:

> I told Mr. Gorbachev—again in Reykjavik as I had in Geneva—we Americans place far less weight upon the words that are spoken at meetings as these, than upon the deeds that follow.[93]

Only two months later, the president unveiled his latest deed on behalf of the MX. The new proposal resurrected the discredited "rail garrison" option. Although the details remain to be worked out, initial plans call for 25 six-car trains with each train carrying two MX missiles, thus constituting the additional 50 missiles.[94] The trains would remain at air bases (10 possible sites already have been selected) until a time of national emergency, when they would be dispersed along domestic rail lines. It is unreasonable, of course, to expect that the Pentagon would yet come forward with its plans for resolving the tricky old "public interface" problem, as well as the assorted dilemmas of environmental impact, vulnerability (if that still merits any official attention), and the like. Review of such matters commenced in January 1988, the same year the 50 original MX missiles in Minuteman silos became fully operational. The only certainty is that when the time comes, the effort will be made to railroad the new scheme as essential to our "national security."

Frank C. Carlucci, Weinberger's replacement as Secretary of Defense, began this process in early 1988, arguing before Congress that the entire MX missile force, including the 50 silo-based weapons, should be based on rail cars because of the vulnerability of missile silos. In May he authorized full-scale development of a rail-based launching system and the Air Force awarded two development contracts for the construction and testing of the mobile missile. His actions put the administration at odds with many in Congress, especially Democrats, who favor the small mobile Midgetman system. Some oppose the mobile MX as too costly given the Reagan legacy of massive budget deficits. Others view the single-warhead Midgetman as the more flexible and less vulnerable of the two mobile missile options, given the proposed 4,900 warhead limit on the total number of land- and sea-based ballistic missiles under START.[95] While these types of issues do constitute a "debate," it hardly can be considered one that does anything other than point out disagreement over the narrow specifics of a policy whose ends remain largely, if not wholly, intact.

The future of national security and arms control thus remains unclear. For the moment, cold war tensions between the superpowers have moderated somewhat. Both sides seem intent on ratifying an agreement calling for 50 percent "deep cuts" in the strategic forces, which would complement the Intermediate-range Nuclear Forces Treaty signed in Washington in December 1987. Neither that Washington summit nor the Moscow summit in late May 1988 produced an agreement on whether and how to limit mobile land-based ICBMs. And the entire START process, with proposed 50 percent reductions, already has intensified debates over U.S. and Soviet force structure and reinvigorated disagreements over such topics as the phantom "window of vulnerability," Soviet intentions and capabilities, and the implications of strategic force modernization.[96] Indeed, even with some future START accord, the basic interests behind and perceptions of national security are likely to endure, albeit at a potentially reduced quantitative level of overall weaponry. Qualitatively, though, it remains to be seen whether the fledgling detente at the end of the Reagan era will be sustained, but it bears reiteration that the cold war has seen its share of valleys, as well as peaks, since the Second World War.[97]

Moreover, the issue of President Reagan's Star Wars program presents problems that remain long after his departure from the White House. The Reykjavik talks ran into the Star Wars juggernaut and Reagan's unwillingness to consider serious restrictions on its development and deployment. Subsequently the Senate placed restraints on space testing in the near future and the Reagan administration accepted them, in part because no such tests would be ready to proceed so quickly. Yet the issue remains unsettled, even though differences between U.S. and Soviet positions have narrowed. First announced in Reagan's March 1983 address to the nation, the strategic defense initiative (SDI) is being marketed as a protective shield that will "make nuclear weapons obsolete." "How does a defense of the United States threaten the Soviet Union or anyone else?" the president wondered aloud after the summit. In fact, no one takes the idea of SDI as a leakproof astrodome very seriously. But as the Scowcroft Commission confirms, it is commonly understood within the defense establishment that short of an impenetrable shield, a Star Wars ballistic missile defense (BMD) system would have enormous value in offering "point defense" for U.S. strategic nuclear weapons.[98] These "intermediate utilities," as they are called, like point defense, could among other things provide cover for vulnerable weapons systems like the MX. Thus they would enhance the security not of people, but of counterforce weapons.

An SDI-MX link would underscore something that already is an accomplished fact: the complete disappearance of meaningful distinction between "offense" and "defense" in nuclear warfare. While counterforce weapons continue to be researched, designed and built, we will be subject to ever more presidential rhetoric about their contribution to "national security" and "deterrence." The public rationalizations for weapons such as the MX will get increasingly thin, as the clamour for them thickens. In 1981 then Defense Secretary Weinberger made the following pitiful plea as he initiated the Townes Committee investigation into MX basing modes: "We need the MX missile, please tell us where to put it."[99] This plea illustrates the nature of the MX as a "technical folly," in the words of physics professor and defense expert Freeman Dyson—a super-technical weapon whose design and mission have been "stymied by the comparatively simple job of building a base for it."[100] Two terms later, the Reagan administration still had no publicly credible idea of how to overcome this folly.

Conclusion: The structural inertia of national security

It is almost incredible, until you ponder the routineness of it, that 50 MX missiles are fully operational. Their deployment now cannot be stopped. And the others are on the way. Their existence stands as testimony to the structural inertia of a weapons system flying under the all-purpose, one-threat-fits-all banner "national security." The title of this chapter reads, in part, "The MX Missile Confronts Two Presidencies." Weapons like the MX appear as life, as if they live and breathe, requiring that we do the only thing humanely justifiable and find them a comfortable home. Presidents are rhetorical gardeners whose job it is to nurse these little saplings to health with stock phrases about "security" and "defense." As one arms analyst has written of Reagan's MX plan:

> The MX, it appears, will be deployed in silos, for no other reason than the sheer momentum of its production process. The production and deployment of the weapon have become ends in themselves, serving no larger plan or purpose than the Administration's diffuse and inchoate desire for "strength."[101]

The argument about momentum and structural inertia can be taken too far, however. For there *is* a larger purpose to the MX. The MX project is viewed as one step in the overall strategy of reasserting the U.S. hegemonic international role, and likewise nuclear superiority, in the face of Soviet attainment of rough nuclear parity. Soviet strategic parity has been seen as a direct threat to the ability of the U.S. to project its power on a global basis, as this quote from Reagan arms negotiator Paul Nitze indicates:

> For many years U.S. strategic nuclear preponderance has made it possible to offset Soviet military superiority at the periphery and to deter its offensive employment. It has also made it possible for the U.S confidently to use the seas for projection of its supportive power despite the Soviet Union's always very real sea-denial capabilities.[102]

For Nitze and others within the militarist current of defense advisers, the MX will bolster U.S. attempts to gain political leverage in global conflicts *below* the nuclear threshold. "I'm always worried less about what would happen in actual nuclear exchange than the effect that the nuclear balance has on our willingness to take risks in local situations," commented Richard Perle, President Reagan's Assistant Secretary for International Security Policy. He continued, ". . . I worry about an American President feeling he cannot afford to take actions in a crisis because Soviet nuclear forces are such that, if escalation took place, they are better poised than we are to move up the escalation ladder."[103] These political and psychological dimensions of the decline of U.S. hegemony underlie much of the continuing debate about our national security posture.

Yet pure nuclear concerns are also at the heart of the MX. The goal of the MX is to complement the ambitions of counterforce doctrine, which seek to provide the U.S. with the ability to fight limited nuclear wars, or launch a successful preemptive first strike against the Soviet Union. It is within this (largely private) overall framework that programs like the MX take on their (largely public) appearance of inevitability. If the MX confronted Presidents Carter and Reagan, and not the other way around, it is because neither one of them wanted to confront the logic of national security driving the missile toward deployment.

President Carter came to office intending, at least rhetorically, to question this logic. As I have indicated, he was mindful of the "shadow over the earth," and saw as a contributory factor the weapons procurement process, about which he observed that "once it gains momentum, it is almost impossible to stop." But as the political climate of the country grew darker, particularly around the midpoint of his term, he could do nothing to lighten things up. Indeed, even as he signed an arms control agreement, he was lengthening the "shadow over the earth." The factors contributing to the shift toward militarism had little to do with the "Soviet threat," with the sole exception of the Soviet invasion of Afghanistan, whose linkage to arms control is of dubious value and which, at any rate, postdated the rightward turn in U.S. foreign policy.

Without an alternative logic, without a desire and a program to challenge conventional notions of national security—steeped in a presumed connection between nuclear weapons and security, and fueled by a visceral hatred for something called "communism" and vigilance against the "Soviet threat"—Carter was swamped by a tide of belligerence. By the end of his term it seemed as natural for him to be endorsing an MX scheme as it always would seem for his successor. In his memoirs Carter offers this reflection on Soviet foreign policy: "[T]he fact was that when violence occurred in almost any place on earth, the Soviets or their proxies were most likely to be at the center of it."[104] Save for intensity, this statement rivals any of Reagan's assertions that the Soviets are "the focus of evil in the modern world." President Reagan, for his part, did not undergo quite as abrupt a shift on defense matters and certainly not on the MX. As with his consistent belief that regulation inhibits the great talisman of economic growth, he had no intention of questioning the fundamental assumptions of "national security." For him, "national security" needs are everywhere, always.

Congress also remained under the spell of "national security." That body accepted wholeheartedly the definitions and goals of U.S. security needs underlying the various MX decisions. Legislators found themselves, along with the president, debating and ultimately ratifying the details of what kind of MX system we would have. But *we would have* the system. As one MX-watcher notes, "Congress has consistently authorized and appropriated funds requested for MX research and development, and it has rejected amendments to delete funding."[105] This fact should give pause to political scientists wedded to conventional theories of the presidency, and their overdrawn emphasis on the balance of power between the executive and legislative branches. Concern for this institutional balance assumes that one branch conceivably would do something different than the other if the balance tipped in their direction, something at odds with the fundamental beliefs and aims of the branch disadvantaged by the imbalance. But this is not a reasonable assumption within the current configuration of the two institutions.

Finally, it must be said that the MX dilemma is much larger than just the MX missile and the assorted national security rationalizations for its deployment discussed herein. National security is big business. The imperatives of corporate profitability bring a whole different but related set of pressures to bear on these military-technical decisions. With the Reagan administration, and particularly with its advocacy of a Star Wars program, the economics of defense were glaringly obvious. The torrent of defense contracts associated with Star Wars, the MX, and a host of other military projects showed no sign of abating. Indeed, the entire edifice of the "Reagan recovery" was built upon a military foundation. Perhaps the single most significant sectoral investment trend in the economy over the last few years has been toward military investment, as key industries such as manufacturing and transportation seek to restore their economic health under the influence of military Keynesianism or, more appropriately, "deficitary militarism."[106]

Thus we have come full circle. Today more than ever, the imperatives of the state—economic growth and national security—and hence the imperatives of the presidency, are indissolubly intertwined. And this bond makes the structural exigencies just that much more dangerous for the presidency. As presidents press ahead in their pursuit of national security—along with the attendant ambiguities inherent in counterforce weaponry and the apparent bounties of military spending—the self-defeating logic of that pursuit will become clearer and more acute. The escalation and refinement of counterforce weapons, and nuclear weapons generally, accelerates the arms race and makes nuclear war more likely. The quest for national security, therefore, increasingly undermines itself. It may well be that as Dyson has argued, the doctrine of nuclear deterrence as a guarantor of security, which lies at the root of all other strategies, including counterforce weaponry, is itself "the greatest technical folly of all."[107] This self-defeating logic tightly confines the thoughts and actions of the president. Relaxing this logic should be the most urgent political priority of the nuclear age.

CHAPTER FIVE

Restructuring the Bounds
of the Presidency

There have been five considerable crises in
American history .... So far, it is clear, the hour
has brought forth the man.
> —Harold Laski, 1940

The threat is nearly invisible in ordinary ways.
It is a crisis of confidence. It is a crisis that strikes
at the very heart and soul and spirit of our
national will. We can see this crisis in the growing
doubt about the meaning of our own lives and in
the loss of a unity of purpose for our Nation.
> —Jimmy Carter, 1979

As we came to the decade of the 80's, we faced
the worst crisis in our postwar history.
The heart of America is strong, good, and true.
The cynics were wrong—America never was a sick
society. We're seeing a rededication to bedrock
values of faith, family, work, neighborhood, peace,
and freedom—values that help bring us together as
one people, from the youngest child to the most
senior citizen.
> —Ronald Reagan, 1984

Beyond the balance of power

Once again, the American presidency is in crisis. In 1987, the year
of the bicentennial celebration of the Constitution, the presidency
of Ronald Reagan was held up to the light of scrutiny not seen
since the days of the Watergate hearings. Accordingly, we were
treated to a flurry of political scientists postulating about the office,
its strengths, its weaknesses, its future.

One theorist saw his stock swiftly rise, as he weighed in with a predictable "I told you so." Arthur Schlesinger, Jr., a leading proponent of what I have called the restrictivist school of thought, finds in the Iran-contra scandal confirmation of his thesis on the "imperial presidency." Recall Schlesinger's argument that the presidency becomes imperial when the constitutional balance between presidential power and presidential accountability (especially vis-a-vis Congress) is upset in favor of an overzealous exercise of the former. Schlesinger sees the constitutional balance fluctuating in a cyclical fashion throughout history. This danger of systemic imbalance—"the perennial threat to the constitutional balance"—resides largely in the sphere of foreign affairs, where "the imperial temptation" is always just one international crisis away.[1] While Congress, the courts, the press and the public strenuously exercise their role as countervailing centers of power in the domestic sphere, they "generally lack confidence in their own information and judgement" when it comes to foreign policy[2] So the imperial temptation lies in waiting, surfacing as the *political will* to challenge the chief executive ebbs.

President Reagan succumbed to the urge, engaging in activities Schlesinger characterizes as "foolish," such as the "Iran-Nicaragua flimflam." On this reading, then, the Iran-contra hearings represented a healthy reassertion of Congress' rightful duty to check excesses of power occurring within our system of separation of powers. To those critics of the hearings who believe a tough congressional inquiry into misdeeds of the Reagan administration will cripple the office, resulting in another "failed presidency," Schlesinger responds that "No one need fear that the recurrent uproar against the imperial presidency will inflict permanent damage on the office. For the American presidency is indestructable."[3]

Every day of the congressional probe brought with it compelling new evidence of the deficiency of Schlesinger's widely-acclaimed thesis. Covered with a thick overlay of apology for the existence of the investigatory committee, deference to the witnesses, and hopelessly misframed questions (eg. "Richard Secord: patriot or profiteer?") the hearings verily shouted out the daydream-like quality of the argument that Congress can be expected to restore balance to a foreign policy apparatus tilted toward the president. Columnist Alexander Cockburn put it well with his observation: "True to gloomy predictions, Republicans, with the slack-jawed acquiescence and even vociferous support of most Democrats, have turned the joint congressional investigation into a pro-contra rally."[4]

We should have expected this bipartisan cheerleading for the *essence* of Reagan's policy, of course. Only days before the hearings commenced, Senate Intelligence Committee Chair David Boren (D.-Oklahoma) expressed what he considered to be the crux of the Iran-contra affair:

> The American people should understand that the worst thing that happened here, and the most dangerous thing that happened, is that the whole constitutional *process* was perverted. Did the president faithfully carry out the letter and spirit of the law ... or was he ignoring it, and, in fact, did he subvert the *process?* (my emphasis)[5]

This is a prime example of the distinction between *pragmatic* opposition to a policy, as in Boren's case, and *principled* opposition.[6] Important as laws such as the Boland amendments are, crucial though cooperation and consultation between the executive and legislative branches surely is, the fact remains that Congress as a body does not seriously question the notion that the United States has the right to sit in judgment over the internal affairs of a sovereign nation "in our backyard." The gist of Reagan's case against the "Communist menace" in our hemisphere, the assertion that Nicaragua suffers under the heal of a cruel Sandinista dictatorship, goes unquestioned on Capitol Hill. The policymaking process was at issue before the joint committee, not the policy itself. Schlesinger's contention that an invigorated Congress offers the remedy for America's occasional lapse into global messianism thus is wide of the mark. There is no *substantive* policy balance to be restored; only a *procedural* imbalance exists, as Boren's comments indicate. The presidency may on occasion become more or less procedurally imperial, but the historic, defining character of the substance of U.S. foreign policy always has been steeped in the imperial urge, and given the geographic proximity, particularly so toward Central America.[7]

One of the central purposes of my study has been to fundamentally challenge the way political science examines and theorizes about the presidency. Schlesinger's restrictivist perspective is but one example of the dominant theoretical orientation of the field of presidential studies to which I take exception. In this book I have surveyed major works in the discipline, breaking them down into two schools of thought. The expansivist school argues for vigorous presidential leadership of the political system. With the image of Franklin Roosevelt's tenure firmly in mind, expansivists stake out a position which commends the active, power-wielding, and programmatic chief executive, a perspective that perhaps finds its ultimate expression in Richard Neustadt's equation of the good of the country with the good of the presidency.

The danger inherent in the expansivist logic fueled the alternative orientation, the restrictivist perspective, which adopted a much more cautious approach to presidential power. To be sure, there were some political scientists who blamed the decline of the office on the pathological personality of Richard Nixon and character flaws of Lyndon Johnson. These theorists longed for the day of a renewed expansivist chief executive, albeit one with the "right" blend of personality traits, whatever that might be. In the wake of Vietnam and the fallout from Watergate, though, political scientists more commonly began to perceive the shortcomings of unchecked presidential initiative, particularly the constitutional deformation rampant in the many facets of Nixon's secretive presidential war.

When it considers the presidency, political science tends to vacillate between versions of these two dominant perspectives. In opposition to this orthodoxy, I have proposed a structural alternative. To differentiate a structural theory in the deep sense that I intend from what are often termed the "structural" concerns of mainstream views, I explained that the two traditional theories think of structure in a shallow way, exclusively in terms of *constitutional* structure.[8] Thus the *political* structure often is explored, leaving us with discussions of the relative balance of power between the president and Congress, as if tilting one way or the other would throw the system in a direction at odds with the basic beliefs of the nation's orthodox consensus. But such studies are advanced without a corresponding analysis of the fundamental interests and assumptions *underlying both* government institutions, analysis which, in the words of presidency theorist Bruce Miroff, would move the inquiry "beyond Washington."[9] Structure understood in this deeper sense of the word, by comparison, would focus analysis on these core assumptions which normally are taken for granted by mainstream political scientists indebted to the ideology of liberal democratic capitalism and its pluralist model of explanation. It would critically question prevailing assumptions about the contextual priorities of corporate capitalism, the foreign policy that supports its worldwide operation, and the presumed need to regain America's postwar hegemony.

Moreover, a structural theory places the imperatives of the capitalist state at the center of its analysis, seeing in those imperatives an underlying continuity among presidencies which transcends differences of party, policy and personality usually accorded primacy by conventional theories. Although few analysts have attempted to uncover the dynamics of the office by forcing an explicit encounter between state theory and theories of the presidency, when such efforts do occur, the most convincing ones focus on two issue areas that dominate the president's agenda as the leading state actor—promoting economic growth and national security. As Alan Wolfe has claimed, "there are only two issues at work in American politics most of the time: economic growth and military strength.[10] Wolfe's assessment of these imperatives explores the political implications for all administrations of the decline of postwar U.S. hegemony. Accompanying this decline was the intensification of the dilemma of promoting economic growth and security, which in the absence of the unprecedented postwar economic expansion made it increasingly difficult for presidents to meet the demands of varying constituencies. The "impasse" between public expectations of economic prosperity and military supremacy, and the waning ability of the state to furnish them, has produced declining confidence in government generally, and in the president as head of government.

The case studies in Chapters Three and Four obviously do not ignore the kinds of details about governmental processes and inside administrative maneuverings that mark the case studies conventional theories of the presidency draw upon. But these details hopefully have been marshalled in a way that clarifies and underscores the fundamental *continuities* between the two presidencies. Structural theory must engage the *means* of presidential policy, if for no other reason than to emphasize the basic agreement about the *ends* of policy. For the point of the story behind the Carter and Reagan administrations is that when all the internal disputes, policy proposals, and competing interests have run their course, the core imperatives of national security and economic growth—as defined by corporate and defense establishment elites—emerge from the fray. While conventional accounts of the chief executive would focus on the differences, to whatever degree they exist, as ends in themselves, structural theory looks to and questions the deeper principles and interests that shape and confine the activities of all presidents, regardless of their party affiliation.

Furthermore, it bears notice here that the institutional balance of power between the executive and legislative branches is in no way decisive or even particularly illuminative on OSHA or MX policy in these cases. Congress was just as willing as Carter and Reagan to exempt firms from OSHA regulations and to see the OMB gather power over regulatory decisions. And congressional action on the MX can only be described as wholesale capitulation to the idea that the MX would go on in some shape or form. The presidencies of Carter and Reagan—different though they have been in terms of their strength vis-a-vis Congress—thus stand as testaments to the shared ends of presidents, as central state actors. The structure of the presidency is most forcefully constrained by, but is not reducible to, the pursuit of a favorable business climate and national security. Other issues surely are of concern. But on no other matters are chief executives as nearly imprisoned by structure as on the two major imperatives.

The foregoing discussion is not meant to imply that a structural theory of the presidency is without need of refinement. Two aspects seem to me to merit attention. First, but of secondary import, theories of the state—whether instrumental, structural-functional or social struggle—would benefit from greater stress on a *temporal* dimension. As the political, social and economic climate changes, social struggle brings more or less pressure to bear on the state for concessions. A dramatic rise in such movement activity accounts for a large part of the pressure on the state to adopt social regulations in the late 1960s. Yet as the economy worsened and the imperative of business profitability became exigent, social struggle had less impact and eventually little at all on regulatory matters. Understanding the conditions for these shifts is absolutely crucial to understanding the parameters within which presidents operate. Too often, theories of the state are viewed as either/or propositions. One either studies the elites holding state power, or studies the functional provision of growth as structurally bound, or studies social movements and their efficacy. A conclusion of this study, however, is the need to situate these components of the theories in time.[11] For as the climate of the political economy changes, the component of state theory that has primacy may change as well, as it did in the 1970s. *Primacy* is the issue, though. The drive to select which theory definitively captures the essence of the state in capitalist democracy seems futile, and needlessly devisive.[12]

Second, and finally, a structural theory of the presidency must provide a fuller, more nuanced analysis of public expectations than do conventional theories. Presidential scholars increasingly point to the disjuncture between what people expect from their president and what reasonably can be delivered. But this very real gulf between expectation and performance can be posed in ways that wind up blaming the people for holding irrational desires. Such accounts can view the public with disdain, as a mass of illusioned complainers who shun political participation and thus bring their problems on themselves. Harold Barger's text falls into such a trap. Postulating that the presidency has become "impossible," that there is no way to rid people of their hopeless illusions about the nature of executive power, and noting the potential danger to systemic legitimacy, he concludes that the hope for a more realistic public is slim:

> Few governments, of course, ever live up to the ideal [of representative government] because most people lack the knowledge, skills, or motivation to make rational judgments about those who rule them.
> Citizens ought to act more rationally and realistically, but we might just as well argue that sin or greed should be eradicated from human nature.[13]

Blaming the people for the persistence of "illusions" about presidential efficacy distorts the relationship between the citizen and the state. The work of political theorist William Connolly has helped put this relationship into clearer perspective.[14] People have a need, even a will, to believe that they live in a country that does good things in the world and can provide something like "the good life" for them. Moreover, our notion of ourselves as free people living in a free society is intimately connected to our belief that the state—and the president as head of state—has within its range of *currently available* tools the means to effectively deal with society's problems. As Connolly argues, "We define our grievances and policy agendas as falling within the limits of action available to the welfare state so that we can see the state, and ourselves, as free"[15] This need to construe ourselves as free helps ossify our political dialogue within very narrow but close-at-hand parameters, with "credible" options for the political economy, for example, usually straying no farther than variations on a relatively free-market approach to the economy, or a slightly more interventionist approach. Obviously the policy planning network and the national media play a key role here in orchestrating a limited range of "acceptable" thought (what the renowned journalist and political commentator Walter Lippmann referred to as the "manufacture of consent"), but the quest for personal identity establishes the necessary precondition for such management.

In an era of declining U.S. hegemony and concomitant economic transformation, however, the state finds itself unable to generate the kind of economic growth in accordance with previous notions of "the good life." Constrained by the confines of a range of options narrowly drawn, the state is in a bind, and so are the people. This helps explain the appeal of Reagan as a candidate. As the quotes that frame this chapter suggest, Jimmy Carter's diagnosis of the nations's ills was complex (or it had the appearance of complexity), calling for sacrifice, soul searching and at an early point even a different way of looking at international relations. But the reality of his program was nothing more than relatively tepid liberalism. When domestic and foreign policy crises (real, imagined, and manufactured) mounted, his only recourse was to move more fully into the orbit of conservative political and economic thought, foreshadowing Reaganism. But Reagan, by contrast, was the real article, offering a very reassuring message. And the country bought the messenger, if not fully the message. As Garry Wills observes about the relationship between President Reagan the political performer, and the American people:

> He wrests from us something warmer than mere popularity, a kind of complicity. He is, in the strictest sense, what Hollywood

promoters used to call "fabulous." We fable him to ourselves, and he to us. We are jointly responsible for him[16]

To overcome our ills, all we need do is what we have always done. Hard work and faith will make us prosper; more sophisticated weapons will make us strong.

Presidents naturally have a reservoir of good will and deference amongst the public, stemming in part from the awe commensurate with being a head of state as well as a more earthly head of government. Reagan's own reservoir was very deep; he has been popularly characterized as wearing a "teflon coat" or having a certain "magic." And these impressions have persisted (the Iran-contra scandal notwithstanding) even though the majority of Americans often disagreed with specific policies he pursued.[17] It was his overarching approach—familiar and reassuring—that was appealing. But the fundamental problems of the political economy are unrelenting. And the crises the U.S. faces in international affairs have not abated after two terms of Reaganism. Indeed they have been exacerbated. The luster of simple solutions certainly will grow dimmer as the need to reconfigure the world economy, and the U.S. role in it, grows more apparent.[18] Reagan has bought some time, much more than Carter ever could hope to have. But that time will run out on his successors.

Whose president is it, anyway?

The lesson here, I think, for those endorsing a structural approach to the presidency, is that if the presidency is ever to break the grip of the imperatives of the state, which if left unattended threaten a crisis of state legitimacy, the imperatives themselves must be recast. The quest for economic growth must be loosened from the strictures of business confidence and corporate designs. The economy must be brought under more democratic planning and control. Only then will the president, and the state, actually have within their reach the policy tools necessary to come closer to fulfilling the expectations that accompany their democratic accountability.

One way to begin thinking about such changes is to consider the need for democratic accountability in economic institutions that wield enormous power over our lives without a commensurate degree of citizen input. For instance, the Federal Reserve Board, whose nominal "independence" is belied by the composition of its members and the interests it responds to, should be subject to democratic control, along with the money supply, through the appointment of all members to four year terms coinciding with presidential elections, instead of the current 14-year terms. And they should report directly to either Congress or the executive branch. Similarly, corporations should be subject to controls on their ability to move nationally and internationally, to respond to the unaccountable and undemocratic nature of "capital flight." And the pressures of "capital strike" could be addressed through national programs to facilitate worker ownership and control of plants threatened by closure, along with local and federal public investment programs to offset the decline of private investment.[19]

Additionally, the spiraling logic of consumption and corporate product priorities must be slowed and countered. For a more democratically-controlled economy would not have escaped the escalatory logic of growth—the consumptive equivalent of the arms race—if the "more is better" logic goes unquestioned. In the absence of such changes, the public likely will be consigned to frustration over the intractability of the problems which emerge in these times of economic dislocation and crisis.[20] I am not pretending here to dissect the specifics of such ideas, ideas which would engender critically-needed discussion of the ends of social life. Rather, the point is to argue generally that measures such as these—which challenge the prevailing policy assumptions of all presidents and policy elites, Democratic and Republican alike—need to be incorporated into public debate *if* the president is to marshall the democratic power of the state to actually formulate and implement a truly *public* policy.

Likewise, ideas about national security must be freed from their moorings in the arms race, and especially the growing reliance on counterforce weaponry. The equation of nuclear arms and security, while always dubious, is even less true, and even more dangerous, today. Moreover, as suggested in the previous chapter, the issue of the arms race leads right back into the issues of economic growth and the national security state's global projection of power. They are inseparable concerns. Of course, to even speak of redefining our notions of growth and security sets the head spinning. Yet who knows if the seeds for radical changes in the U.S. perception of *its* options have been sewn in the ongoing changes in the Soviet Union, as Mikhail Gorbachev attempts to implement policies of glasnost (openness) and perestroika (restructuring) against entrenched resistance. Such complex, far-reaching possibilities may contradict and diminish the short-term appeal of President Reagan's simple messages; they may undermine the pragmatic messages of his plodding successor George Bush. But the problems of state crisis, presidential crisis, and public expectations are intimately connected. To begin to come to grips with how difficult the solution to them would be, is to begin to move toward such a solution. Wolfe's insight on the future of presidency is appropriate here, and applies to more than just the economy:

> The American people will either have to accept a presidency as contained and narrow-based as their economic system or they will have to democratize their economy to match their grandiose vision of presidential leadership.[21]

The vision people hold of the president and the state is not irrational or unreasonable. But it is demanding, and increasingly so in an era of rising international challenges to America's global position.

A presidency empowered to more closely meet those demands in the ways admittedly barely sketched above would in fact be a strong—even "expansivist"—chief executive. But it would be a democratic strength, not a plebiscitary one. This distinction cannot be overemphasized. As we've seen, the issue of the nature of presidential strength has pervaded debates about the chief executive throughout the twentieth century. For much of the century the liberal agenda of Franklin Roosevelt was celebrated as the essence of the active, expansivist chief executive. But the expansivist perspective proved to be malleable and open to competing claims. Later presidency scholars, such as Neustadt, would carry the banner of the active Rooseveltian president but without his agenda, often reducing FDR to personality and administrative technique.

Following the turmoil of the 1960s and early 1970s, conservatives attempted to claim FDR's kind of presidency as their own in an historical irony that saw the emergence of what might be

called a "Roosevelt in reverse,"[22] perhaps culminating in Ronald
Reagan, whose campaign in 1980 often drew on the memory of
FDR even though his stated mission was to undo much of the
New Deal legacy. One group of establishment elites—the
internationally-oriented corporate, political and academic leaders
of the Trilateral Commission, founded in 1973—saw the decline
of the legitimacy of the presidency in the wake of Vietnam and
Watergate as a troubling outgrowth of the "democratic surge" of
protest that threatened the "governability of American
democracy." In the 1975 report to the Trilateral Commission on
the governability of democracies, entitled *The Crisis of Democracy*,
political scientist Samuel Huntington, author of the section on
the United States, lamented the profusion of civic protest of the
1960s. This protest presented "the danger of overloading the
political system with demands which extend its functions and
undermine its authority."[23] The chief institutional casualty of this
societal "excess of democracy" was the presidency:

> Probably no development of the 1960s and 1970s has greater
> import for the future of American politics than the decline in the
> authority, status, influence, and effectiveness of the presidency.[24]

From the Trilateral perspective, the crisis of democracy stimulated
by an overly-engaged citizenry also posed a treat to capitalism
and corporate power. "Truman had been able to govern the
country with the cooperation of a relatively small number of Wall
Street lawyers and bankers," Huntington observed. "By the
mid-1960s, the sources of power in society had diversified
tremendously, and this was no longer possible."[25] The presidency
needed to be relegitimized and active, but in opposition to, not
with, popular demands.

A trace of the Trilateral anxiety about challenges to presidential
authority can be found in the proposals of a newer group, the
Committee on the Constitutional System (CCS). Formed in 1982,
this organization of prominent citizens from a variety of government, business, financial, academic and other backgrounds has
as its aim promoting "the effectiveness and accountability of
government."[26] Included as one of three Committee co-chairs is
Lloyd Cutler, a Washington lawyer, former White House counsel
to President Carter and Trilateral member. The CCS essentially
looks to formulate proposals to overcome the deadlock and

incoherence that result from a constitutional system of balanced but divided powers. They offer a series of constitutional amendments, federal statutes and party rule reforms to modernize the political structure to facilitate competence in government, particularly a closer, parliamentary-style coordination of power between Congress and the president.

What is striking about the committee's "structural reforms" is the disjuncture between the seemingly innocuous nature of such tinkering with the machinery of government and the potential implication of such elite strategies.[27] The CCS says nothing about the substantive ends of political and economic life toward which its procedural proposals would move the polity. Indeed, the Committee evinces little care, and even a whiff of disdain, for the views of the public concerning these matters, instead choosing to see its program as a mere technical correction to the designs of the framers. As political scientist and CCS member James Sundquist contends:

> Structural amendments, in the absence of governmental breakdown that is indisputably traceable to institutional rather than individual failure, are inherently technical and abstract, not likely to arouse emotion. But the very fact that government has not broken down attests, in the popular mind, to the wisdom of the constitutional design. The absence of criticism surely reflects a faith that the structure that has survived so long without formal alteration must have served the country well since the beginning and can be counted on to serve it no less well in times to come.[28]

The committee assumes citizen quiescence toward governmental structure and correspondingly regards the citizens' role as little more than a voter. Moreover, it is virtually silent about the changing context of political economy within which such elite strengthening measures would be implemented and the implications of more centralized political power for citizen power. And there seems to be a presumption within the CCS that public discussion about the purposes of political life should come after (if at all?) the ratification of elite plans for the mechanisms of government.

The agenda for change offered by the CCS puts the cart before the horse. What are the stakes involved for the people if a more coordinated, powerful, Hamiltonian presidency emerges from such reform? What should the state do with its clout? Does the American political system, with modification, adequately serve the interests of the people, or is the political-economic system itself a problem? The CCS and the Trilateral Commission equate a lack of citizen arousal with satisfaction, and they view vigorous direct popular involvement as either a threat (Trilateral Commission) or as, at best, a peripheral issue (CCS). But perhaps apathy signals resignation or disgust with the system. A centralized, efficient, sheer "Neohamiltonian" type of strength wed to the interests of corporate-military power would be no improvement over the drift and delay that so concerns mainstream elites. Meaningful democratization of the political economy would have to entail the simultaneous expansion of popular avenues of participation, including the emergence of a truly progressive-left party. In the absence of lively public debate over the direction and control of the American political economy, calls to unify a divided government will primarily serve to freeze the status quo as it strengthens the institutions that sustain it.

Critics undoubtedly will charge that the kind of system-challenging changes suggested here are impractical and unrealistic. They certainly do not meet the standards of "viable" public policy advanced in Neustadt's discussion of presidential power and expertise necessarily committing the chief executive to working within the parameters of the established system.[29] Yet one of the enduring lessons of history is that systems change, structures change. Sociologist Robert Bellah and his associates remind us of this important fact in *Habits of the Heart*, their widely-acclaimed critique of liberal individualism in American culture. "Structures are not unchanging," Bellah writes. "They are frequently altered by social movements, which grow out of, and also influence, changes in consciousness, climates of opinion, and culture."[30] Bellah's focus is on the interplay between character and society and how our mores affect, and reflect, our cultural and moral life. He looks there to find "new flights of the social imagination" that may guide society onto new paths.

Might not the presidential candidacies of the Rev. Jesse Jackson in 1984 and 1988 be indicators that new flights of social, political and economic imagination are possible in the U.S. as the twenty-first century approaches? Setting aside questions of personality which have preoccupied so many analysts, the *issues*

he has raised—a decidedly non-elite politics of inclusion, transformation of the war economy of the national security state into
a peace economy, wholesale overhaul of the nation's budgetary
priorities, explicit criticisms of the ability of multinational captial
to dominate the lives of workers at home and abroad, and
others—all draw on a critique of American society which has a
class-based appeal near its heart. And he did achieve a remarkable
increase in citizen support, white and black, in his second run
for the White House with his radical reform agenda, an agenda
from which the Democratic party and its overwhelmingly better-
financed candidates had to distance themselves, while appearing
to treat Jackson with respect. Regardless of how he personally
fares as a political candidate in the future, he has provided a
glimmer of hope that an alternative politics can succeed in the U.S.

This book has focused primarily on explaining incarceration—
the president as a prisoner of a structure of economic power and
national security interests that dominate the landscape of the
American political economy. It has devoted scant attention to
liberation, yet the two projects obviously are intimately connected.
To understand one is to have a more realistic shot at the other.
Prisons need not hold us forever. Again, structures can change.

This book also has centered on an even more specific
dimension of this incarcertion, namely the extent to which the
discipline of political science has contributed to our intellectual
misunderstanding of the nature and possibilities of the office of
the presidency. Having surveyed the terrain of presidential
scholarship we are left, in the final analysis, with a paradox. The
more we desire to understand the presidency and the many
dilemmas it currently confronts, the more we need to cast our
vision beyond the procedural confines of the office, and the
personalities of those holding it, and into the broader realm of
theories of the state and political economy. For until the twin
structural imperatives of the state are rethought, challenged and
tamed, we can expect the presidency to remain in crisis, and
imprisoned.

Introduction

1."What's In Store At The Fed," cover story, *Business Week*, June 15, 1987, pp. 26–30.

2. William Greider, *Secrets of the Temple: How the Federal Reserve Runs the Country* (New York: Simon and Schuster, 1987), p. 12. For an analysis of the antidemocratic nature of the Federal Reserve Board, see also Robert Lekachman, "The FED In Fact And Fiction," *Dissent* (Winter, 1988). An excellent account of the tight money, anti-inflation policies of the Fed under Paul Volcker, and its dramatic impact on President Carter's chances in the 1980 presidential election, can be found in Gerald Epstein, "Domestic Stagflation and Monetary Policy: The Federal Reserve and the Hidden Election," in Thomas Ferguson and Joel Rogers, eds., *The Hidden Election* (New York: Pantheon, 1981).

3. Greider, *Secrets of the Temple*, p. 12.

4. The phenomenon of "capital strike" will receive fuller attention in Chapter Two. For an analysis of capital strike and the ability of business generally to punish the economy, see, among others, Charles E. Lindblom, "The Market As Prison," in Thomas Ferguson and Joel Rogers, eds., *The Political Economy: Readings in the Politics and Economics of American Public Policy* (Armonk, NY: M.E. Sharpe, 1984), originally published in *The Journal of Politics*, Vol. 44, No. 2 (May, 1982); Fred Block, "The Ruling Class Does Not Rule: Notes on the Marxist Theory of the State," in Ferguson and Rogers, *The Political Economy*, originally published in *Socialist Revolution*, Number 33, Vol. 7, No. 3 (1977); and Samuel Bowles and Herbert Gintis, *Democracy and Capitalism* (New York: Basic Books, 1986), especially pp. 87–91.

5. Lindblom, "The Market As Prison," p. 4.

6. Ibid., p. 6.

7. Lindblom, "The Market As Prison." For his discussion of the privileged position of business, see his seminal work *Politics and Markets* (New York: Basic Books, 1977). An interesting and spirited critique of this privileged position thesis can be found in G. William Domhoff, "State Autonomy and the Privileged Position of Business: An Empirical Attack on a Theoretical Fantasy," *Journal of Political and Military Sociology*, Vol. 14 (Spring, 1986). Domhoff argues the point that the position of business is not so privileged and certain as to preclude the need for big business to continually fight to maintain and defend its interests vis-a-vis the state.

8. For the clearest presentation of this "demand constraint" of capitalist democracy, see Joshua Cohen and Joel Rogers, *On Democracy* (New York: Penguin, 1983), chapter 3, and especially pp. 51–53. A probing look at the limits of reformist governments, particularly in Europe, can be found in Ralph Miliband, *The State in Capitalist Society,* (New York: Basic Books, 1969).

9. For a brief look at Hamilton's role in the creation of the presidency, see Donald L. Robinson, "The Inventors of the Presidency," *Presidential Studies Quarterly,* Vo. XIII, No. 1 (Winter, 1983). For a more analytic and critical account of Hamilton's larger project—his central role in defining the "origin, character, and ultimate meaning of the American Constitution"—see Kenneth M. Dolbeare and Linda Medcalf, "The Dark Side of the Constitution," in John F. Manley and Kenneth M. Dolbeare, eds., *The Case Against the Constitution: From the Antifederalists to the Present* (Armonk, NY: M.E. Sharpe, 1987). A critique (albeit to me an unsatisfying one) of the notion of the centrality of Hamilton to the modern presidency can be found in Richard Loss, "Alexander Hamilton and the Modern Presidency: Continuity or Discontinuity?" *Presidential Studies Quarterly,* Vol. XII, No. 1 (Winter, 1982). On Hamilton's role, see also Bert A. Rockman, *The Leadership Question* (New York: Praeger, 1984), pp. 36–43.

10. These objectives are explored in some depth by William Appleman Williams, *Empire As A Way Of Life* (New York: Oxford University Press, 1980); Douglas F. Dowd, *The Twisted Dream* (Cambridge, MA: Winthrop, 1977); and Saul Landau, *The Dangerous Doctrine: National Security and U.S. Foreign Policy* (Boulder, CO: Westview Press, 1988). Hamilton's thoughts on economic expansion can be found in his reports on public credit, a national bank and manufacturers. See his *Papers on Public Credit, Commerce, and Finance,* ed. Samuel McKee, Jr. (New York: Bobbs-Merrill, 1957).

11. James MacGregor Burns, *Presidential Government,* Sentry Ed. (Boston: Houghton Mifflin, 1973); and Theodore J. Lowi, *The Personal President* (Ithaca, NY: Cornell University Press, 1985).

12. Woodrow Wilson, *Congressional Government* (Boston: Houghton, Mifflin, 1985), p. 6.

13. Ibid., p. 23.

14. Ibid., pp. 253–254.

15. Woodrow Wilson, *Constitutional Government in the United States* (New York: Columbia University, 1908), p. 70. This shift in Wilson's thinking has been pointed out by others, notably Edward S. Corwin, *The President: Office and Powers,* 4th Rev. Ed. (New York: New York University Press, 1957), pp. 26–30; and Burns, *Presidential Government,* pp. 88–97.

16. Ibid., pp. 78–79.

17. Ibid., pp. 202–203.

18. William E. Leuchtenburg, *Franklin D. Roosevelt and the New Deal, 1932–1940* (New York: Harper and Row, 1963), p. 327. A short hisotry of the presidency as an academic field of study can be found in George Reedy, "Discovering the Presidency," *The New York Times Book Review,* January 20, 1985.

19. Lowi, *The Personal President,* p. 58.

20. William E. Leuchtenburg, *In The Shadow of FDR* (Ithaca, NY: Cornell University Press, 1985).

21. Clinton Rossiter, *The American Presidency,* Revised Ed. (New York: Mentor Books, 1960), p. 14.

22. Jimmy Carter, *Why Not The Best?* (Nashville, TN: Broadman, 1975), p. 154.

23. Jimmy Carter, "Crisis of Confidence Televised Address," *President Carter 1979* (Washington, D.C.: Congressional Quarterly, 1980), p. 46–A.

24. Arthur M. Schlesinger,Jr., *The Imperial Presidency* (New York: Popular Library, 1974); Thomas E. Cronin, *The State of the Presidency,* 2nd Ed. (Boston: Little, Brown, 1980); Hugh Heclo and Lester M. Salamon, eds., *The Illusion of Presidential Government* (Boulder, CO: Westview, 1981); James Ceasar, Glen E. Thurow, Jeffrey Tulis, and Joseph M. Bessette, "The Rise of the Rhetorical Presidency," in Thomas E. Cronin, ed., *Rethinking the Presidency* (Boston: Little, Brown, 1982); Harold M. Barger, *The Impossible Presidency* (Glenview, IL: Scott, Foresman, 1984); and Lowi, *The Personal President.*

25. Among the very best analyses of the structure of the American political economy is Cohen and Rogers' cogent book *On Democracy,* specially chapters 3–5. See also Samuel Bowles and Herbert Gintis, *Democracy and Capitalism;* and Samuel Bowles, David M. Gordon, and Thomas W. Weisskopf, *Beyond the Waste Land* (New York: Anchor/Doubleday, 1983).

26. Lowi, *The Personal President,* pp. 96, 174, and 180. An insightful and lively overview of the literature on theories of the state is provided in Martin Carnoy, *The State and Political Theory* (Princeton: Princeton University Press, 1984). Bert Rockman senses the importance of understanding the nature of the state within the American political economy, but offers little help in exploring the relationship between the state and the presidency, beyond noting America's antistatist ideology. See his *The Leadership Question,* chapter 3, and especially pp. 49–58. For a more revealing and critical analysis of the complex relationship between the nation's antistatist ideology of limited government and the economy's developing need for "big government," see Edward S. Greenberg, *Capitalism and the American Political Ideal* (Armonk, NY: M.E. Sharpe, 1985).

27. For a detailed development of this position see Alan Wolfe, *America's Impasse: The Rise and Fall of the Politics of Growth* (New York: Pantheon, 1981); and Wolfe, "Presidential Power and the Crisis of Modernization," *democracy,* Vol. 1, No. 2 (April, 1981). This kind of structural account of the presidency,

although with less explicit development of the presidency-state connection, also can be found in Bruce Miroff's penetrating critique of the Kennedy administration, *Pragmatic Illusions: The Presidental Politics of John F. Kennedy* (New York: David McKay Co., 1976). Many structural themes also can be discerned in an excellent theoretical overview of a radical approach to the presidency provided in Michael A. Genovese and Robert J. Welch, S.J., "The Radical/Critical Approach To The Presidency," paper delivered at the 1987 Annual Meeting of the American Political Science Association, Chicago, IL, September 3–6, 1987. See also Douglas J. Hoekstra's brief comments on the "Radicals' Presidency" in "The 'Textbook Presidency' Revisited," *Presidential Studies Quarterly*, Vol. XII, No. 2 (Spring, 1982).

28. Richard Neustadt exemplifies the common lack of serious attention to the decline of U.S. hegemony with his blithe comments on the ability (and implicit desirability) of the U.S. to regain its postwar position of preeminence in the Preface to the 1980 edition of his seminal book *Presidental Power*:

> If there was an "American Century," as Henry Luce proclaimed after the Second World War, it lasted only twice as long as Adolph Hitler's Thousand Year Reich. Tantalizingly, unlike the Reich, conditions favoring this country's sense of independence and security—if not quite the old substance—could return with a few well-placed technological breakthroughs.

See his *Presidential Power: The Politics of Leadership From FDR to Carter* (New York: John Wiley, 1980), p. xiii.

29. There is a large body of work specifying the institutional developments of the postwar domestic and international accords which sustained U.S. hegemony, the details of which cannot be explored here. See Bowles, Gordon and Weisskopf, *Beyond the Waste Land*, chapters 2–4; Samuel Bowles and Herbert Gintis, "The Crisis of Liberal Democratic Capitalism: The Case of the United States," *Politics and Society*, Vol. 11, No. 1 (1982); Cohen and Rogers, *On Democracy*, chapter 4; and Greenberg, *Capitalism and the American Political Ideal*, chapters 8–9.

Chapter One

1. James MacGregor Burns, *Presidential Government*, Sentry Ed. (Boston: Houghton Mifflin, 1973), originally published in 1965; George Reedy, "Discovering the Presidency," *The New York Times Book Review*, January 20, 1985.

2. Among the many who make this point, see Burns, ibid., pp. 57–66; and Clinton Rossiter, *The American Presidency*, Revised Ed. (New York: Mentor Books, 1960), pp. 96–98.

3. For an analysis of the connection between the presidency and the rise of Progressive Era state intervention into the economy, see Gabriel Kolko's classic

The Triumph of Conservatism (New York: The Free Press, 1963). A more succinct account can be found in Edward S. Greenberg, *Capitalism and the American Political Ideal* (Armonk, NY: M.E. Sharpe, 1985), chapters 5 and 6. Woodrow Wilson captured the feel of this modern conception of the role of the state in a campaign speech in 1912 where he contrasts the traditional laissez-faire notion of limited government with the Progressive Era idea of the positive state:

> But I feel confident that if Jefferson were living in our day he would see what we see: that the individual is caught in a great confused nexus of all sorts of complicated circumstances, and that to let him alone is to leave him helpless as against the obstacles with which he has to contend; and that, therefore, law in our day must come to the assistance of the individual. . . . Freedom to-day is something more than being let alone. The program of a government of freedom must in these days be positive, not negative merely.

See Wilson's *The New Freedom* (New York: Doubleday, Page, 1913), p. 284.

4. Theodore Roosevelt, *An Autobiography* (New York: Macmillan, 1913), pp. 388–389.

5. Ibid., pp. 420–421.

6. Ibid., p. 395. See pp. 349–399 for the full account of the contending approaches to the presidency. The importance of the contrast between Theodore Roosevelt's view of the president and the view of William Howard Taft has been cited by many scholars of the presidency, notably Rossiter, *The American Presidency*, pp. 96–99; Burns, *Presidential Government*, pp. 57–66 and 108–110; Edwards S. Corwin, *The President: Office and Powers*, 4th Ed. (New York: New York University Press, 1957), pp. 150–151; Arthur M. Schlesinger, Jr., *The Imperial Presidency* (New York: Popular Library, 1974), pp. 90–92; and Raymond Tatalovich and Byron W. Daynes, *Presidential Power in the United States* (Monterey, CA.: Brooks/Cole, 1984), pp. 373–376. For an account of FDR's indebtedness to Theodore Roosevelt's conception of the presidency, see Arthur M. Schlesinger, Jr., *The Crisis of the Old Order* (Boston: Houghton Mifflin, 1956), pp. 482–484.

7. William Howard Taft, *Our Chief Magistrate and His Powers* (New York: Columbia University Press, 1916) p. 144.

8. Ibid., pp. 139–140. For Taft's view of the executive presented in somewhat different terms, see his *The Presidency* (New York: Charles Scribner's Sons, 1916), pp. 121–142, especially pp. 138–139.

9. Roosevelt's view is here taken from Schlesinger, *The Crisis of the Old Order*, p. 483.

10. George Reedy, "Discovering the Presidency," p. 22.

11. I have chosen the label "restrictivist" as opposed to the "revisionist" label used by some contemporary scholars. It seems to me that a "revisionist"

work—think of revisionist history—sets out to *rewrite* and *reinterpret* a body of previously accepted knowledge. Analysts of the presidency who are sometimes called revisionists, though, really have not offered a new interpretation of the office or its occupants. Most of them simply have had second thoughts about presidential power in the wake of Vietnam and Watergate. I do not think that second thoughts, or some degree of a change of heart, are enough to merit the term "revisionist" in any meaningful sense. A frontal challenge to an orthodox body of scholarship would be needed for that. For a look at some recent work that explores what it calls the "revisionist" perspective on the presidency, see Harold Barger, *The Impossible Presidency* (Glenview, IL: Scott, Foresman, 1984); John Hart, "Presidential Power Revisited," *Political Studies*, Vol. XXV, No.1 (1977); and Tatalovich and Daynes, *Presidential Power in the United States.*

12. Burns, *Presidential Government*, p. 29. For his full development of the Hamiltonian model, see chapter 1 and pp. 112–117.

13. James MacGregor Burns, *The Deadlock of Democracy* (Englewood Cliffs, NJ: Prentice-Hall, 1963).

14. Burns, *Presidential Government*, p. 338.

15. Ibid., p. 66

16. For accounts of the arrogance of Roosevelt, Taft and Wilson toward nations that seemingly threatened the interests of American empire, see William Appleman Williams, *Empire As a Way of Life* (New York: Oxford University Press, 1980), chapter 6; and Noam Chomsky, *Turning the Tide* (Boston: South End Press, 1985), especially chapters 2 and 3.

17. Burns, Presidential Government, p. 346.

18. Even political scientists who take a very different approach to the study of the presidency can wind up endorsing the expansivist school. Perhaps the best example is the subgroup of presidency scholars who study personality and character as key variables. Both James David Barber and Erwin Hargrove have the expansivist-restrictivist range of debate in mind in their work (albeit with different language and categorization), and they clearly prefer the former type of president. See Barber, *The Presidential Character: Predicting Performance in the White House*, 2nd Ed. (Englewood Cliffs, NJ: Prentice-Hall, 1977); and two works by Hargrove, *Presidential Leadership: Personality and Political Style* (New York: Macmillan, 1966), and "What Manner of Man? The Crisis of the Contemporary Presidency," in James David Barber, ed., *Choosing the President* (Englewood Cliffs, NJ: Prentice-Hall, 1974).

19. He was thinking in particular of his fellow countryman James Bryce and his book *The American Commonwealth* (London: The Macmillan Co., 1888).

20. *The American Presidency: An Interpretation* (New York: Harper and Brothers, 1940), p. 11. In 1980, Transaction Books published a new edition of

Laski's text as part of its "Social Science Classics Series," with an introduction by James MacGregor Burns. The pagination is consistent in the two books.

21. Ibid., p. 90.

22. Ibid., p. 123.

23. Ibid., p. 235.

24. Ibid., p. 61.

25. Ibid., p. 165.

26. Ibid., p. 268.

27. Ibid., p. 274.

28. Ibid., p. 278.

29. Ibid., p. 182.

30. Quoted in Arthur M. Schlesinger, Jr. *The Politics of Upheaval* (Boston: Houghton Mifflin, 1960), p. 620.

31. Among the many works adopting the corporate liberal approach to history are Kolko, *The Triumph of Conservatism:* James Weinstein, *The Corporate Ideal in the Liberal State* (Boston: Beacon, 1968); and Kim McQuaid, *Big Business and Presidential Power: From FDR to Reagan* (New York: William Morrow, 1982). For critiques of the approach see Theda Skocpol, "Political Response to Capitalist Crisis: Neo-Marxist Theories of the State and the Case of the New Deal," *Politics and Society,* Vol. 10, No. 2 (1980); and Fred Block, "Beyond Corporate Liberalism," *Social Problems,* No. 24 (1977).

32. Rossiter, *The American Presidency,* p. 14.

33. A friend and fellow presidency scholar Richard Neustadt explains that one of Rossiter's goals in writing *The American Presidency* was to improve general citizenship. See Richard Neustadt, "What Did I Think I Was Doing?" in *Presidency Research*, Vol. VII, No. 2 (Spring, 1985), pp.. 3–14.

34. David L. Paletz, "Perspectives On The Presidency," *Law and Contemporary Problems*, Vol. 35, No. 3 (Summer, 1970). For a perspective deeply indebted to Rossiter's roles approach, but which argues that he confuses what should be the distinct categories of "roles" and mere "obligations", see Tatalovich and Daynes, *Presidential Power in the United States,* chapter 1. One theorist argues that because of the positivist, normative blindness of post-Watergate textbook treatments of the president, Rossiter's focus on roles, or "hats," unfortunately remains all too prevalent, forcing students "to maintain a kind of agnosticism about the proper ends of government or the presidency." See Douglas J. Hoekstra, "The 'Textbook Presidency' Revisited," *Presidential Studies Quarterly*, Vol. XIII, No. 2 (Spring, 1982), p. 165.

35. Rossiter, *The American Presidency,* p. 28.

36. Two recent analysts take issue with the inclusion of four of these five as true "roles," viewing them as obligations (chief of party is the exception). See note 34.

37. Rossiter, *The American Presidency*, p. 28.

38. Ibid., p. 39.

39. Ibid., p. 66.

40. Ibid., p. 69.

41. Ibid., p. 102.

42. For a look at how historians and political scientists have ranked U.S. presidents in surveys spanning more than 20 years, see Tatalovich and Daynes, *Presidential Power in the United States*, pp. 2–3; Burns' views on such rankings can be found in *Presidential Government*, pp. 78–88.

43. Rossiter, *The American Presidency*, p. 140.

44. The quality of mercy can be seen in Rossiter's treatment of Harry Truman as among the eight "great" chief executives. He defends this rating on the grounds that despite his many controversial decisions in foreign affairs, none, not the use of atomic weaponry nor the Korean War, "has been proven wrong, stupid, or contrary to the best judgement and interests of the American people." Rossiter sees in him proof of the democratic principle that a person of average abilities can fulfill the obligations of the toughest job in the world.

45. Indeed, one of the reasons Rossiter rates Rutherford B. Hayes among the six "notable" (near great) presidents is his dispatch of federal troops to crush the first nationwide strike in U.S. history—the railroad strike of 1877. Ultimately more than 100 strikers were killed in the struggle, a fact which Hayes dryly notes in his dairy: "The strikers have been put down by force." Rossiter does not tell us why such carnage should enhance the status of a chief executive. For an account of this mass strike see, among others, Jeremy Brecher, *Strike!* (Boston: South End Press, 1972), chapter 1; and Richard Boyer and Herbert Morais, *Labor's Untold Story* (New York: United Electrical, Radio and Machine Workers of America, 1955), pp. 58–63.

44. Rossiter, *The American Presidency*, p. 228.

47. Ibid., p. 229.

48. Ibid., p. 246.

49. He clearly has Rossiter in mind when he acknowledges his intent to move beyond the functional, role-oriented approach. See *Presidential Power* (New York: John Wiley and Sons, 1980), p. vi. Recently he reaffirmed this goal and added that he had sought to move beyond Edward Corwin's classic constitutional perspective as well. See "What Did I Think I was Doing?"

pp. 4–10. Corwin will be dealt with in the next section on restrictivist approaches. For additional thoughts on Neustadt's break with traditional orientations to the presidency, see Hart, "Presidential Power Revisited," pp. 48–61; and Ira Katznelson and Mark Kesselman, *The Politics of Power*, 2nd Ed. (New York: Harcourt Brace Jovanovich, 1979), pp. 264–265.

50. Neustadt, *Presidential Power*, p. v.

51. Ibid., p. 28–29.

52. For a critique of Neustadt's exclusive emphasis on instrumental motivations as the ones that move people the president would persuade and bargain with, see Peter W. Sperlich, "Bargaining and Overload: An Essay on *Presidential Power*," in Aaron Wildavsky, *Perspectives on the Presidency* (Boston: Little, Brown, 1975), pp. 406–430. Sperlich argues against the Neustadtian view that the president must assume everyone he or she deals with, even the closest of advisers, is a kind of opponent who must be manipulated with rewards and punishments having a direct impact on the person's self-interest. Given the enormous popularity of Neustadt's book, it is surprising how little critical attention it has received. Sperlich's is probably the most widely known and oft-cited review.

53. Neustadt, *Presidential Power*, p. 89.

54. Ibid., p. 114.

55. Ibid., 118–119.

56. For a discussion of Neustadt's lack of concern for the ends of presidential power, see Thomas Cronin, *The State of the Presidency*, 2nd Ed. (Boston: Little, Brown, 1980), chapter 4. I critique Cronin at length later in the chapter.

57. Ibid., p. 142.

58. Ibid., p. 136.

59. Hargrove, "What Manner of Man? The Crisis of the Contemporary Presidency," p. 7. It should be kept in mind, though, that Hargrove tends to reduce the woeful performance of expansivist presidents to defects in LBJ and Nixon's personality and character, minimizing flaws in the political system itself. (See note 18, too.) Among the *numerous* analysts who cite Vietnam and Watergate as the points of origin for this new outlook, see Hart, "Presidential Power Revisited"; Schlesinger, *The Imperial Presidency*; and Tatalovich and Daynes, *Presidential Power in the United States*.

60. Lester M. Salamon, "Beyond the Presidential Illusion—Toward a Constitutional Presidency," in Hugh Heclo and Lester M. Salamon, eds., *The Illusion of Presidential Government* (Boulder, Co.: Westview, 1981), pp. 287–288.

61. Corwin, *The President: Office and Powers*, p. 29–30 and p. 307.

62. Ibid., p. 30.

63. Chomsky is referring to Schlesinger's *A Thousand Days* (Boston: Houghton Mifflin, 1965). Chomsky's critique of Schlesinger's history—which he finds to be subservient to the powers that be—and liberal scholarship in general, can be found in numerous works. Among them, *American Power and the New Mandarins* (New York: Pantheon, 1967), especially "Bitter Heritage" and "The Responsibility of Intellectuals," but passim as well; and "The Bounds of Thinkable Thought," *The Progressive,* October, 1985. Schlesinger served as a special assistant to JFK.

64. Schlesinger, *The Imperial Presidency,* pp. 10 and 129.

65. Ibid., p. 465.

66. Ibid., p. 105.

67. Ibid., p. 164. For a probing look at the constituent elements of world politics and the cold war that explores the interests and motives untouched by Schlesinger's analysis, see Fred Halliday, *The Making of the Second Cold War,* 2nd Ed. (London: Verso, 1986). Anticommunism and the cold war climate in the postwar period receive unusually insightful examination in Ralph Miliband, John Saville and Marcel Liebman, eds., *Socialist Register 1984: The Uses of Anti-Communism* (London: Merlin, 1984), particularly essays by Miliband and Liebman, "Reflections on Anti-Communism," and Alan Wolfe, "The Irony of Anti-Communism: Ideology and Interest in Post-war American Foreign Policy." On the fraudulent nature of the Soviet "threat" to the Straits of Dardanelles, Iran and Greece, particularly Dean Acheson's role in promoting the threat as a cold war strategy, see also Noam Chomsky, *On Power and Ideology* (Boston: South End Press, 1987), chapters 1 and 2.

68. Schlesinger, *The Imperial Presidency,* p. 187.

69. Ibid., p. 196.

70. Ibid., p.289.

71. Ibid., p. 316.

72. An earlier version of the central theme of his book—his critique of "the textbook presidency"—was delivered in a paper entitled "The Textbook Presidency and Political Science" at the American Political Science Association Convention in September, 1970. This predated Schlesinger's work by three years. For a 1974–1980 update of Cronin's thesis see Hoekstra, "The 'Textbook Presidency' Revisited."

73. Cronin, *The State of the Presidency,* p. 2.

74. Ibid., p. 4.

75. Ibid., p. 24.

76. Ibid., p. 76.

77. Cronin does recognize Neustadt's as perhaps the central work on the presidency. He devotes an entire chapter (albeit a short one) to a review of Neustadt's *Presidential Power*. Though counting it as "among the best analytical treatments we have," he finds it generally "too worshipful of power" and sees an elitist thread running through it. Neustadt mirrors the prevailing view which contains "an implicit, if not explicit, fear of the masses juxtaposed with a robust faith in the great leader" (p. 132).

78. Cronin, *The State of the Presidency,* pp. 76–77.

79. Ibid., p. 138.

80. This section draws on pp. 84–100.

81. For the Johnson presidency (with explicit implications for all presidencies), see *The Twilight of the Presidency* (New York: Mentor, 1970), written by George Reedy, LBJ's former Special Assistant. Nixon's presidency receives a most probing examination in Jonathan Schell's *The Time of Illusion* (New York: Vintage, 1975). Concerning the relationship between Nixon and the rest of America, Schell writes that "it became our fate to live for half a decade inside the head of a waking dreamer."

82. Cronin, *The State of the Presidency,* p. 115.

83. Ibid., p. 376.

84. Ibid., p. 379.

85. Theodore J. Lowi, *The Personal President* (Ithaca, NY: Cornell University Press, 1985), p. 20.

86. Ibid., p. 11.

87. This development of the ethic of service delivery is a variation of Lowi's concept of "interest-group liberalism" developed in his widely acclaimed book *The End of Liberalism: The Second Republic of the United States* (New York: Norton, 1979), originally published in 1969. His thesis there is that liberalism has become a system in which the primary public philosophy of government is the satisfaction of various competing private interests of organized groups.

88. Lowi, *The Personal President,* p. 96.

89. Ibid., p. 115.

90. Ibid., p. 151.

91. Ibid., p. 178.

92. Ibid., p. 180.

93. Lowi's discussion of the nine myths can be found on pp. 196–203. It is not necessary here to delve into the specifics.

Chapter Two

1. See Woodrow Wilson, *The New Freedom* (New York: Doubleday, Page, 1913). The introductory quotation is from p. 4.

2. Ibid., p. 57.

3. Ibid., pp. 164–165. It should be noted that here I use the concept of fetishism as it is used in Marxist discourse, to express the conflation of man-made relations with natural processes, so that big business or market relations (surely human constructs) are imbued with natural properties. This notion of fetishism differs from the more common usage in which objects or people are ascribed tremendous, or even magical, powers that are the object of irrational regard or devotion. It is this second sense of the word that I intend in my title to the first chapter, "The Rise and Decline of Presidency Fetishism."

4. Ibid., p. 44. Note the similarity between Wilson's notion of "progressive" politics and Franklin Roosevelt's thoughts on the connection between liberal reform and conservatism, as seen in a quote from his 1936 bid for reelection, cited herein on p. 36 of Chapter One. The two best analyses of the conservative nature of progressive reforms remain the work of Gabriel Kolko, *The Triumph of Conservatism* (New York: The Free Press, 1963); and James Weinstein, *The Corporate Ideal in the Liberal State* (Boston: Beacon, 1968). More recently, such analysis has been carried forward to include a critique of the conservative nature of the supposedly progressive presidency of John F. Kennedy. See Bruce Miroff's excellent study *Pragmatic Illusions* (New York: David McKay Co., 1976).

5. James MacGregor Burns, *The Power To Lead: The Crisis of the American Presidency* (New York: Simon and Schuster, 1984), p. 11.

6. See ibid., pp. 202–211, and chapter 9, for a sustained sense of Burns' notion of structure, but references to the concept are sprinkled throughout.

7. Among the many works devoted to assessing various theoretical approaches to studying the presidency are George C. Edwards III and Stephen J. Wayne, eds., *Studying the Presidency* (Knoxville: University of Tennessee Press, 1983); Aaron Wildavsky, ed., *Perspectives on the Presidency* (Boston: Little, Brown, 1975); Norman C. Thomas, "Studying the Presidency: Where And How Do We Go From Here?" *Presidential Studies Quarterly*, Vol. VII (1977); and David Paletz, "Perspectives On The Presidency," *Law and Contemporary Problems*, Vol. 35, No. 3 (Summer, 1970).

8. Donald L. Robinson, ed., *Reforming American Government* (Boulder, CO: Westview Press, 1985).

9. Stephen J. Wayne, "Approaches," in Edwards and Wayne, *Studying the Presidency*.

10. David F. Prindle, "Toward A Comparative Science of the Presidency: A Pre-Theory," *Presidential Studies Quarterly*, Vol. XVI, No. 3 (Summer, 1986).

11. Thomas E. Cronin, *The State of the Presidency,* 2nd Ed. (Boston: Little, Brown, 1980), p. 377.

12. The 1986 contra aid debate occurred *before* the Iran-contra story broke. If contra aid resulted in the U.S. eventually getting bogged down in a full-scale deployment of U.S. troops, Neustadt might revise such a view. But since the assistance to the contras was obtained through the method of persuasion, through bargaining relationships with Congress, Reagan's victory cannot be construed as Pyrrhic in nature. For the failure inherent in Truman and Eisenhower's presidential "victories" was rooted in their use of the persuasive method of command, instead of bargaining. Process was the issue, not substance.

13. A structural view would seek to do for the concept of "national security" what Jonathan Schell did for the concept of "credibility" as used by the Nixon administration in connection to its policies in Vietnam—only a *thorough* structural analysis would include more than even Schell does, especially in relation to the economic aspects of policy and the uses of anticommunist appeals. See Schell's *The Time of Illusion* (New York: Vintage, 1975).

14. Senator Kerry's arguments against contra aid can be found in the *Congressional Record,* 99th Congress, Second Session, August 12, 1986, pp. 11375-11379. Kerry opposes the means selected by the Reagan administration to overthrow the Sandinistas, but shares the end itself. Indeed he accepts uncritically most of the major administration interpretations of controversial Sandinista behavior, despite much evidence undermining those interpretations—and this, remember, from someone who is arguably the most liberal member of the Senate, and certainly its most outspoken opponent of contra aid. The nature of this shared consensus among liberals and conservatives can be seen further in 1988 congressional debates over funding for the contras. Concerning a proposed Democratic contra aid plan in the House, eventually defeated on March 3, liberal Democratic Representative James A. Traficant, Jr. of Ohio remarked, "I'm not going to sink any more money down a washtub of malfeasance, misfeasance and nonfeasance. In seven years the record is clear. The contras have not overthrown an outhouse and they don't even control a crossroads as far as I can tell." (*New York Times,* March 4, 1988, p. A4). Equally clear is the implication that if the contras *had* overthrown an outhouse and controlled crossroads, Rep. Traficant (and presumably other liberals) would have taken a more supportive view of funding for contra violence and terror. Moreover, the entire funding debate in February and March of 1988 took place within a climate of congressional and media silence on U.S. efforts to sabotage the Central American peace agreement signed in Guatemala City on August 7, 1987. On the nature of liberal and conservative positions on the contras, and congressional debates over funding for them, see Noam Chomsky's two-part essay, "Is Peace At Hand?" *Zeta Magazine,* Vol. 1, No. 1 (January, 1988), and "Central America: The Next Phase," *Zeta Magazine,* Vol. 1, No. 3 (March, 1988); and Alexander Cockburn, "Legends of Antaeus," *Zeta Magazine,* Vol. 1, No. 4, (April, 1988). The most penetrating critique of twentieth century U.S. policy toward Central America in general, and Nicaragua in particular, can be found

in Noam Chomsky's two powerful books *Turning the Tide* (Boston: South End Press, 1985); and *On Power and Ideology* (Boston: South End Press, 1987). See also Peter Kornbluh, *Nicaragua: The Price of Intervention* (Washington, D.C.: Institute for Policy Studies, 1987).

15. For an attempt (albeit an unsatisfying one) to defend mainstream theories from the charge that they are overly descriptive and atheoretical, see Thomas, "Studying the Presidency: Where And How Do We Go From Here?"

16. Ira Katznelson and Mark Kesselman, *The Politics of Power,* 2nd Ed. (New York: Harcourt Brace Jovanovich, 1979), p. 265. For some reason, the authors have omitted the final sentence of this passage from their 3rd edition, (1987), p. 111. For his part, Neustadt maintains that he simply was concerned with the "problem of statecraft" in his book, and that his many critics ignore this problem in their analyses. And ironically, he points out that many analysts have criticized his work as being too prescriptive in nature, out of step with "science." See "What Did I Think I Was Doing?" *Presidency Research,* Vol. VII, No. 2 (Spring, 1985).

17. Miroff, *Pragmatic Illusions,* p. xiii. See also John Hart, "Presidential Power Revisited," *Political Studies,* Vol. XXV, No. 1 (1977). I have taken issue with the term "revisionist" as used to describe this school of thought on the presidency; see note 11 in Chapter One.

18. Ibid., p. xv.

19. For an example of the former, see Paletz, "Perspectives On The Presidency"; for an example of the latter, see Thomas, "Studying The Presidency: Where And How Do We Go From Here?"

20. Theodore J. Lowi, *The Personal President* (Ithaca, NY: Cornell University Press, 1985), pp. 134–137.

21. See note 18, Chapter One, dealing with the expansivist inclinations of the two leading proponents of the psychological approach to the presidency, James David Barber and Erwin Hargrove.

22. Lowi, *The Personal President,* p. 174. Lowi's view of the president as the personification of the state is woven into the fabric of the book, but appears explicitly on pp. 96, 174, and 180. In an interesting related argument, W. Wayne Shannon refers to presidents as the "reification of the nation's meaning." Quoted in Harold M. Barger, *The Impossible Presidency* (Glenview, IL: Scott, Foresman, 1984), p. 16. See also Bert A. Rockman, *The Leadership Question* (New York: Praeger, 1984). On p. xvi Rockman comments: "In the United States, especially, the presidency has come to be considered in contemporary mythology to be the nearest thing to a concrete embodiment of the state." For his discussion of the American state, which actually ends up being a variant of pluralist view, see chapter 3, especially pp. 49–58.

23. The literature on pluralist democracy is enormous. Three seminal works in this vast body are Robert A. Dahl, *A Preface to Democratic Theory* (Chicago:

University of Chicago Press, 1956); Dahl, *Who Governs?* (New Haven: Yale University Press, 1961); and David B. Truman, *The Governmental Process*, 2nd Ed. (New York: Knopf, 1971, originally 1951).

24. On the epistemological presuppositions of theorists of the presidency, see Douglas J. Hoekstra, "The 'Textbook Presidency' Revisited," *Presidential Studies Quarterly*, Vol. XII, No. 2 (Spring, 1982); and Michael A. Genovese and Robert J. Welch, S.J., "The Radical/Critical Approach To The Presidency," paper delivered at the 1987 Annual Meeting of the American Political Science Association, Chicago, IL, September 3–6, 1987.

25. The classic critique of the democratic pluralist conception of the state is offered in Ralph Miliband, *The State in Capitalist Society* (New York: Basic Books, 1969). See also William E. Connolly, ed., *The Bias of Pluralism* (New York: Atherton Press, 1969).

26. Joshua Cohen and Joel Rogers, *On Democracy* (New York: Penguin, 1983). The brief discussion here is particularly indebted to their third chapter entitled "Structure." This is simply the best short account of the structure of American democracy—what they term "capitalist democracy"—that I know of.

27. Ibid., p. 50.

28. The capital strike argument will receive more attention when I discuss structural-functional theories of the state. For a clear explanation of capital strike, see Samuel Bowles and Herbert Gintis, *Democracy and Capitalism* (New York: Basic Books, 1986), pp. 87–91.

29. Cohen and Rogers, *On Democracy*, p. 53.

30. There are a number of good overviews of the literature on theories of the state, among them Martin Carnoy, *The State and Political Theory* (Princeton: Princeton University Press, 1984); David A. Gold, Clarence Y.H. Lo, and Erik Olin Wright, "Recent Developments in Marxist Theories of the Capitalist State," *Monthly Review*, Vol. 27, Nos. 5 and 6 (October, November, 1975); and Bob Jessop, "Recent Theories of the Capitalist State," *Cambridge Journal of Economics*, Vol. 1, No. 4 (December, 1977).

31. Miliband, *The State in Capitalist Society*; G. William Domhoff, *Who Rules America Now?* (Englewood Cliffs, NJ: Prentice-Hall, 1983); and C. Wright Mills, *The Power Elite* (New York: Oxford University Press, 1956). For an interesting critique of instrumentalism, as well as the other approaches to state theory, see Theda Skocpol, "Political Response to Capitalist Crisis: Neo-Marxist Theories of the State and the Case of the New Deal," *Politics and Society*, Vol. 10, No. 2 (1980).

32. Domhoff, *Who Rules America Now?*, p. 1.

33. These relationships are explored by Domhoff in his many works, especially *Who Rules America Now?*, and by Thomas R. Dye, *Who's Running America? The Conservative Years*, 4th Ed., (Englewood Cliffs, NJ: Prentice-Hall, 1986).

34. For an insightful discussion of the growing part played by business PACs and business policy planning organizations in the rightward drift of American politics, see Thomas Edsall, *The New Politics of Inequality* (New York: Norton, 1984). See also Thomas Ferguson and Joel Rogers, *Right Turn* (New York: Hill and Wang, 1986); and Joseph G. Peschek, *Policy-Planning Organizations: Elite Agendas and America's Rightward Turn* (Philadelphia: Temple University Press, 1987).

35. Domhoff, *Who Rules America Now?*, p. 150.

36. Ibid.

37. The debate, first published in *New Left Review*, can be found in Robin Blackburn, *Ideology in Social Science* (New York: Vintage, 1973), including Poulantzas's piece "The Problem of the Capitalist State," and Miliband's "Reply to Nicos Poulantzas." See also Ernest Laclau, *Politics and Ideology in Marxist Theory* (London: New Left Books, 1977), especially chapter 2, "The Specificity of the Political," for a critique of the Miliband-Poulantzas debate.

38. Poulantzas, "The Problem of the Capitalist State," p. 245.

39. Ibid., p. 246.

40. Fred Block, "The Ruling Class Does Not Rule," in Thomas Ferguson and Joel Rogers, eds. *The Political Economy: Readings in the Politics and Economics of American Public Policy* (Armonk, NY: M.E. Sharpe, 1984), p. 40.

41. Samuel Bowles and Herbert Gintis, *Democracy and Capitalism* (New York: Basic Books, 1986), p. 88.

42. Ibid., 88–89.

43. See, for example, James O'Connor, *The Fiscal Crisis of the State* (New York: St. Martin's, 1973).

44. Two of the most probing texts on the issue of legitimacy are Jurgen Habermas, *Legitimation Crisis* (Boston: Beacon, 1973), and William Connolly, ed., *Legitimacy and the State* (New York: New York University Press, 1984).

45. Samuel Bowles and Herbert Gintis, "The Crisis of Liberal Democratic Capitalism: The Case of the United States," *Politics and Society*, Vol. 11, No. 1 (1982), p. 52. Bowles and Gintis suggest that the contradictory nature of this relationship is perhaps most evident when popular struggles strive to extend into the sphere of capitalist production (where *property* rights reign) the rights vested in *persons* by democracy.

46. Ibid., p. 60.

47. Two insightful and creative attempts to bring instrumental analysis to bear on the institution are found in Kim McQuaid, *Big Business and Presidential Power: From FDR to Reagan* (New York: William Morrow, 1982); and Laurence H. Shoup, *The Carter Presidency and Beyond* (Palo Alto, CA: Ramparts, 1980).

The former examines the influence of the Business Council (and its sister organization the Business Roundtable) on presidential policy-making since the New Deal, while the latter traces the formidable connections between the "Eastern Establishment" (especially through the Trilateral Commission) and a single president, Carter. Of the handful of critical introductory American government textbooks, the most illuminating structural analysis of the presidency is presented in Katznelson and Kesselman, *The Politics of Power*, 3rd Ed., chapter 4. David Paletz does deserve mention for including the "Power Elite" category of analysis (with Mills, Domhoff and Chomsky as its representatives) as an "emerging perspective" among the six key perspectives on the office. See his brief survey of the literature, "Perspectives On The Presidency." The problem, of course, is that this "emerging perspective" has not emerged very far since he wrote in 1970. See also Hoekstra, "The 'Textbook Presidency' Revisited," for his comments on the "Radicals' Presidency"

48. Miroff, *Pragmatic Illusions*, p. 272.

49. Ibid., p. xv.

50. Ibid., p. 279. Miroff also claims that the president must stabilize the nation on the social front too, as evident in Kennedy's handling of the disorder stemming from the civil rights upheaval. But he maintains that the stabilization of the economy is the president's "paramount domestic duty." There is no discussion of legitimacy, per se, in the book. For another, briefer analysis of the president that complements Miroff's thesis, see Katznelson and Kesselman, *The Politics of Power*, 3rd Ed., chapter 4. They argue that the president has three main functions: to assist corporate production domestically, to defend corporate capitalism abroad and to maintain social control. The authors link each sphere with particular constitutional grants of authority and particular agencies within the Executive Office of the President.

51. For an assessment of the importance of, and differences between, the foreign and domestic aspects of the presidency by a leading conventional presidency scholar, see Aaron Wildavsky, "The Two Presidencies," in Wildavsky, ed. *Perspectives on the Presidency*. Wildavsky does not, however, acknowledge the crucial connection between these two spheres, instead seeing only the more minor point that the president has more power in the sphere of foreign affairs.

52. Alan Wolfe, *America's Impasse: The Rise and Fall of the Politics of Growth* (New York: Pantheon, 1981), p. 237.

53. Alan Wolfe, "Presidential Power and the Crisis of Modernization," *democracy*, Vol. 1, No. 2 (April, 1981), p. 22. This discussion also draws on Wolfe's essay "Perverse Politics and the Cold War," in E.P. Thompson, ed., *Exterminism and Cold War* (London: Verso, 1982).

54. Wolfe, "Presidential Power and the Crisis of Modernization," pp. 27–28.

55. Wolfe, *America's Impasse*, p. 10.

56. Wolfe, "Presidential Power and the Crisis of Modernization," p. 31.

Chapter Three

1. Kenneth B. Noble, "Union Carbide Faces Fine of $1.4 Million On Safety Violations," *New York Times*, April 2, 1986, p. A1. Union Carbide is no stranger in the area of safety and health violations. The company was involved in some of this century's worst work/environment-related catastrophes, including the 1930 Gauley Bridge disaster in West Virginia, in which some 476 workers died from exposure to silica dust, and the 1984 methyl isocyanate leak in Bhopal, India that killed more than 2,300 people. For an account of the history of occupational safety and health disasters, see Joseph A. Page and Mary Win O'Brien, *Bitter Wages* (New York: Grossman, 1973).

It should be noted that Union Carbide vigorously contested the *proposed* penalty in court. Companies routinely have their fines reduced through litigation. A typical settlement in a case involving a large fine is for less than a third of the original amount. Also noteworthy is that in July 1987 OSHA imposed a larger fine of $1,576,100 against Chrysler Corporation for 811 alleged violations, including willfully exposing 131 auto workers at its Newark, Delaware assembly plant to hazardous levels of lead and arsenic. The company said it would not contest the penalty, its second major fine of the year, the other one being the nearly $300,000 it paid in February, on assessed fines of $910,000. OSHA followed its July fine against Chrysler with an even larger fine of $2.59 million—the record largest proposed fine on a single company in the agency's history—against IBP, Inc., the nation's largest meatpacker. For a discussion of why OSHA's headline-grabbing big cases do not necessarily signal an agency on the rebound, see William Glaberson, "Is OSHA Falling Down on the Job? *New York Times*, August 2, 1987, section 3, p. 1; and Kenneth B. Noble, "For OSHA, Balance Is Hard to Find," *New York Times*, January 10, 1988, Week in Review, p. 5. The bulk of OSHA's high-profile 1987 fines were for record-keeping violations, as opposed to job hazard offenses, and do not reflect a resurgent policy with the capability and intention to make and vigorously enforce health and safety standards.

2. For speculation on whether the nomination of Pendergrass to head OSHA signaled a new life for the agency after "a five-year snooze in the Reagan era," see Richard Corrigan, "Rekindling OSHA?" *National Journal*, May 3, 1986. For a 1987 follow-up, see Glaberson, "Is OSHA Falling Down on the Job?"

3. "Deregulation: A Fast Start For the Reagan Strategy," *Business Week*, March 9, 1981, p. 66.

4. It is not my intention to delve into the pre-OSHA history of state and voluntary industry safety and health plans. Suffice to say that these plans collectively were of little or no value in combating the problem of workplace safety and health. It was their woeful inadequacy that led, in large part, to the assertion of a strong federal role in this area. Among the many sources of information on this matter, see Nicholas A. Ashford's voluminous report to the Ford Foundation, *Crisis in the Workplace* (Cambridge, MA: MIT Press, 1976); Daniel M. Berman, *Death On The Job* (New York: Monthly Review, 1978);

Office of Technology Assessment (OTA), *Preventing Illness and Injury in the Workplace* (Washington, D.C.: U.S. Government Printing Office, 1985); Charles Noble, *Liberalism at Work: The Rise and Fall of OSHA* (Philadelphia: Temple University Press, 1986); and Page and O'Brien, *Bitter Wages*.

5. The most detailed account of this coalition of forces pushing for passage for the OSH Act can be found in Berman, *Death On The Job*, and Noble, *Liberalism at Work*, chapter 3.

6. On Nixon's ambivalent, somewhat confused approach toward economic policy, see Herbert Stein, *Presidential Economics*, Rev. Ed. (New York: Simon and Schuster, 1985), chapter 5; Alan Wolfe, *America's Impasse* (New York: Pantheon, 1981), pp.73–79; and Thomas Ferguson and Joel Rogers, *Right Turn* (New York: Hill and Wang, 1986), pp. 68–77.

7. Charles Noble, "Class, State, and Social Reform in America: The Case of the Occupational Safety and Health Act of 1970," in Paul Zarembka and Thomas Ferguson, eds. *Research in Political Economy*, Vol. 8 (Greenwich, CT: JAI Press, 1985), p. 155.

8. The most insightful analysis of the failure of business to prevent the passage of an OSH Act — analysis to which I am indebted in this paragraph— can be found in two works by Charles Noble, *Liberalism at Work*, chapter 3; and "Class, State, and Social Reform in America."

9. During the debate over the OSH Act, there was no business organization that played the directive, negotiating role with labor and government along the lines of the roles assumed by the National Civic Federation or the Business Council historically on crucial issues. For a look at the power of these two groups in the policy formation process see, for the NCF, James Weinstein, *The Corporate Ideal in the Liberal State* (Boston: Beacon, 1968); and for the BC, Kim McQuaid, *Big Business and Presidential Power: From FDR to Reagan* (New York: William Morrow, 1982).

10. *Public Papers of the Presidents of the United States: Richard Nixon, 1970* (Washington, D.C.: U.S. Government Printing Office, 1971), p. 1161. For Labor Secretary James D. Hodgson's remarks preceding Nixon's at the signing cermony, see *Weekly Compilation of Presidential Documents*, Vol. 7, No. 1 (Washington, D.C.: Office of the Federal Register, 1971), pp. 4–5.

11. As Charles Noble has argued, the OSH Act "codified a new, more radical vision of worker rights," making it "a remarkable piece of legislation." See his *Liberalism at Work*, p. 94. He then goes on to demonstrate why OSHA has yet to realize its potential as a "radical liberal reform." Much the same sense of the OSH Act as long on promises and short on results can be gotten from Berman, *Death On The Job*, although Noble's account of why OSHA has not achieved its potential is considerably more nuanced than is Berman's.

12. OSH Act of 1970 (Public Law 91-596), Sec. 5(a).

13. OSH Act of 1970, Sec. 6(b)(5).

14. Stein, *Presidential Economics*, pp. 194–195.

15. The literature on the economic crisis of the early 1970s is enormous. Little would be gained by exhaustively citing it here. I will simply point out a few of the sources that have been particularly helpful to me: Wolfe, *America's Impasse*; Paul Sweezy, "The Crisis of American Capitalism," *Monthly Review*, Vol. 32, No. 5 (October, 1980); Paul Sweezy, "The Deepening Crisis of American Capitalism," *Monthly Review*, Vol. 33, No. 5 (October, 1981); Arthur MacEwan, "World Capitalism and the Crisis of the 1970s," in Richard Edwards, et al, eds., *The Capitalist System*, 2nd Ed. (New York: Prentice-Hall, 1978); "Special Issue: Inflation," *Dollars and Sense* (October, 1979); Gerald Epstein, "Domestic Stagflation and Monetary Policy: The Federal Reserve and the Hidden Election," in Thomas Ferguson and Joel Rogers, eds., *The Hidden Election* (New York: Pantheon, 1981); Joshua Cohen and Joel Rogers, *On Democracy* (New York: Penguin, 1983); Micheal H. Best and William E. Connolly, *The Politicized Economy*, 2nd Ed. (Lexington, MA: D.C. Heath, 1982); Samuel Bowles, David M. Gordon and Thomas E. Weisskopf, *Beyond the Waste Land* (New York: Anchor/Doubleday, 1984); Samuel Bowles and Herbert Gintis, "The Crisis of Liberal Democratic Capitalism: The Case of the United States," *Politics and Society*, Vol. 11, No. 1 (1982); Mike Davis, "The Political Economy of Late-Imperial America," *New Left Review*, No. 143 (January-February, 1984); and James O'Connor, *The Fiscal Crisis of the State* (New York: St. Martin's 1973).

16. By far, the two most compelling accounts of the rightward shift in U.S. public policy are found in Thomas Byrne Edsall, *The New Politics of Inequality* (New York: Norton, 1984), and Ferguson and Rogers, *Right Turn*. Both books, but especially the latter, are careful to point out that the recent shift overwhelmingly has been a *policy* shift, *not* a shift in public attitudes.

17. This distinction is now widely accepted in the literature on regulation. Sources from which I've drawn insight on this distinction include Steven Kelman, "Regulation that Works," in *The Big Business Reader*, Mark Green and Robert Massie, Jr., eds. (New York: The Pilgrim Press, 1980); Joan Claybrook, *Retreat From Safety* (New York: Pantheon, 1984); William Lilley III and James C. Miller III, "The New 'Social Regulations,'" *The Public Interest*, No. 47, (Spring, 1977); William K. Tabb, "Government Regulations: Two Sides to the Story," *Challenge*, (November-December, 1980); Andrew Szasz, "The Reversal of Federal Policy Toward Worker Safety and Health," *Science & Society*, Vol. 1, No. 1 (Spring, 1986); Edsall, *The New Politics of Inequality*; and Noble, *Liberalism at Work*.

18. Alan Stone, "State and Market: Economic Regulation and the Great Productivity Debate," Ferguson and Rogers, *The Hidden Election*. Stone's article is very useful for drawing distinctions between different meanings of the word "deregulation," and for making clear the crucial differences between "deregulation" and "overregulation," and how these ideas affected the Carter and Reagan administrations.

19. In "The Reversal of Federal Policy Toward Worker Safety and Health," Szasz offers a solid analysis of "social deregulation," while Stone, in "State and

Market: Economic Regulation and the Great Productivity Debate," comes up with the possibility of "de-overregulation."

20. Szasz, "The Reversal of Federal Policy Toward Worker Safety and Health," makes this argument forcefully.

21. *Public Papers of the Presidents of the United States: Jimmy Carter, 1977,* Vol. I (Washington, D.C.: U.S. Government Printing Office, 1977), p. 105.

22. Ibid.

23. Ibid., "The Environment," Message to Congress, May 23, 1977, p. 970.

24. *Public Papers of the Presidents of the United States: Jimmy Carter, 1977,* Vol. II (Washington, D.C.: U.S. Government Printing Office, 1978), p. 1330.

25. This internal administrative discord permeates the private documents of the Carter administration. I have gotten a solid sense of this tension from my research at the Jimmy Carter Presidential Library in Atlanta, Georgia. My two major sources of manuscript material there are the *Stuart Eizenstat Papers,* Domestic Policy Staff, Subject File for various categories; and the *White House Central File,* Subject File for various categories.

26. The American National Standards Institute was, ironically, dominated by the companies and industry trade associations that established it to ensure corporate control over safety and health standard-setting.

27. Many analysts have made this point. See, in particular, John Mendeloff, *Regulating Safety* (Cambridge, MA: The MIT Press, 1979), especially chapter 6; Noble, *Liberalism at Work*; and OTA, *Preventing Illness and Injury in the Workplace.* Injury rates are extremely sensitive to changes in the business cycle. As employment expands and more inexperienced workers are hired, accident rates rise. As unemployment increases, injury rates tend to decline. The actual impact of OSHA safety standards on the accident rate probably has been minimal. But more on this latter.

28. Best and Connolly, *The Politicized Economy,* p. 103; and Berman, *Death On The Job,* p. 34.

29. Two thorough, standard examinations (and endorsements) of the "injury tax" approach to OSHA issues can be found in Robert Stewart Smith, *The Occupational Safety and Health Act: Its Goals and Achievements* (Washington, D.C.: American Enterprise Institute, 1976); and James Chelius, *Workplace Safety and Health* (Washington, D.C.: American Enterprise Institute, 1977).

30. Smith, *The Occupational Safety and Health Act.* See also Carter CEA chairman Charles Schultze, *The Public Use of Private Interest* (Washington, D.C.: Brookings Institution, 1977), p. 18 and chapter 2 in general, in which he echoes the praise for such market-like taxes and incentives because they accord with the logic of "harnessing the 'base' motive of material self-interest to promote the common good," thereby promoting economic efficiency while endorsing a " 'devil take the hindmost' approach to questions of individual equity."

31. Best and Connolly make this point lucidly in their critique of the market approach to environmental management. See *The Politicized Economy*, chapter 3. See also Noble, *Liberalism at Work*, pp. 208–215.

32. Memorandum To The President From Charles L. Schultze, Stu Eizenstat and Bert Lance, "Reform of OSHA," May 27, 1977, OSHA [O/A 6465] [1], Box 248, *Stuart Eizenstat Papers*, Jimmy Carter Library, Atlanta, GA., p. 1.

33. Ibid., p. 2.

34. Ibid.

35. The Carter Presidential Library has an entire folder devoted to the flap over the Schultze memorandum. See OSHA [CF, O/A 41], Box 248, *Stuart Eizenstat Papers*, Jimmy Carter Library, Atlanta, GA.

36. On the role of AEI in the business offensive against social regulations, see two works by Joseph G. Peschek: *Policy-Planning Organizations: Elite Agendas and America's Rightward Turn* (Philadelphia: Temple University Press, 1987); and his " 'Free the Fortune 500!' The American Enterprise Institute and the Revival of Free-Market Conservatism in the 1970s," paper delivered at the 1986 Annual Convention of the Western Political Science Association, Eugene, OR, March 20-22, 1986. See also Richard Kazis and Richard L. Grossman, *Fear at Work: Job Blackmail, Labor and the Environment* (New York: Pilgrim Press, 1982), especially chapters 5 and 9; Noble, *Liberalism at Work*, chapter 4; and Ronald Brownstein, "Making the Worker Safe for the Workplace," *The Nation*, June 6, 1981.

37. Schultze, *The Public Use of Private Interest*, pp. 17–18. The insight on the Schultze-AEI connection comes from Peschek, *Policy-Planning Organizations*, p. 194.

38. For details of the executive summary of the Interagency Taskforce see, Memorandum For The President From Ray Marshall and James T. McIntyre, Jr., "Strengthening the Federal Role in Protecting Workplace Safety and Health," July 19, 1978, HE 4–2, 1/20/77–12/31/78, Box HE-7, *White House Central File*, Subject File, Jimmy Carter Library, Atlanta, GA.

39. *Weekly Compilation of Presidential Documents*, Vol. 13, No. 51 (Washington, D.C.: Office of the Federal Register, 1977), p. 1858.

40. Ibid., p. 1861.

41. For the text of E.O. 12044 and related presidential announcements, see the *Public Papers of the Presidents of the United States: Jimmy Carter, 1978*, Vol. I (Washington, D.C.: U.S. Government Printing Office, 1979), p. 556–564. It bears notice that President Ford really began executive oversight of the regulatory process with his E.O. 11821 of 1974, requiring that major proposals for legislation, regulations and rules be accompanied by an inflationary impact statement. For an overview of all White House review programs related to regulatory reform, see Noble, *Liberalism at Work*, chapter 6; and Christopher C. DeMuth, "The White House Review Programs," *Regulation* (January-February, 1980).

42. For the text of President Carter's March 26, 1979 message to Congress on his program for further regulatory reform, see "Regulatory Reform," *President Carter: 1979* (Washington, D.C.: Congressional Quarterly, 1979), pp. 16-A and 17-A.

43. Memorandum For Stu Eizenstat From Kitty Bernick, "Cost-Benefit Analysis and OSHA," January 31, 1980, FG 21–5, 1/20/77–1/20/81, Box FG–131, *White House Central File*, Subject File, Jimmy Carter Library, Atlanta, GA.

44. A good brief discussion of the cotton dust case can be found in DeMuth, "The White House Review Programs." He provides some insight into what he appropriately terms the "furious interagency dispute" over OSHA's 1978 revision of the standard, but his account is hampered by the lack of internal Carter administration documents relating to the matter at the time he wrote—1980. And he and I diverge sharply in our general assessment of the value of White House review, since he contends that such review does not go far enough in giving power to the executive to reduce the costs of regulation, a position that is obsessed with regulatory costs, to the exclusion of a host of other important considerations.

45. Memorandum For The President From Stuart Eizenstat and Simon Lazarus, "Marshall and Schultze Memorandum on OSHA Cotton Dust Regulations," May 29, 1978, OSHA [O/A 6465] [3], Box 248, *Stuart Eizenstat Papers*, Jimmy Carter Library, Atlanta, GA., p.3.

46. Ibid.

47. For a solid overview of the large body of current opinion on the merits of engineering controls v. personal protective equipment, see OTA, *Preventing Illness and Injury in the Workplace*, pp. 7–10 and chapter 9.

48. Memorandum For The President From Charles Schultze, "OSHA's Cotton Dust Regulation," June 4, 1978, OSHA [O/A 6465] [2], Box 248, *Stuart Eizenstat Papers*, Jimmy Carter Library, Atlanta, GA., p. 3.

49. Memorandum For Hamilton Jordan From Stu Eizenstat, "Critique of Cotton Dust Decision—At Your Request," June 8, 1978, OSHA [O/A 6465] [2], Box 248, *Stuart Eizenstat Papers*, Jimmy Carter Library, Atlanta, GA., p. 2.

50. This quote, and a collection of newspaper articles—some with White House staff markings and comments on them—are contained on OSHA [O/A 6465] [2], Box 248, *Stuart Eizenstat Papers*, Jimmy Carter Library, Atlanta, GA.

51. Memorandum For The President From Stu Eizenstat and Charlie Schultze, "Cotton Dust; Further Troubles," June 10, 1978, OSHA [O/A 6465] [1], Box 248, *Stuart Eizenstat Papers*, Jimmy Carter Library, Atlanta, GA., p. 3.

52. Memorandum For Hamilton Jordan From Stu Eizenstat, June 8, 1978, p. 3.

53. Memorandum For Stu Eizenstat From Si Lazarus, "Perception of the cotton dust decision: next steps," June 10, 1978, OSHA [O/A 6465] [2], Box 248, *Stuart Eizenstat Papers*, Jimmy Carter Library, Atlanta, GA., p. 1.

54. Memorandum For Hamilton Jordan From Stuart Eizenstat, "Eula Bingham's remarks on inflation and regulation at Steelworkers conference on lead regulations," December 6, 1978, OSHA [O/A 6465] [1], Box 248, *Stuart Eizenstat Papers*, Jimmy Carter Library, Atlanta, GA. The memo contains long excerpts from a Bureau of National Affairs publication, which quotes Bingham extensively. All quotes in this paragraph are drawn from this memo.

55. Noble, *Liberalism at Work*, p. 188, and 188–193.

56. Memorandum For The President From W. Michael Blumenthal, untitled, May 25, 1979, with attached memorandum to the Economic Policy Group Steering Group, BE 4, 1/20/77–1/20/81, Box BE-13, *White House Central File*, Subject File, Jimmy Carter Library, Atlanta, GA.

57. Ibid, p. 4.

58. For President Carter's personal account of the abrupt Camp David skull session and subsequent TV address, see his memoirs, *Keeping Faith* (New York: Bantam, 1982), pp. 114–121. On the whole I view Carter's memoirs as a disappointment, carefully written to a fault, and revealing little about domestic policy. They are—understandably, I suppose—given over mainly to foreign policy issues.

59. Memorandum For The President From Stuart Eizenstat, "Economy," March 26, 1980, BE 4, 1/20/77–1/20/81, Box BE-13, *White House Central File*, Subject File, Jimmy Carter Library, Atlanta, GA.

60. These statistics, and my sketch of the context of economic decline in this section of the chapter, were taken from Epstein, "Domestic Stagflation and Monetary Policy: The Federal Reserve and the Hidden Election"; Bowles, Gordon and Weisskopf, *Beyond the Waste Land*, chapter 2; Ferguson and Rogers, *Right Turn*, chapter 3; and Stein, *Presidential Economics*, chapter 6 and Afterword. For a wide-ranging chronology and analysis of the economic crisis of global capitalism in the 1970s and 1980s, see Joyce Kolko, *Restructuring the World Economy* (New York: Pantheon, 1988), especially chapters 1 and 2.

61. Myra MacPherson, "The First Salvos: Ronald Reagan Takes Over and Takes Aim, *Washington Post*, June 5, 1980, p. D3.

62. Claybrook, *Retreat From Safety*, p. 99.

63. "President Reagan's Economic Proposals Text," February 18, 1981, in *President Reagan* (Washington, D.C.: Congressional Quarterly, 1981), p. 115.

64. Among the many critics of Weidenbaum's figures, see Tabb, "Government Regulations: Two Sides to the Story;" OTA, *Preventing Illness and Injury in the Workplace*, pp. 263–24; Kazis and Grossman, *Fear at Work*, chapter 9; Szasz, "The Reversal of Federal Policy Toward Worker Safety and Health;" Noble, *Liberalism at Work*, pp. 114–116; and *Business Week*, "Deregulation: A fast start for the Reagan strategy," p. 66.

65. *Business Week*, "Deregulation: A fast start for the Reagan strategy."

66. David Stockman, *The Triumph of Politics* (New York: Avon, 1986), pp. 104–108.

67. Noble eloquently makes this argument about the redefinition of the general and particular interests at stake on the OSHA controversy, in his *Liberalism at Work*, pp. 111–114.

68. Ibid., pp. 151–152; and see the sources cited in note 64.

69. The most flagrant example of this can be found in Harold M. Barger, *The Impossible Presidency* (Glenview, IL: Scott, Foresman, 1984), pp. 310–313. While making his general case that the public holds unattainable expectations about the president's ability to solve domestic problems, Barger includes a section on regulatory policy in which he rails against social regulations that by the 1970s had "become so extensive and widespread that few activities in American life were exempt from the watchful eye of a regulatory Big Brother" (p. 311). He goes on basically to applaud the coming of President Reagan to "disarm" the regulatory monster."

70. Philip J. Simon, *Reagan in the Workplace: Unraveling the Health and Safety Net* (Washington, D.C.: Center For Study of Responsive Law, 1983), p. 3.

71. *The President's Report on Occupational Safety and Health for 1982* (Washington, D.C.: U.S. Department of Labor, 1983), p. 1.

72. Philip Shabecoff, "Toward a 'Neutral' Role for OSHA," *New York Times*, March 29, 1981.

73. Linda Greenhouse, "U.S. Pulls a Switch on High Court," *New York Times*, April 5, 1981.

74. American Textile Manufacturers Institute v. Donovan, 452 U.S. 490 (1981). OSHA's resolve to continue to use cost-benefit criteria despite the Supreme Court's ruling is reflected in Labor Secretary Donovan's assertion that "OSHA does not intend to take action unless it can be shown that the positive effects at the workplace outweigh its negative effects," quoted in *The President's Report on Occupational Safety and Health for 1982*, p. 1.

75. For the text of E.O. 12291, see *Public Papers of the Presidents of the United States: Ronald Reagan, 1981* (Washington, D.C.: U.S. Government Printing Office, 1982), pp. 104–108.

76. For the importance of the distinction between cost-benefit criteria as a decision *tool*, and those criteria as a decision *rule*, see OTA, *Preventing Illness and Injury in the Workplace*, chapter 14. This chapter also provides an excellent discussion and critique of the whole issue of cost-benefit analysis and regulation.

77. Murray L. Weidenbaum, "The Changing Relationship Between Government and Business," *Vital Speeches of the Day*, Vol. XLVII, No. 14, May 1, 1981.

78. Three excellent sources for discussion of the technical and ethical problems with cost-benefit analysis are Steven Kelman, "Cost-Benefit Analysis: An Ethical Critique," *Regulation*, (January-February, 1981); OTA, *Preventing Illness and Injury in the Workplace*, pp. 289–293; and two articles by Edward Greer, "Lives in the Balance Sheet," *The Nation*, May 19, 1979; and "Deregulation Fever Hits the Supreme Court," *The Nation*, December 29, 1980.

79. Kelman, ibid., p. 36.

80. For the thorough account of OSHA's vinyl chloride policy, see David D. Doniger, *The Law and Policy of Toxic Substances Control* (Baltimore: Johns Hopkins University, 1978).

81. Quoted in Brownstein, "Making the Worker Safe for the Workplace," p. 694.

82. Ibid.

83. See OTA, *Preventing Illness and Injury in the Workplace*, pp. 221–223 for the data on both OSHA and NIOSH budgets.

84. Ibid., p. 293.

85. Mark Green, "The Faked Case Against Regulation," *Washington Post*, January 14, 1979.

86. W. Kip Viscusi, "Presidential Oversight: Controlling the Regulators," *Journal of Policy Analysis and Management*, Vol. 2, No. 2 (1983), pp. 161–163.

87. The most thorough accounts of these reductions can be found in Claybrook, *Retreat From Safety*: Noble, *Liberalism at Work*; OTA, *Preventing Illness and Injury in the Workplace*; and Simon, *Unraveling the Health and Safety Net*.

88. Simon, *Unravelling the Health and Safety Net*, p. 21.

89. For a discussion of the relationship between the business cycle and occupational injury rates, see OTA, *Preventing Illness and Injury in the Workplace*, pp. 5–6 and 34–36; and Noble, *Liberalism at Work*, pp. 61–66 and 150–151.

90. Corrigan, "Rekindling OSHA?"

91. Wolf, *America's Impasse*, p. 204.

92. Noble, *Liberalism at Work*, p. 151.

93. See Best and Connolly, *The Politicized Economy*, chapter 6, for a helpful discussion of the bind currently confronting the liberal democratic state.

Chapter Four

1. Jimmy Carter, *Keeping Faith: Memoirs of a President* (New York: Bantam, 1982), p. 212. The Carter quote that frames the chapter is from a diary entry dated June 4, 1979, in ibid., p. 241.

2. Gaddis Smith, *Morality, Reason & Power: American Diplomacy in the Carter Years* (New York: Hill and Wang, 1986), pp. 4–5.

3. For an alternative interpretation of Reagan's bombing remark, see Garry Will's, *Reagan's America: Innocents at Home* (New York: Doubleday, 1987), chapter 18, note 2, p. 416–417. Wills views the remark as an expression of Reagan's background as an actor, especially his experience with the tactic of the "faked 'blooper.'" He contends we should view it in the same vein as the saying "break a leg," and not look upon it as an instance of the president's ideological aversion to the Soviet Union,.

4. For accounts of Reagan's admission of his lack of knowledge of this important point, see Kurt Anderson, "A View Without Hills or Valleys," *Time*, February 6, 1984; and Steven R. Weisman, "Clark's Move to Interior Makes External Waves," *New York Times*, October 16, 1983.

5. "Inaugural Address of President Jimmy Carter," *Public Papers of the Presidents of the United States: Jimmy Carter, 1977*, Vol. 1 (Washington, D.C.: U.S. Government Printing Office, 1977), p. 3.

6. These excerpts from Carter's speeches are quoted in Jerry Sanders, *Peddlers of Crisis* (Boston: South End Press, 1983), pp. 235–236. Chapter 7 of this excellent study of the Committee on the Present Danger presents an illuminating, compelling account of Carter's "odyssey from global interdependence to global confrontation."

7. "[Reagan] Has harsh words for Soviet Union," Thomas Oliphant, *Boston Globe*, January 30, 1981, p. 1.

8. Alan Wolfe, "Perverse Politics and the Cold War," in E.P. Thompson, ed., *Exterminism and Cold War* (London: Verso, 1982), p. 237. Wolfe obviously includes the Soviet Union in his observation on the accumulation of super amounts of power.

9. The most thorough account of the importance of Jimmy Carter's association with the Trilateral Commission, for the evolution of both his ideas and his electability, can be found in Laurence H. Shoup, *The Carter Presidency and Beyond* (Palo Alto, CA: Ramparts Press, 1980). See also various selections from Holly Sklar's comprehensive anthology *Trilateralism* (Boston: South End Press, 1980). Also of value, particularly for understanding Carter's foreign policy shift to the right, is Joseph G. Peschek's *Policy-Planning Organizations* (Philadelphia: Temple University Press, 1987), especially chapter 4.

10. Smith, *Morality, Reason & Power*, p. 9.

11. David Gold, Christopher Paine and Gail Shields, *Misguided Expenditure: An Analysis of the Proposed MX Missile System* (New York: Council on Economic Priorities, 1981), p. 21. *Strategic* nuclear forces like the MX missile include those weapons which are long-range in nature, capable of reaching the opponent's home territory, and designed for use during a major superpower confrontation. They stand in contrast to *tactical* nuclear weapons, designed for a variety of shorter-range objectives usually limited to a particular theater of battle, such as Europe.

12. Gold, et al, *Misguided Expenditure*, pp. 57–61. For another version of the argument that the strategic triad is not based on any logical necessity, see Herbert Scoville, Jr., *MX: Prescription for Disaster* (Cambridge, MA: MIT Press, 1981), pp. 210 and 218, and chapters 17 and 18 in general. For a solid yet brief examination of the politics of interservice rivalries, and their contribution to the perpetuation of the perception of "the Soviet threat," see Alan Wolfe, *The Rise and Fall of the Soviet Threat* (Boston: South End Press, 1984), chapter 5.

13. Scoville, *MX: Prescription for Disaster*, p. 210.

14. Carter, *Keeping Faith*, p. 213.

15. For Carter's account of the B-1 cancellation, see ibid., pp. 80–83, and for the neutron bomb decision, pp. 225–229.

16. For discussions of the early history of the MX and related shifts in U.S. nuclear doctrine, see Gold, et al, *Misguided Expenditure*, chapters 2 and, especially, 3; and Robert C. Aldridge, *First Strike!: The Pentagon's Strategy for Nuclear War* (Boston: South End Press, 1983), chapter 1. I draw liberally from these outstanding—and in the case of Aldridge, courageous—works.

17. My purpose here is not to uncover every nuance of strategic nuclear doctrine, but to make the general point that the MX has been developed as a counterforce, first strike weapon, in line with the concomitant development of this war-fighting doctrine. Among the many insightful discussions of the changes in U.S. strategic doctrine, I rely on Aldridge, *First Strike!*; Robert C. Aldridge, *The Counterforce Syndrome* (Washington, D.C.: Institute for Policy Studies, 1980); Fred Kaplan, *Dubious Specter: A Skeptical Look at the Soviet Nuclear Threat* (Washington, D.C: Institute for Policy Studies, 1980); Fred Kaplan, *The Wizards of Armageddon* (New York: Simon and Schuster, 1983); Paul Joseph, "From MAD to NUTs: The Growing Danger of Nuclear War," *Socialist Review*, No. 61, (Vol. 12, No. 1, January-February, 1982); and the invaluable journal *The Bulletin of the Atomic Scientists*.

18. On the distinction between these two senses of the term "first strike," see Aldridge, *First Strike!*, pp. 24–25; and Fred Halliday, *The Making of the Second Cold War*, 2nd Ed. (London: Verso, 1986), pp. 74–75.

19. This is not the place to discuss the various absurdities of the idea of "limited" nuclear war, with its sterile, morally debased calculations of "acceptable" deaths. As Robert Aldridge, former design engineer for the Polaris

and Trident missile systems at Lockheed, has argued, "[T]he chances of it [limited nuclear war] remaining limited are practically zero," a proposition that is now widely accepted, outside the Pentagon. See Aldridge, *First Strike!*, p. 33. When the Congressional Office of Technology Assessment studied the effects of "limited" nuclear war, limited to attacks on ICBM sites, they concluded that the Soviet Union could expect between 3.7 and 27.7 million civilian deaths in the first day alone. The comparable figures for the U.S. were between 2 and 22 million prompt deaths, depending in part on which way the wind is blowing. These casualty estimates do not include deaths over the long term due to injuries and exposure to radiation. I thus agree with Paul Warnke, onetime head of Carter's Arms Control and Disarmament Agency, that such talk of limited nuclear war (here referring to plans within the Carter administration) amounts to "apocalyptic nonsense." More on these Carter plans later. For the details of the OTA study, see *The Effects of Nuclear War* (Washington, D.C.: U.S. Government Printing Office, 1979). See also Eric Chivian, Susanna Chivian, Robert Jay Lifton, and John E. Mack, eds. *Last Aid: The Medical Dimensions of Nuclear War* (San Francisco: W.H. Freeman, 1982).

20. Aldridge, *First Strike!*, p. 27 and all of chapter 1; and Michio Kaku and Daniel Axelrod, *To Win A Nuclear War: The Pentagon's Secret War Plans* (Boston: South End Press, 1987), p. 3 and pp. 184–186.

21. Quoted from a 1956 issue of the prestigious journal *Foreign Affairs*, in Aldridge, *First Strike!*, p. 26. Nitze was Deputy Secretary of Defense at the time.

22. *U.S. Foreign Policy for the 1970s: A New Strategy for Peace*, a report to Congress by President Richard M. Nixon, (February 18, 1970), p. 122, quoted in Aldridge, ibid., p. 30.

23. Gold, et al, *Misguided Expenditure*, p. 29; and Aldridge, ibid., pp. 30–32.

24. For Schlesinger's role in the development of counterforce doctrine, including his secretly drafted national directive, National Security Decision Memorandum-242 (NSDM-242), signed by Nixon in 1974, see Kaku and Axelrod, *To Win A Nuclear War*, pp. 175–182; Aldridge, *First Strike!*, pp. 30–33; and Scoville, *MX: Prescription for Disaster*, pp. 54–57.

25. In this section I am most indebted to the very detailed account of the early history of the MX found in Gold, et al, *Misguided Expenditure*, chapter 3.

26. There are many excellent sources that discuss the various proposals for basing the MX. For an exceptionally detailed version, see Office of Technology Assessment (OTA), *MX Missile Basing* (Washington, D.C.: U.S. Government Printing Office, 1981). Two useful short versions are The Center For Defense Information's "MX: The Weapon Nobody Wants," *The Defense Monitor*, Vol. X, No. 6 (1981); and Thomas B. Cochran, William M. Arkin and Milton M. Hoenig, *Nuclear Weapons Databook*, Vol. 1, "U.S. Nuclear Forces and Capabilities" (Cambridge, MA: Ballinger, 1984), pp. 120–133.

27. Cochran, et al, *Nuclear Weapons Databook*, Vol. 1, p. 128.

28. Cited in Gold, et al, *Misguided Expenditure*, p. 41.

29. Ibid.

30. Ibid., p. 47.

31. By far, the most in depth examination of the CPD can be found in Sanders, *Peddlers of Crisis*.

32. Halliday, *The Making of the Second Cold War*, p. 54. Chapter 3 of this book provides an excellent discussion of the decline of U.S. military superiority. While Halliday eschews single cause explanations of the rise of the second cold war, he clearly considers the decline of U.S. military superiority and relative evening out of the arms race to be a primary constituent element. On the decline of U.S. power, and alleged Soviet leads in important components of military strength, see also Richard Barnet, *Real Security* (New York: Simon and Schuster, 1981), especially chapters 1 and 2; and Gary L. Olson, ed., *How the World Works* (Glenview, IL: Scott, Foresman, 1984), chapters 16–20.

33. Among the many accounts of the Team B panel, see Arthur Macy Cox, "The CIA's Tragic Error," *New York Review of Books*, November 6, 1980; Sanders, *Peddlers of Crisis*, pp. 197–204; Barnet, *Real Security*, pp. 56–59; and Peschek, *Policy-Planning Organizations*, pp. 60–62 and p. 139. Lest anyone think the CPD was the only policy-planning group offering influential conservative views on foreign policy issues at the time, Peschek's perceptive book analyzes the agendas of five such leading groups that span the center-right of the policy spectrum, including the Brookings Institution, the Trilateral Commission, the American Enterprise Institute, the Heritage Foundation, and the Institute for Contemporary Studies.

34. Smith, *Moralilty, Reason & Power*, p. 15.

35. Ibid., p. 245.

36. Carter, *Keeping Faith*, 51–53.

37. Ibid., p. 52. In his memoirs, Vance writes that at the time of the transition, Carter asked him if he had any objections to Brzezinski for the post of National Security Adviser. Vance recalls: "I said that I did not know Brzezinski well, but I believed we could work together." Cyrus Vance, *Hard Choices* (New York: Simon and Schuster, 1983), p. 34.

38. Vance, ibid., pp. 35–36.

39. Halliday, *The Making of the Second Cold War*, pp. 214–233. See also all of chapter 8 for a thorough analysis of the demise of detente, of which Carter's years are only part of the story.

40. For Carter's private 1977 meeting with the JCS, see Kaku and Axelrod, *To Win A Nuclear War*, pp. 184–186.

41. For an account of the legislative and budgetary history of the MX through mid-1983, see Kenneth N. Ciboski, "Taking the 'X' out of MX or Finding a Home for the Missile," in David C. Kozak and Kenneth N. Ciboski, eds. *The American Presidency: A Policy Perspective from Readings and Documents* (Chicago: Nelson-Hall, 1985). While Ciboski's version of the legislative skirmishes over the MX is generally on the mark, his overall conceptual framework for thinking about the MX issue is woefully inadequate. For other histories of the legislative process on the MX, see the perennially useful *Congressional Quarterly* and the *National Journal*.

42. For accounts of the March 1977 "deep cuts" fiasco, see Carter, *Keeping Faith*, pp. 215–219; Vance, *Hard Choices*, pp. 47–55; and Smith, *Morality, Reason & Power*, pp. 76–77.

43. Carter, *Keeping Faith*, p. 219.

44. See Scoville, *MX: Prescription for Disaster*, p. 8 and pp. 99–109; and Gold, et al, *Misguided Expenditure*, pp. 42–43.

45. Department of Defense *Annual Report*, FY 1979, pp. 63–64, cited in Gold, et al, *Misguided Expenditure*, p. 55. See also Scoville, *MX: Prescription for Disaster*, p. 56; Smith, *Morality, Reason & Power*, pp. 81–82; and "MX: The Missile We Don't Need," *The Defense Monitor*, Vol. VIII, No. 9 (October, 1979), p. 7. For more on the idea of a first strike being a cosmic roll of the dice, see Kaku and Axelrod, *To Win A Nuclear War*, pp. 212–21.

46. Smith, *Morality, Reason & Power*, pp. 81–82; and Richard Burt, "Brown Says ICBM's May Be Vulnerable To The Russians Now," *New York Times*, August 21, 1980.

47. *Fiscal Year 1979 Arms Control Impact Statements*, June 1978, p. 21, cited in Aldridge, *First Strike!*, p. 129.

48. Reprinted in *Vital Speeches of the Day*, June 15, 1978, pp. 515–51, and cited in Shoup, *The Carter Presidency and Beyond*, pp. 153–154.

49. Vance, *Hard Choices*, pp. 101–102; and Carter, *Keeping Faith*, pp. 229–230. Vance had urged the president to make a major address on U.S.-Soviet relations at this time, to combat what Vance saw as the growing domestic mood of hostility toward the Soviet Union.

50. "Deployment of the MX Missile," *Public Papers of the Presidents of the United States: Jimmy Carter, 1979*, Vol. I (Washington, D.C.: U.S. Government Printing Office, 1980), p. 1016.

51. Quoted in Gregg Herken, *Counsels of War* (New York: Alfred A. Knopf, 1985), p. 291.

52. Vance, *Hard Choices*, p. 135.

53. "MX Missile System," *Public Papers of the Presidents of the United States: Jimmy Carter, 1979*, Vol. II (Washington, D.C.: U.S. Government Printing Office, 1980), p. 1601.

54. For explanations of the Carter MPS plan, see OTA, *MX Missile Basing*, especially chapters 1 and 2; "MX: The Missile We Don't Need," *The Defense Monitor*, Vol. VIII, No. 9 (August, 1979); and "MX: The Weapon Nobody Wants," *The Defense Monitor*, Vol. X, No. 6 (1981).

55. This MPS configuration sometimes is referred to as a multiple aim points (MAPS) system, which is an earlier name for the same thing.

56. Gold, et al, *Misguided Expenditure*, pp. 117–129, and generally all of Part II.

57. Christopher E. Paine, "MX: the public works project of the 1980s," *The Bulletin of the Atomic Scientist*, (February, 1980), p. 13.

58. For the definitive critique of the escalatory logic of military planners, see Dr. Seuss, *The Butter Battle Book* (New York: Random House, 1984).

59. "Interview With The President," *Public Papers of the Presidents of the United States: Jimmy Carter, 1979*, Vol. II (Washington, D.C.: U.S. Government Printing Office, 1980), p. 1612.

60. "MX: The Weapon Nobody Wants," *The Defense Monitor*, Vol. X, No. 6 (1981), p. 1.

61. "Letter To Congressman John F. Seiberling from William J. Perry," October 12, 1979, ND 18 9/1/79–12/31/79, Box ND–51, *White House Central File*, Subject File, Jimmy Carter Library, Atalant, GA., p. 2.

62. Aldridge, *First Strike!*, p. 109. For a thorough critique of Carter's MPS system, see Gold, et al, *Misguided Expenditure*, pp. 94–102.

63. Governor Matheson's "opposition" to Carter's plan is an especially revealing example of how opponents typically limit their differences to the details of defense plans, sidestepping the larger issue of whether such plans have anything to do with real national security. See "Statement By Governor Scott M. Matheson," June 16, 1980, plus attached Memorandum For The President from Defense Secretary Harold Brown, outlining his objections to Matheson's statement, ND 18, 1/1/80–6/30/80, Box ND–52, *White House Central File*, Subject File, Jimmy Carter Library, Atlanta, GA.

64. Curiously, L.A. Times reporter Robert Scheer, in his otherwise exhaustive and absolutely revealing study of the Reagan administration's attitude toward nuclear war, places Carter's advocacy of the multiple shelter MX system in the aftermath of events in Iran and Afghanistan. This clearly is chronologically incorrect. The pro-MX arguments Scheer cites were being made by Carter well before any shift in the public mood in response to these two events. See Scheer, *With Enough Shovels: Reagan, Bush and Nuclear War*, Updated Ed. (New York: Vintage, 1983), pp. 69–70.

65. George F. Kennan, Op Ed, *New York Times*, February 1, 1980, quoted in Smith, *Morality, Reason & Power*, p. 247.

66. Aldridge, *First Strike!*, pp. 35–36; Kaku and Axelrod, *To Win A Nuclear War*, pp. 191–192; Smith, ibid., pp. 234–237; and Fred Kaplan, " 'New look' from the Pentagon," *Inquiry*, September 22, 1980.

67. From a transcript of the CBS Evening News with Dan Rather, March 29, 1982, as quoted in Kaku and Axelrod, *To Win A Nuclear War*, p. 229.

68. Colin S. Gray and Keith Payne, "Victory Is Possible," *Foreign Policy*, No. 39 (Summer, 1980), quoted in Jeff McMahan, *Reagan and the World* (New York: Monthly Review Press, 1985), p. 35; and Scheer, *With Enough Shovels*, pp. 12–13, and pp. 34–35. Chapter 2 of McMahan's book solidly critiques the notion that superiority in nuclear weaponry confers the power of political coercion.

69. Colin Gray, "The MX ICBM: Why We Need It," *Air Force Magazine*, Vol. 69, No. 8 (August, 1979), p. 71.

70. Quoted from an extensive interview with Scheer, *With Enough Shovels*, pp. 18 and p. 21.

71. "Excerpts From President Reagan's Speech on Foreign Policy and Congress," *New York Times*, April 7, 1984, p. A6.

72. For analyses of trends in U.S.-Soviet military spending, see Robert W. Komer, "What 'Decade of Neglect'?" *International Security*, Vol. 10, No. 2 (Fall, 1985), pp. 70–83; Halliday, *The Making of the Second Cold War*, pp. 55–59; and Joshua Cohen and Joel Rogers, *Inequity and Intervention: The Federal Budget and Central America*, (Boston: South End Press, 1986), chapters 1 and 2.

73. See notes 31 and 33.

74. This figure is taken from Halliday, *The Making of the Second Cold War*, pp. 56–57, and is based on estimates from the Stockholm International Peace Research Institute, a widely-respected independent source. The corresponding CIA estimate of Soviet expenditures, from their 1980 study, is about three percent per year, average annual rate, which does not contradict Halliday's assertion of the Soviet's slow steadiness in this regard and is, in fact, the same rate as the U.S. and most of its NATO allies from 1976–1980. See Cox, "The CIA's Tragic Error."

75. Concerning the charge that Carter was in some way "soft" on the Soviets, Brzezinski has said:

It was President Carter who, for the first time in peacetime, increaseed the defence budget. It was President Carter who ordered the creation of a Rapid Deployment Force. It was President Carter who decided on the deployment of the MX missile. It was he who shaped a regional security framework in the Persian Gulf.

George Urban, "A Conversation with Zbigniew Brzezinski," *Encounter*, May, 1981, as cited in Halliday, *The Making of the Second Cold War*, p. 233.

76. Komer, "What 'Decade of Neglect'?" p. 79.

77. Charles Mohr, "Irate Carter Rebuts Reagan on Military And Security Policy," *New York Times*, March 2, 1986, p. A1.

78. "Remarks at a White House Meeting With Private Sector Leaders," March 6, 1985, *Weekly Compilation of Presidential Documents* (Washington, D.C.: Office of the Federal Register, 1985), p. 261.

79. Mohr, "Irate Carter Rebuts Reagan on Military And Security Policy," p. A30.

80. Scheer, *With Enough Shovels*, p. 66.

81. For the details of the mobility of the "window of vulnerability," see Christopher Paine, "Running in circles with the MX," *The Bulletin of the Atomic Scientists* (December, 1981).

82. *FAS Public Interest Report*, February 1974, cited in Gold, et al, *Misguided Expenditure*, p. 34.

83. Clear and thorough explanations of the technical uncertainties of nuclear weaponry can be found readily in a number of places, notably J. Edward Anderson, "First Strike: myth or reality," *The Bulletin of the Atomic Scientists* (November, 1981), and generally in the journal; Aldridge, *First Strike!*; Gold, et al, *Misguided Expenditure*; numerous issues of the Center For Defense Information's *The Defense Monitor*; and Kaplan, *Dubious Specter*.

84. Paine, "Running in circles with the MX," p. 7.

85. For examinations of Soviet vulnerability, see Howard Morland, "Are We Readying A First Strike?" *The Nation*, March 16, 1985; Halliday, *The Making of the Second Cold War*, pp. 70–8–; "The $100 Million Mobile Missile: The MX And The Future Of U.S. Strategic Forces," *The Defense Monitor*, Vol. VI, No. 6 (August, 1977); and "MX: The Missile We Don't Need," *The Defense Monitor*, Vol. VIII, No. 9 (October, 1979).

86. For a discussion of the Townes Committeee, see Ciboski, "Taking the 'X' out of MX or Finding a Home for the Missile."

87. "Address to the Nation on Strategic Arms Reduction and Nuclear Deterrence," *Public Papers of the Presidents of the United States: Ronald Reagan, 1982*, Vol. II (Washington, D.C.: U.S. Government Printing Office, 1983), p. 1506. The text of the president's address runs on pp. 1505–1510.

88. See the *Report of the President's Commission on Strategic Forces* (Washington, D.C.: U.S. Government Printing Office, April, 1983).

89. Ibid., p. 6. For a penetrating analysis of nuclear weapons as instruments of political coercion, and the U.S. drive to gain the capacity to "prevail" in a nuclear war, see McMahan, *Reagan and the World*, chapter 2.

90. Ibid., p. 8.

91. See David B. Ottaway and Walter Pincus, "MX Vulnerability 'No Longer An Issue'," *Manchester Guardian Weekly*, March 17, 1985.

92. "Radio Address to the Nation," *Weekly Compilation of Presidential Documents* (Washington, D.C.: Office of the Federal Register, 1985), p. 275.

93. "Text of Reagan's Broadcast Address On Talks With Gorbachev in Iceland," *New York Times*, October 14, 1986, p. A10.

94. For details of the "rail garrison" proposal, I have drawn on "Recent Developments With The MX Missile: Still The Wrong Way To Go," a 1987 MX missile update report from the Center for Defense Information, in Washington, D.C.; and "10 Possible Sites Selected For MX," *New York Times*, February 12, 1987.

95. While President Reagan has proposed a ban on land-based mobile missiles under START, pending agreement on strict verification procedures, he is under pressure to ensure that any future treaty does not prohibit mobile missiles.

96. For a taste of the emerging defense establishment debate on the implications of a proposed 6,000 strategic warhead limit under a START agreement, see for example, Stansfield Turner, "Winnowing Our Warheads," *New York Times Magazine*, March 27, 1988; Michael R. Gordon, "Reagan's Missile-Cut Offer Throws Open 'Window of Vulnerability' Debate," *New York Times*, December 7, 1987; and Robert C. McFarlane, "Risking Double Defeat: No Arms Treaty and Bad Arms," *New York Times*, July 1, 1988.

97. On the cyclical nature of the cold war, see Halliday, *The Making of the Second Cold War*, and Wolfe, *The Rise and Fall of the Soviet Threat*.

98. For a critique of the offensive implications of a Star Wars ballistic missile defense (BMD) system within the overall U.S. nuclear strategy, see E.P. Thompson, "The Real Meaning of Star Wars," *The Nation*, March 9, 1985; and E.P. Thompson, ed. *Star Wars* (New York: Pantheon, 1985). A thorough overview of BMD technology can be found in Office of Technology Assessment (OTA), *Ballistic Missile Defense Technology* (Washington, D.C.: U.S. Government Printing Office, 1985).

99. Cited in Aldridge, *First Strike!*, p. 103.

100. Freeman Dyson, *Weapons and Hope* (New York: Harper, 1984), p. 63 and chapter 5. Dyson argues that the MX actually is a relatively small technical folly lodged within the much larger technical folly of nuclear missile forces, which is itself lodged within the grandest technical folly of all—the folly of nuclear deterrence. See also his "Demystifying The Bomb," *New York Times Magazine*, April 5, 1987, as part of a symposium entitled "A World Without Nuclear Weapons?"

101. Paine, "Running in circles with the MX," p. 10.

102. Paul H. Nitze, "Nuclear Strategy: Detente and American Survival," in *Defending America: Toward a New Role in the Post-Detente World* (New York: Basic Books, 1977), edited and co-published by the Institute for Contemporary Studies, as cited in Peschek, *Policy-Planning Organizations*, p. 129.

103. Quoted in Halliday, *The Making of the Second Cold War*, p. 49.

104. Carter, *Keeping Faith*, p. 256.

105. Ciboski, "Taking the 'X' out of MX or Finding a Home for the Missile," p. 398.

106. The phrase is borrowed from Mike Davis, "The Political Economy of Late-Imperial America," *New Left Review*, No. 143 (January-February, 1984), p. 36. For an analysis of the sectoral investment trend toward the defense sector, see Davis' "Reaganomics' Magical Mystery Tour," *New Left Review*, No. 149 (January-February, 1985). See also E.P. Thompson, "Look Who's Really Behind Star Wars," *The Nation*, March 1, 1986; Gold, et al, *Misguided Expenditure*, part 2; and Aldridge, *First Strike!*, chapter 11.

107. Dyson, *Weapons and Hope*, p. 64.

Chapter Five

1. Arthur Schlesinger, Jr., "The Imperial Temptation," *The New Republic*, March 16, 1987, pp. 17-18. The full version of this thesis is contained in his classic, *The Imperial Presidency* (New York: Popular Library, 1974), which I critique in Chapter One. For an explication of his current thoughts about his original thesis (nothing has been modified, really), see his *The Cycles of American History* (Boston: Houghton Mifflin, 1986), chapter 11.

2. Schlesinger, *The Cycles of American History*, p. 276; and "The Imperial Temptation," p. 17.

3. Schlesinger, "The Imperial Temptation," p. 18.

4. Alexander Cockburn, "Ashes and Diamonds," *In These Times*, June 10-23, 1987. Cockburn's comments can be found in this column, as well as his "Beat the Devil" column in *The Nation*.

5. Adam Pertman, "Checks, Balances: Iran-contra hearings should reveal if constitution's promises were kept," *Boston Sunday Globe*, May 3, 1987, p. 1.

6. For a powerful discussion of this distinction, see Noam Chomsky, "The Bounds of Thinkable Thought," *The Progressive*, October, 1985; and Chomsky's *On Power and Ideology: The Managua Lectures* (Boston: South End Press, 1987). In these works he discusses the constrained and ultimately power-serving "debates" between opposing groups, usually characterized by the media as some variant of the "hawks" vs. the "doves," on a range of issues such as the Vietnam

War, President Nixon's "secret bombing" of Cambodia, aid to the contras, President Reagan's Star Wars program, and the general threat of nuclear war. In each of these cases the "debate" takes place within the bounds of permissible discourse centered on two positions of pragmatic concern, and thus further legitimizes the premises of U.S. state policy—premises which are deemed beyond the bounds of "reasonable" debate.

7. Of the many solid critiques of the nature of U.S. foreign policy as an imperial, expansionary quest for empire, especially in Central America, see William Appleman Williams, *Empire As A Way Of Life* (New York: Oxford University Press, 1980); two of Noam Chomsky's numerous devastating critiques: *Turning the Tide* (Boston: South End Press, 1985), and *On Power and Ideology*; and Saul Landau, *The Dangerous Doctrine: National Security and U.S. Foreign Policy* (Boulder, CO: Westview Press, 1988).

8. In addition to the examples of this phenomenon cited in Chapter Two, we can add Larry Berman's text *The New American Presidency* (Boston: Little, Brown, 1987), which situates the "structural" dangers of constitutional insolvency, created when the framers wrought the separation of powers, at the center of his analysis of the presidency.

9. Bruce Miroff, "Beyond Washington," *Society*, Vol. 17, No. 5 (July/August, 1980).

10. Alan Wolfe, *America's Impasse: The Rise and Fall of the Politics of Growth* (New York: Pantheon, 1981), p. 237. Another text that undertakes a structural account of the presidency is Bruce Miroff, *Pragmatic Illusions* (New York: David McKay Co., 1976), discussed in Chapter Two. Lest one think Wolfe's focus on the imperatives of economic growth and national security is overdrawn, it is worth pointing out that even analysts far to the right of him find these issues at the root of the state's agenda. For example, as the authors of a study for the elite Trilateral Commission wrote in the introduction to their 1975 Report on the Governability of Democracies, "Governments, after all, have traditionally existed to deal with problems of security and economics, and, individually and collectively, to adapt their policies in these areas to changing environments." See Michael J. Crozier, Samuel P. Huntington and Joji Watanuki, *The Crisis of Democracy* (New York: New York University Press, 1975), pp. 1–2.

11. For an analysis of the development of the American political economy that creatively employs such a temporal dimension, see Edward S. Greenberg, *Capitalism and the American Political Ideal* (Armonk, NY: M.E. Sharpe, 1985). Greenberg uses the concept of "policy regimes" to explain the "continuous reformulations" of government response to the stages of transformation of American capitalism. As he explains, "Each of these stages, defined in terms of intertwined sets of problems, constraints, political coalitions, and public-policy packages existing in temporary equilibrium, will be understood . . . as "policy regimes" (p. 48).

12. G. William Domhoff seems to be moving toward a more synthetic approach to theories of the state in his article "State Autonomy and the Privileged Position of Business: An Empirical Attack on a Theoretical Fantasy," *Journal of Political and Military Sociology*, Vol. 14 (Spring, 1986). His effort to correctly point out the structural dimensions of Ralph Miliband's work—usually characterized as instrumental—is hopeful on this score, although Domhoff does adopt a self-consciously combative tone in the paper. The basic thrust would seem to be the need to emphasize the points of contact between power structure research and structural-functional concerns.

13. Harold M. Barger, *The Impossible Presidency* (Glenview, IL: Scott, Foresman, 1984), p. 44. See especially chapters 1 and 10.

14. Here I am drawing on two essays by Connolly: "Personal Identity, Citizenship, and the State," in William E. Connolly, *Appearance and Reality in Politics* (New York: Cambridge University Press, 1981); and "The Dilemma of Legitimacy," in William E. Connolly, ed., *Legitimacy and the State* (New York: New York University Press, 1984).

15. Connolly, "Personal Identity, Citizenship, and the State," p. 167.

16. Garry Wills, *Reagan's America: Innocents At Home* (New York: Doubleday, 1987), p. 2.

17. See, for example, Steven V. Roberts, "Many Who See Failure in His Policies Don't Blame Their Affable President," *New York Times*, March 2, 1984; and Steven R. Weisman, "Can The Magic Prevail?" *New York Times Magazine*, cover story, April 29, 1984. This disjuncture between Reagan's personal popularity and his policy popularity leaves the door ajar for candidates and ideas that draw Americans away from the "right turn" espoused by corporate elites. For a pathbreaking analysis of the origins and implications of this personal/policy split, see Thomas Ferguson and Joel Rogers, *Right Turn* (New York: Hill and Wang, 1986).

18. For an exhaustive account of the crisis of the world economy, and strategies of reconstruction, see Joyce Kolko, *Restructuring the World Economy* (New York: Pantheon, 1988).

19. For a complete version of some of these proposals for democratic control of the economy, and responses to potential counterarguments, see Samuel Bowles, David M. Gordon, and Thomas E. Weisskopf, *Beyond the Waste Land* (Garden City, NY: Anchor/Doubleday, 1983); Joshua Cohen and Joel Rogers, *On Democracy* (New York: Penguin, 1983); Kenneth M. Dolbeare, *Democracy at Risk*, Revised Ed. (Chatham, NJ: Chatham House, 1986); and Robert Lekachman, "The FED In Fact And Fiction," *Dissent* (Winter, 1988). For a more international focus to similar concerns, see Alec Nove, *The Economics of Feasible Socialism* (London: George Allen & Unwin, 1983).

20. Among the many books I have found useful in exploring the need to challenge the priorities of corporate capitalism, see Michael H. Best and William

E. Connolly, *The Politicized Economy* (Lexington, MA: D.C. Heath, 1982); Cohen and Rogers, *On Democracy*; Bowles, Gordon and Weisskopf, *Beyond the Waste Land*; and Samuel Bowles and Herbert Gintis, *Democracy and Capitalism* (New York: Basic Books, 1986).

21. Alan Wolfe, "Presidential Power and the Crisis of Modernization," *democracy*, Vol. 1, No. 2 (April, 1981).

22. The phrase is borrowed from Richard Neustadt, *Presidential Power* (New York: John Wiley, 1980). Neustadt uses the phrase (twice, on p. 120 and p. 205) in the context of discounting the possibility that a president seeking to lower public expectations could sustain such a call for very long.

23. Huntington, "The United States," in Crozier, Huntington, and Watanuki, *The Crisis of Democracy*, p. 114.

24. Ibid., p. 93.

25. Ibid., p. 98.

26. Donald L. Robinson, ed., *Reforming American Government:* (Boulder, CO: Westview Press, 1985), p. xv. This text is subtitled "The Bicentennial Papers of the Committee on the Constitutional System" and details the CCS analysis of and prescription for constitutional reform to create more unified, coherent and centralized national government. A statement of the "problem" from the CCS perspective can be found on pp. 68–71. See also the related work of CCS member James L. Sundquist, *Constitutional Reform and Effective Government* (Washington, D.C.: The Brookings Institution, 1986).

27. An interesting critique of the Committee on the Constitutional System's set of NeoHamiltonian reform proposals currently percolating in some circles of power and carrying the endorsement of prominent political scientists, can be found in Jeanne Hahn, "NeoHamiltonianism: A Democratic Critique," in John F. Manley and Kenneth M. Dolbeare, eds., *The Case Against The Constitution: From the Antifederalists to the Present* (Armonk, NY: M.E. Sharpe, 1987). I am drawing on Hahn's essay liberally in these paragraphs on the CCS.

28. Sundquist, *Constitutional Reform and Effective Government*, p. 73, as cited in Hahn, "NeoHamiltonianism: A Democratic Critique," p. 170.

29. Neustadt, *Presidential Power*, pp. 135–142.

30. Robert N. Bellah, et al, *Habits of the Heart* (New York: Harper, 1985), p. 275.

INDEX